STUDY GUIDE for

Ralph, Lerner, Meacham, Wood, Hull, and Burns

World Civilizations

Volume 2

NINTH EDITION

by J. Michael Allen

 W · W · NORTON & COMPANY · NEW YORK · LONDON

ISBN 0-393-96883-9 (pbk.)

W. W. Norton & Company, Inc., 500 Fifth Avenue, New York, N.Y. 10110

http://www.wwnorton.com

W. W. Norton & Company Ltd., 10 Coptic Street, London WC1A 1PU

1 2 3 4 5 6 7 8 9 0

Contents

To the Teacher and the Student

This edition of the *Study Guide* is designed specifically to accompany the ninth edition of *World Civilizations*. Though it incorporates material from earlier editions, it has been completely revised and updated. Every chapter has been carefully tailored to correspond to the material as it now stands in the ninth edition, including material that is new to that edition. This applies to the exercises as well as to the readings.

The purpose of this *Study Guide* is to help students master the material in *World Civilizations* and to assist teachers in initiating discussions that will both review and extend the topics covered in the textbook. The guide may also be convenient as the basis for tests. In order to approach the material in a variety of ways to pursue these objectives, each chapter of the guide is divided into several sections. Not every chapter contains every type of section, nor is every chapter the same length. This reflects both the varying lengths of chapters in the textbook, and the author's belief that the most valuable kinds of review and evaluation may vary from topic to topic. The sections into which a chapter may be divided are as follows:

Chronology. Chronological reviews are provided for many, but not all, chapters. These reviews are designed to put the information in the chapter into a broad, chronological perspective. Their value as study aids is to help students remember both specific and relative chronology; that is, in some cases dates are emphasized, whereas in other cases the order of events is more important than specific dates. In no case, however, does the chronology section include every date mentioned in the textbook chapter.

Identifications. Again, the choice of items for the identifications is selective. Identification sections might involve matching, multiple-choice questions, short answers, fill-in-the-blank questions, or a combination. Identifications may cover events, ideas, works of literature and art, people, or all

four. This section is designed not only to allow rapid evaluation (by either teachers or the students themselves) of students' grasp of specific information, but also to assess students' ability to understand the broader historical significance of specific items.

Study Questions. These are found in every chapter. Some of them take the form of multiple-choice questions, but generally they are the type that can be answered by an essay or in a class discussion. They can thus serve either as the basis for essay examinations or as the starting point for class discussions, in addition to providing the student with a way of assessing his or her grasp of material in the textbook. The primary distinction between the study questions and the problems that follow is that the study questions can be answered from the material in the textbook alone. Therefore, if students answer all of the study questions thoroughly, they will have a convenient, point-by-point summary of the textbook.

Problems. These are also included in all chapters. Unlike the study questions, however, they require students to move beyond the material in the textbook. Designed to stimulate students' curiosity and provoke discussion and inquiry, they must be answered on the basis of additional reading and study. In some cases, specific books (both fiction and nonfiction) are recommended. The problems can be used in a variety of ways: as the basis for class discussions, as topics for papers, or as extra reading assignments. They can also, of course, be modified to meet the needs and preferences of particular classes and individual teachers.

Map Exercises. These are included for each of the textbook's major parts, and are taken from the maps in the textbook itself. The map exercises are based on the belief that a certain amount of geographic knowledge is essential for an understanding of the development of human societies. In the map exercises students will identify the stages on which the drama of human history has been enacted. Ideally, students will be able to visualize changes over time more easily by reference to concrete locations and features on maps. The exercises are not comprehensive: unlike the study questions, they do *not* provide a thorough review of all the important geographic information mentioned in the textbook. But they do require students to familiarize themselves with a certain minimal amount of information about cities, rivers, regions, empires, oceans, and other details that will enhance their understanding of the course of human history.

Readings. The readings accompanying each chapter were selected with two primary purposes in mind: to illustrate material discussed in the textbook chapter, and to provide students with the opportunity to "roll up their sleeves" and plunge directly into the stuff of historical research. It is one thing to read *about* Confucius, or the Crusades, or the framing of the American constitution; it is quite another thing to actually read from the *Analects*, or follow a speech of Pope Urban II, or delve into the *Federalist* papers. An attempt has been made to include readings that are both relevant and interesting. To further enhance the value of the readings, a few questions are provided to help tie the readings to the other material in the textbook and the guide.

In every way, this *Study Guide* is designed to enhance students' use of the textbook and their understanding of the topics presented there. This guide is not intended to limit the creativity of teachers or the inquisitiveness of students. On the contrary, it is meant to be a resource for both teachers and students, to be used in a variety of ways and incorporated into the structure of the class as appropriate.

ACKNOWLEDGMENTS

I would like to thank Jon Durbin of W. W. Norton, the point man for this project. His suggestions, patience, and insight were greatly appreciated. Steve Forman and Kate Nash, also at Norton, were most helpful with their timely responses to inquiries. My wife and children, as usual, gave up time with me so that I could spend it with maps and questions, documents and dates. My thanks to them.

CHAPTER 21 | India, East Asia, and Africa During the Early-Modern Era (c. 1500–1800)

CHRONOLOGY

Supply the date or dates for each of the following events bearing on the history of India:

1. Death of Babur, founder of the Mughal Dynasty

_____

2. Beginning of the reign of Akbar, "the Great Mughal"

_____

3. Chartering of the British East India Company

_____

4. Reign of Shah Jahan, builder of the Taj Mahal

_____

5. Acquisition of Bombay by the British

_____

6. Sack of Delhi by Nadir Shah

_____

Below is a list of events from the history of China, Japan, and Africa. For each item, write in the blank the number of the item from the India list to which it corresponds most closely in time.

_____ Beginning of Qing (Manchu) Dynasty

_____ Arrival of first Portuguese vessel at Guangzhou (Canton)

_____ Establishment of Portuguese settlement at Macao

_____ Establishment of Tokugawa Shogunate

_____ Suppression of Christianity in Japan and beginning of policy of isolation

_____ Beginning of reign of Kangxi

_____ Beginning of reign of Qianlong

_____ Portuguese lose enclaves in West Africa to the Dutch

_____ Chartering of Royal Africa Company

IDENTIFICATIONS

You should be able to define or explain the importance of each of the following:

Hamayun	Lord George Macartney
Shivaji	daimyo
Nanak	Hideyoshi
Urdu	samurai
Tulsi Das	"floating world"
Sultan Ibrahim II	Kabuki drama
Seven Years War	Oyo kingdom
Manchu	"New Christians"
Dorgon	jihad
banner units	*Asiento*
White Lotus Society	Boers
Six Records of a Floating Life	Ogboni Society

STUDY QUESTIONS

1. How did the Mughal Dynasty of India get its name? Was the title appropriate? Why or why not?
2. What significant changes in governmental policy were introduced by Akbar? To what extent were they beneficial?
3. What measures did Akbar take to win the allegiance of his Hindu subjects?

1

4. Describe Akbar's unique religious establishment. How successful was it?

5. In spite of impressive achievements, how did the long reign of Aurangzeb weaken the Mughal state?

6. How were the Sikhs and the Marathas, respectively, threats to Mughal power in the seventeenth and eighteenth centuries?

7. Cite specific examples to show that Indian culture of the Mughal period was eclectic and cosmopolitan.

8. What date would you assign to the final ascendancy of the British over the French in India?

9. What policies did the Qing emperors adopt to confirm their legitimacy as rulers of China? In what ways did the Chinese and Manchus remain separate?

10. What was at issue in the "War of the Three Feudatories"? What were its results?

11. Examine tax policies under Kangxi. What were the purposes behind his policies? What were the strengths and weaknesses of his taxation policies?

12. What problems were created by China's swelling population during the Qing period? How did the government deal with these problems?

13. In what respects did the position of women deteriorate during the Qing period? Are there any ways in which it improved?

14. What did the following Jesuits contribute to China: Matteo Ricci, Ferdinand Verbiest, Giuseppe Castiglione?

15. What was the Jesuit approach to missionary work in China? What were its advantages and disadvantages? How did it lead to conflict with other Catholic orders?

16. How did the "School of Han Learning" contribute to Chinese philosophy and learning? What was the contribution of Gu Yanwu?

17. What new problems were posed for the governments of both China and Japan by the coming of European traders to their ports? How did the two governments differ in their attempts to handle these problems?

18. Explain the key features of the government of Japan under the Tokugawa Shoguns. How effective was this government?

19. What specific measures did the Tokugawa Shoguns take to control the daimyo?

20. What important economic changes took place in Japan during the Tokugawa period? How did these changes threaten the survival of the Shogunate?

21. What intellectual and religious trends were at work in Japan that could also undermine the Shogun's position?

22. Describe the Japanese social hierarchy in theory and in practice. Why did theory and practice sometimes diverge?

23. Describe the importance of sugar in the African economy during this period. What was the role of sugar in the development of the Atlantic slave trade?

24. What were the effects of the slave trade on African societies? Give specific examples.

25. When did the shipment of slaves from Africa directly to the Americas begin, and why?

26. What were the Portuguese goals in Africa? How successful were the Portuguese in attaining these goals?

27. Compare the forms of government in the Oyo and Dahomean empires. In what ways were they similar? In what ways did they differ from one another?

28. What was the purpose of claims of divinity by African monarchs? How did this divinity manifest itself?

29. How did the nature of European involvement in Africa change after the opening of the sixteenth century?

30. How do you explain the flourishing of Asante civilization during the first half of the eighteenth century?

31. "History took another, more tragic, course in the extreme southwest corner of Africa." Explain this statement.

PROBLEMS

1. Every one of the Mughal rulers of India between 1526 and 1707 offers an interesting and colorful subject for study. Akbar was undoubtedly one of the most remarkable personalities ever to govern a state. Look into Akbar's intellectual and religious activities, his relations with Portuguese Jesuits, or his building program.

2. Examine the contrasts in character and personality among the first three Mughal rulers who succeeded Akbar.

3. Trace the evolution of the Indo-Muslim style of architecture.

4. Investigate the origins and development of the religion of the Sikhs.

5. Analyze the remarkable population growth in China under the Qing Dynasty and its probable causes.

6. Compare the background, personality, and governing style of Akbar and Kangxi. (For Kangxi, you might start with Jonathan Spence, *Emperor of China: Self-Portrait of K'ang Hsi.*)

7. Examine the writings of Voltaire or other leading exponents of the European Enlightenment for evidence of Western awareness of and reactions to Chinese civilization (actual or imagined).

8. Study the Chinese family system as reflected in the novel *Dream of the Red Chamber* (trans. C. C. Wang).

9. Investigate any of these aspects of Chinese culture during the Qing period: the "School of Han Learning"; scholars; painting; architecture; the drama; the cult of Confucius.

10. "Most specialists now believe that population growth in China had outstripped the carrying capacity of the land at the current level of technology in China by the end of Qianlong's reign." Examine the implications of this statement in light of the English economist Thomas Malthus's famous theory about population growth and resources.

11. Study the suppression of Christianity by the early Tokugawa Shoguns; the origins and development of Kabuki

drama; development of the Japanese wood-block print; or city life in Japan during the Tokugawa period.

12. Read Thomas C. Smith's *The Agrarian Origins of Modern Japan* and evaluate his argument about Tokugawa-period economic changes.

13. Examine African art from this period. Read William Bascom's *African Art in Cultural Perspective*. What does the art tell you about the societies that produced it?

14. Explore the role of the missionary impulse in Africa.

15. Explore in more detail the impact of European rivalries on African history.

16. Investigate the founding and activities of the Royal African Company.

17. Study African religious beliefs. How did these religious beliefs affect daily life? How did they affect art? How did they affect interaction with Europeans?

AIDS TO AN UNDERSTANDING OF INDIA, EAST ASIA, AND AFRICA DURING THE EARLY MODERN ERA

CHARACTER OF AKBAR THE GREAT MUGHAL
V. A. Smith

Akbar, as seen in middle life, was a man of moderate stature, perhaps five feet seven inches in height, strongly built, neither too slight nor too stout, broad-chested, narrow-waisted, and long-armed. His legs were somewhat bowed inwards from the effect of much riding in boyhood, and when walking he slightly dragged the left leg, as if he were lame, although the limb was sound. His head drooped a little towards the right shoulder. His forehead was broad and open. The nose was of moderate size, rather short, with a bony prominence in the middle, and nostrils dilated as if with anger. A small wart about half the size of a pea which connected the left nostril with the upper lip was considered to be a lucky mark. His black eyebrows were thin, and the Mongolian strain of blood in his veins was indicated by the narrow eyes characteristic of the Tartar, Chinese, and Japanese races. The eyes sparkled brightly and were "vibrant like the sea in sunshine." His complexion, sometimes described by the Indian term "wheat-coloured," was dark rather than fair. His face was clean shaven, except for a small, closely trimmed moustache worn in the fashion adopted by young Turks on the verge of manhood. His hair was allowed to grow, not being clipped close in the ancestral manner. His very loud voice was credited with "a peculiar richness." . . .

Akbar was extremely moderate in his diet, taking but one substantial meal in the day, which was served whenever he called for it, not at any fixed hour. The variety of dishes placed at his disposal was of course great, and they were presented with appropriate magnificence and elaborate precautions against poison. He cared little for flesh food, and gave up the use of it almost entirely in the later years of his life, when he came under Jain influence. . . .

He followed the practice of his family for many generations in consuming both strong drink and various preparations of opium, sometimes to excess. His drinking bouts, naturally, were more frequent while he was young than they were in his more mature years, but it is certain that tolerably often he was "in his cups," as his son puts it. When he had drunk more than was good for him he performed various mad freaks, as when at Agra he galloped the elephant Hawai across the bridge of boats, and at Surat tried to fight his sword. . . .

He took special delight in the practice of mechanical arts with his own hands. We are told that "there is nothing that he does not know how to do, whether matters of war, or of administration, or of any mechanical art. Wherefore he takes particular pleasure in making guns and in founding and modelling cannon." Workshops were maintained on a large scale within the palace enclosure, and were frequently visited by him. He was credited with many inventions and improvements. That side of his character suggests a comparison with Peter the Great. . . .

"A monarch," he said, "should be ever intent on conquest, otherwise his neighbours rise in arms against him. The army should be exercised in warfare, lest from want of training they become self-indulgent." Accordingly he continued to be intent on conquest all his life and to keep his army in constant training. He never attained more than a part of the objective of his ambition, which included the conquest of every part of India besides Central Asia. . . .

In 1582 he resolved to attempt the impossible task of providing all sects in his empire with one universal eclectic religion to which he gave the name of Divine Monotheism. He persuaded himself that he was the vicegerent of the Almighty, empowered to rule the spiritual as well as the temporal concerns of his subjects. That audacious attempt was an utter failure, but Akbar never formally admitted the fact, and to the end of his life he persisted in maintaining the farce of the new religion. From the time he proclaimed that creed he was not a Muslim. The formula of initiation required the categorical apostasy from Islam of the person initiated.

His attitude towards religion expressed the queer mixture in his mind of mysticism, rationalism, superstition, and a profound belief in his own God-given powers. His actions at times gave substantial grounds for the reproach that he was not unwilling to be regarded as a God on earth.

From V. A. Smith, *Akbar the Great Mogul (1542–1605)*, Clarendon Press, 1919. Reprinted by permission of the publisher.

CONFUCIAN CLASSICS AND THE CHINESE EXAMINATION SYSTEM
Matteo Ricci

I think it will be as interesting as it is new to the reader to treat somewhat more fully of this phase of their studies. Confucius, called the Prince of Chinese Philosophers, compiled four volumes of the works of more ancient philosophers and wrote five books of his own. These five he entitled "The Doctrines," and they contain the ethical principles of right living, precepts governing the conduct of political life, customs, and examples of the ancients, their rites and sacrifices, and even samples of their poetry and other subjects of this nature. Besides these five books there is another one composed of the precepts of the great philosopher and of his disciples and compiled without particular arrangement. These are chiefly directions for proper moral proceedings, in the light of human reason, with a view to virtuous conduct on the part of the individual, of the family and of the kingdom in general. This volume, being a summary in excerpts from the four books mentioned, is called the Tetrabiblion. The nine books of Confucius, making up the most ancient of Chinese libraries, of which all others are a development, are written mostly in hieroglyphic characters, and present a collection of moral precepts for the future good and development of the kingdom.

There is a law in the land, handed down from ancient kings and confirmed by the custom of centuries, stating that he who wishes to be learned, and to be known as such, must draw his fundamental doctrine from these same books. In addition to this it is not sufficient for him to follow the general sense of the text, but what is far more difficult, he must be able to write aptly and exactly of every particular doctrine contained in these books. To this end he must commit the entire Tetrabiblion to memory, so as to be a recognized authority thereon. Contrary to what has been stated by some of our writers, there are no schools or public academies in which these books are taught or explained by masters. Each student selects his own master by whom he is instructed in his own home and at his personal expense.

The number of such private teachers, of course, is great, partly because it would be hard for one master to teach many at a time, owing to the difficulty of handling the Chinese characters, and partly because it is an old custom here for each home to have a private school for its own children. At times it happens that tutors, other than the one regularly employed, may be called in, as it would seem, to prevent the custom of bidding for the position from interfering with the interest of their profession.

In the field of philosophy there are three degrees, conferred upon those who pass the written examinations assigned for each degree. The first degree is awarded in the larger cities and in a public academy, by some prominent scholar, appointed by the emperor for that purpose. In virtue of his office this dignitary is known as Tihio, and the first degree, corresponding to our baccalaureate, is called Lieucai. The Tihio visits the various cities of his province in which the degree is to be conferred and for which a triple examination is required. Upon the arrival of this chancellor, as we would call him, the candidates assemble for the examinations. The preliminary examination is conducted by the local teachers who have attained to the baccalaureate and are preparing for a higher degree, and they are paid from the royal treasury for these particular examinations. Anyone may be admitted to the preliminary examinations, and sometimes four or five thousand from a single district will take them. Those who pass the first test are recommended by the teachers to the four city prefects, who are themselves learned men, otherwise they would not be in office. The prefects then select the candidates who are to be presented to the chancellor. Not more than two hundred may be thus presented, and these are chosen for the excellence of their written composition.

The third examination is conducted by the chancellor, himself, and is far more rigid than those preceding it. Of the two hundred admitted to this examination, the twenty or thirty obtaining the highest grades are granted the degree, depending upon the size of the district from which the candidates are drawn. They are then known as academic bachelors, a distinguished class representing the advanced citizenry of their particular town, and their company is cultivated by all who hope to attain to the same dignity. Their particular insignia is an ankle-long gown, a cap, and leggings, which no class other than their own is permitted to wear. They are given seats of honor at the conventions of the magistrates, and with them they may employ the more intimate rites of address which the common people are never permitted to use. In their home cities they enjoy a great many civil privileges and are looked upon as inferior to none, save the chancellor and the four city prefects, nor is it easy for other magistrates to pass judgment upon the cases they present or on charges made against them.

From *China in the Sixteenth Century: The Journals of Matthew Ricci: 1583–1610.* pp. 33–34. Louis J. Gallagher, S.J., trans. Random House, New York, 1953.

TOWN LIFE UNDER THE TOKUGAWA (Genroku Period, 1688–1703)
G. B. Sansom

The life of the townspeople, especially in the Genroku period, judged if not by European practice at least by European standards, appears to have been extremely dissolute; though it must be remembered that their numbers were few in comparison with the industrious millions of peasants, and also that we learn from books and pictures chiefly of their more extravagant amusements. Further, their morality was not based upon religious emotion, nor was it conditioned by fear of divine retribution. In the history of Japanese thought little part is played by the personal sense of sin, which in Western men has engendered puritanical complexes and driven them to extremes of restless inquiry and despair. The Japanese have cared little for abstract ideas of Good and Evil, but they have always been concerned with problems of behaviour, as questions of a man's duty not so much to himself as to the society of which he is a member. It is therefore not surprising that the most influential moralists of the period, notably Yamaga Soko and Ogyu

(Butsu) Sorai, held utilitarian views which might have been stated by Hobbes in his *Leviathan*. In general Chinese and Japanese philosophers have tended to the belief that man's disposition is innately good. They have agreed that he needs guidance, and they have set great store by decorum, but they have mostly reprobated only such actions as entail direct evil consequences to society.

One should bear these considerations in mind when studying the life of the Floating World in Yedo, for—the deplorable fact cannot be concealed—its principal figures were the courtesan and the actor, while among its supernumeraries were the disreputable crowd of pandars and procurers who haunted the gay quarters. There had been since the early days of Yedo, at a place on its outskirts called Yoshiwara (Reedy Plain), a pleasure haunt where the citizens gathered to see plays and dancing; and here prostitutes plied their trade until they were suppressed by the Bakufu. In 1617 an enterprising townsman obtained a licence from the authorities, set up the business again, and succeeded in attracting large numbers of citizens to the quarter. Its name, by a change of ideograph, he had altered to mean Happy Fields; but they were soon deserted owing to the competition of a class of female bath-attendants who came into fashion at this time. The bath-houses became gay resorts, whose stylishly dressed clients, both townsmen and the lower orders of samurai, were entertained by the much bedizened bath-girls. One of the most celebrated of these establishments was in front of the mansion of a great daimyo and this open flaunting of illicit prostitution caused the Bakufu to suppress the bath-girls in 1650. After the great fires of 1657–1658 the Yoshiwara was removed to a different district, where the bath-girls and others assembled. By Genroku it was exceedingly flourishing, and is said to have contained some two thousand courtesans. Known as *Fuyajo* or the Nightless City, it was almost self-contained, since it harboured as well as those ladies a numerous population of their attendants, of dancing and singing girls, jesters and other entertainers, together with a most varied collection of trades-people to supply their needs. Hither resorted not only the young townsmen, but also samurai in disguise, and even high officers of the Shogun or his vassals, while rich merchants were known to give costly, fantastic entertainments within its walls. There thus grew up a distinct town, with its own customs, its own standards of behaviour, and even its own language. In this world of licence and disorder, everything was highly regulated. There was a formal etiquette between a house and its clients. There was a strict hierarchy among the courtesans, whose ranks and appellations were solemnly observed. They were treated with forms of great respect, attended by richly-dressed waiting maids and hedged about by an elaborate ritual. From time to time they made public progress through the streets of the quarter, in stately processions which were eagerly witnessed by thousands of spectators from all parts of the city. Everything seems to have been done to make patrons feel that they were sojourning among people of discreet and delicate sentiments. It was, of course, an essentially sordid business, but it does seem to have been invested with glamour and even a certain elegance. The social side of family life was, probably owing to the subordination of women, undeveloped except in its formal aspects, and the townspeople were debarred from public func-

tions: so that it is perhaps not unnatural that they should have flocked to places where they found light and colour and feminine society in luxurious surroundings. However, that may be, the pleasure quarters were a conspicuous feature of city life, not only in Yedo, but in Kyoto, where there was the famous district of Shimabara, in Osaka, which boasted of its Shin-machi, and in many smaller towns, such as the more important stages on the main highways. Many of them were founded in much earlier times, but it was in Genroku, that, to quote from an eighteenth century work, "their splendour was by day like Paradise and by night like the Palace of the Dragon King." Their prosperity encouraged all the crafts of the entertainer, such as instrumental music, dancing and singing, to say nothing of juggling and buffoonery, while their variegated life attracted artists of a Bohemian temperament. The pleasure quarter offered the most tempting models to a painter, in the movement of crowds, the colour of costumes, and the shapes of women who lived by their beauty; the playwright and the novelist could find there all the tragedy and all the comedy they desired; and since the great courtesans and the leading rakes, their patrons, were known by name to all the gossips in the city, books and pictures which depicted their amours or their adventures had a ready sale.

From G. B. Sansom, *Japan: A Short Cultural History*, rev. ed., Appleton-Century, 1929. Reprinted by permission of the publisher.

THE SLAVE TRADE IN AFRICA
J. D. Fage

The buying and selling of slaves on the coast was a complicated business. In the first place, where African political authority extended over Europeans, slaves could usually not be bought or sold without the permission of the African chief. For example, the chiefs of the tribes at the mouths of the Oil Rivers would not allow trade to begin until duties had been paid. At Whydah on the Slave Coast, European factors were required to purchase a trading licence for each visiting ship. They were then required to buy the king's stock of slaves at a price well above the current market price before they were allowed to complete their cargo with slaves bought from private merchants. In addition, the king levied a tax on the purchase price of every slave bought. Even where the Europeans were not subject to African authority, trade was usually impossible unless the European traders gave substantial and frequent presents to the local chiefs and elders.

There was no trading currency in common use throughout the coastal districts. On the Windward Coast, slaves and European imports were commonly valued in relation to bars of iron; on the Ivory Coast, to pieces of cloth; on the Gold Coast, to gold dust; between Accra and Keta, to cowrie shells; on the Slave Coast, to both iron and copper bars; in the Oil Rivers, to brass basins; in the Cameroons, to pieces of cloth. Iron and copper were used by the Africans for making tools and utensils, and were imported from Europe in standard size bars. It was accepted on the Slave Coast that one iron bar was worth four copper bars. Similarly, Europeans imported cloth in standard lengths. Now, except for cowrie shells and gold dust, these media of exchange were all commodities which could be consumed, and their value varied in accordance with the extent of the need for them. As a consequence, the process of bargaining in the slave trade was apt to be unduly complicated and lengthy. An example may help to make this clear. Let us say that on the Slave Coast a European trader who wanted slaves was doing business with an African who wanted guns. They had to agree on the value of a slave and of a gun in terms of bars, and to do this they needed to take into account not only the relative scarcity or abundance of slaves and guns on the coast at the time, but also the relative scarcity or abundance of iron and copper bars. Where the large trading companies were strongly established, possessing depots in which they kept adequate stocks of the imports most in demand, they tried to fix prices, saying, for example, that the price of a certain kind of gun was so many bars. But these prices could easily be upset by the arrival on the coast of an interloper whose trading might result in a temporary glut either of guns or of bars. In addition, the maintenance of stocks was apt to be a chancy business because African tastes for European goods were apt to change. For example, in one year blue cloth might be in great demand on one part of the coast and quite unsaleable on another only a few miles away, while a year later, for no reason apparent to the Europeans, the position might be reversed.

Once acceptable prices had been agreed upon, the slaves on sale were inspected by a surgeon from the ship or factory, and the old and infirm slaves weeded out. In general only about one-third of the slaves taken by Europeans were women. This was partly because less women were offered for sale, partly because the effects of child-bearing meant that the ages between which women could be considered fit for plantation slavery were more narrowly limited than for men. Men were usually taken between the ages of ten and about thirty-five; women usually only up to the age of twenty-five. The selected slaves were then usually branded with the mark of their purchaser and shipped, or confined within forts or factories awaiting shipment. . . .

The goods brought to West Africa by the European traders varied slightly according to the period, the nationality of the traders, and the place where they were trading, but the following commodities found a pretty steady sale: textiles (woollens and linens manufactured in Europe, cottons manufactured mostly in India until the nineteenth century, and silks manufactured either in Europe or in Asia); all kinds of firearms, powder, and shot; knives and cutlasses; many kinds of European-made ironmongery and hardware; iron, copper, brass, and lead in bar form; spirits (rum, brandy, or gin, according to the country of origin of the trader); and many kinds of provisions.

We do not have enough information to be able to state exactly how many African slaves were carried across the Atlantic to America. However, on the basis of the information we do possess, it seems likely that the number of slaves imported into America, from the time the trade began in the sixteenth century until it was eventually brought to an end in the nineteenth century, was at least fifteen million, and unlikely to have been much greater than twenty million. It should be noted that these figures are for the slaves *landed in America*. The number *leaving Africa* must have been considerably greater, since it was rare for a slave ship to complete a voyage without the death from disease of at least a part of its human cargo. It seems reasonable from what we know of the mortality on slaving voyages to assume that *on an average* at least a sixth of the slaves shipped from Africa never lived to see America. On occasions the mortality was very much higher than this. Thus in all probability, somewhere between eighteen and twenty-four million Africans were carried away from West Africa by the European Slave trade.

It has been stated that the number of slaves imported into America in the sixteenth century was at least 900,000. The subsequent growth of the demand for slaves on the plantations, and the intensive competition between European traders to supply this demand, soon made the sixteenth-century trade seem insignificant. In the seventeenth century the number of slaves reaching America was more than three times as great, at least 2,750,000, or an average of 27,500 a year. The eighteenth-century trade was on an even greater scale, at least 7,000,000 slaves reaching America, or 70,000 a year on the average. During the nineteenth century, the demand for slaves continued to increase at first, and it did not finally cease until by the 1880's all the American nations had at length abolished the status of slavery. The efforts made to stop the trade prevented a steady expansion as in the previous centuries; nevertheless, by the time the trade had finally come to an end, a further 4,000,000 slaves had arrived in America.

From J. D. Fage, *An Introduction to the History of West Africa*, 3rd ed., Cambridge University Press, 1962. Reprinted by permission of the publisher.

ANALYSIS AND INTERPRETATION OF THE READINGS

1. Which of the personality traits attributed to Akbar would be most valuable to him as a ruler?
2. What was the connection between education and the social order in China, judging from the journal of the Jesuit Matteo Ricci?
3. What light does the description of the Japanese "Floating World" of pleasure throw on the relations between the feudal classes and the townsmen?
4. Were any limitations imposed upon the Europeans who traded on the slave coast? If so, what kinds of limitations, and why would they have accepted them?

CHAPTER 22 | The Economy and Society of Early-Modern Europe

CHRONOLOGY

1607	1694	1649
1720	1651	1747
1657	1769	1666
1807		

From the list above, select the correct date for each of the following items:

First English Navigation Act _____

Dissolution of French East India Company _____

Bubonic plague in Seville _____

Founding of the Bank of Sweden _____

Founding of the Bank of England _____

Ending of the slave trade in England _____

South Sea and Mississippi Bubbles _____

Establishment of first English colony in
   North America _____

Road and Bridge Corps of civil engineers
   originated in France _____

Great Fire of London _____

IDENTIFICATIONS

In the blanks, write the appropriate names from the following list:

Fuggers
John Law
Jean Baptiste Colbert
John Wesley

Viscount Charles Townshend
John Kay
Duke of Bridgewater

Inventor of the fly-shuttle _____

Developer of French sugar-producing
   colonies _____

Promoter of the Mississippi
   Company _____

English canal builder _____

German banking house _____

Founder of Methodism _____

Advocate of turnip husbandry _____

You should be able to define or explain each of the following terms:

open-field system
sharecropping
putting-out system
regulated company
joint-stock company

chartered company
"middle passage"
corvée
"deserving" poor

STUDY QUESTIONS

1. How do you explain the relatively late age of marriage in early-modern Europe?
2. What was the purpose of the enclosure movement in agriculture? What were its social effects? How did the movement in England differ from that in France?
3. What innovations contributed to the increasing efficiency of agriculture in the eighteenth century? In which European countries was scientific progress in agriculture most evident?

4. Explain the "putting-out" system that developed in the textile industry. What were its advantages both for entrepreneurs and for workers? What were its disadvantages?
5. What industries other than textiles were developing in rural areas during the time period considered here?
6. What were the obstacles to efficient and economical transportation, and what attempts were made in the eighteenth century to overcome them?
7. What were the causes of the recurrent population crises of the seventeenth and eighteenth centuries?
8. What was the connection between population shifts and changes in agriculture and industry?
9. What factors help explain Europe's unprecedented population increase after 1750?
10. Why are maize and potatoes described as "miracle crops"?
11. What is meant by the term "proto-industrialization"? What were its manifestations in early-modern Europe?
12. Define capitalism. Define mercantilism.
13. What assumptions did mercantilism and capitalism have in common? In what respects did they differ?
14. What was the primary source for the early capital that helped fuel the Commercial Revolution?
15. What advantages did joint-stock companies have over other forms of business organization?
16. What medieval social or institutional patterns were evident in mercantilism?
17. What was the relationship between the Commercial Revolution and overseas colonization?
18. How did Spain's colonial policy illustrate the objectives of mercantilism, and in what respects was its policy deficient?
19. What variations on the mercantilist theme did the Dutch employ, and how successful were they in competition with their rivals?
20. How do you account for the outstanding success of France and England in the age of mercantilism?
21. Why were the growth of banks and improvement in the monetary system essential to the success of the Commercial Revolution?
22. Chartered companies were "an example of the way capitalist and mercantilist interests might coincide." How is this demonstrated by the British and French East India companies?
23. Why were the early English colonial settlements less strictly regulated than the Spanish colonies? Why did English colonial policy change in the late seventeenth century?
24. During the seventeenth and eighteenth centuries what were the most prized agricultural products from America? From East Asia?
25. Explain the notorious "triangular" trade pattern that proved so profitable to British merchants.
26. About how many African slaves were transported from Africa during the history of the slave trade? What percentage of this total came during the eighteenth century? Where did most of these slaves go?
27. How was the concept of "freedom" interpreted in a "society of orders"?
28. What are sumptuary laws? Why were they passed?
29. What legal and economic disabilities rested on the European peasantry? Why were the peasants of western Europe generally more free than those in eastern Europe?
30. Name three European cities that had attained populations of 200,000 or more by 1800.
31. What change in the structure of society, especially in France, is represented by the rise of the *bourgeoisie*?
32. How did the decay of the guild system affect the status of workers?
33. Describe briefly the nature of education during this period.
34. Describe the social functions of Carnival and other such celebrations.

PROBLEMS

1. "The pattern of life for most Europeans centered on the struggle to stay alive." Explore further how this simple fact affected the daily life of Europeans during the period covered in this chapter.
2. Investigate further any of the following topics:
   a. The social and economic effects of the enclosure movement
   b. The role of the potato and maize in improving the European diet
   c. The African slave trade
   d. Canal building in England and France
   e. Living conditions in populous cities
   f. The changing status of labor accompanying the decay of the guilds
   g. Village festivals, folklore, and pastimes
3. Explore the relationship between the Commercial Revolution and the Protestant and Catholic Reformations.
4. In what respects is mercantilism still an influential force?
5. Trace the changes in the structure of society, the changes in beliefs concerning the "social orders," and the relationships between them.
6. Support or refute this proposition: "The Commercial Revolution was of substantial benefit to the inhabitants of western Europe."
7. Read the diary of Samuel Pepys (or selections from it). What sorts of things did he choose to record? What insights do you gain with regard to life in seventeenth-century England?

AIDS TO AN UNDERSTANDING OF THE ECONOMY AND SOCIETY OF EARLY-MODERN EUROPE

SOME RESULTS OF THE ENCLOSURE MOVEMENT IN ENGLAND
Sir Thomas More

But yet this is not only the necessary cause of stealing. There is another, which, as I suppose, is proper and peculiar to you Englishmen alone. What is that, quoth the Cardinal? forsooth my lord (quoth I) your sheep that were wont to be so meek and tame, and so small eaters, now, as I hear say, be become so great devourers and so wild, that they eat up, and swallow down the very men themselves. They consume, destroy, and devour whole fields, houses, and cities. For look in what parts of the realm doth grow the finest and therefore dearest wool, there noblemen and gentlemen, yea and certain abbots, holy men no doubt, not contenting themselves with the yearly revenues and profits, that were wont to grow to their forefathers and predecessors of their lands, nor being content that they live in rest and pleasure nothing profiting, yea much annoying the weal public, leave no ground for tillage, they inclose all into pastures; they throw down houses; they pluck down towns, and leave nothing standing, but only the church to be made a sheep-house. And as though you lost no small quantity of grounds by forests, chases, lawns, and parks, those good holy men turn all dwelling-places and all glebeland into desolation and wilderness. Therefore that one covetous and insatiable cormorant and very plague of his native country may compass about and inclose many thousand acres of ground together within one pale or hedge, the husbandmen be thrust out of their own, or else either by cunning and fraud, or by violent oppression they be put besides it, or by wrongs and injuries they be so wearied, that they be compelled to sell all: by one means therefore or by other, either by hook or crook they must needs depart away, poor, silly, wretched souls, men, women, husbands, wives, fatherless children, widows, woeful mothers, with their young babes, and their whole household small in substance and much in number, as husbandry requireth many hands. Away they trudge, I say, out of their known and accustomed houses, finding no place to rest in all. All their household stuff, which is very little worth, though it might well abide the sale: yet being suddenly thrust out, they be constrained to sell it for a thing of nought. And when they have wandered abroad till that be spent, what can they then else do but steal, and then justly pardy be hanged, or else go about a begging.

From Sir Thomas More, *Utopia*, Maurice Adams ed.

POLITICAL CONSEQUENCES OF THE GROWTH OF BANKING
R. H. Tawney

Nourished by the growth of peaceful commerce, the financial capitalism of the age fared not less sumptuously, if more dangerously, at the courts of princes. Mankind, it seems, hates nothing so much as its own prosperity. Menaced with an accession of riches which would lighten its toil, it makes haste to redouble its labors, and to pour away the perilous stuff, which might deprive of plausibility the complaint that it is poor. Applied to the arts of peace, the new resources commanded by Europe during the first half of the sixteenth century might have done something to exorcise the specters of pestilence and famine, and to raise the material fabric of civilization to undreamed-of heights. Its rulers, secular and ecclesiastical alike, thought otherwise. When pestilence and famine were ceasing to be necessities imposed by nature, they reestablished them by political art.

The sluice which they opened to drain away each new accession of superfluous wealth was war. "Of all birds," wrote the sharpest pen of the age, "the eagle alone has seemed to wise men the type of royalty—not beautiful, not musical, not fit for food, but carnivorous, greedy, hateful to all, the curse of all, and, with its great powers of doing harm, surpassing them in its desire of doing it." The words of Erasmus, uttered in 1517, were only too prophetic. For approximately three-quarters both of the sixteenth and of the seventeenth centuries, Europe tore itself to pieces. In the course of the conflict the spiritual fires of Renaissance and Reformation alike were trampled out beneath the feet of bravos as malicious and mischievous as the vain, bloodyminded and futile generals who strut and posture, to the hateful laughter of Thersites, in the most despairing of Shakespeare's tragedies. By the middle of the sixteenth century the English Government, after an orgy of debasement and confiscation, was in a state of financial collapse, and by the end of it Spain, the southern Netherlands including Antwerp, and a great part of France, including the financial capital of southern Europe, Lyons, were ruined. By the middle of the seventeenth century wide tracts of Germany were a desert, and by the end of it the French finances had relapsed into worse confusion than that from which they had been temporarily rescued by the genius of Colbert. The victors compared their position with that of the vanquished, and congratulated themselves on their spoils. It rarely occurred to them to ask what it would have been, had there been neither victors nor vanquished, but only peace.

It is possible that the bankruptcies of Governments have, on the whole, done less harm to mankind than their ability to raise loans, and the mobilization of economic power on a scale unknown before armed the fierce nationalism of the age with a weapon more deadly than gunpowder and cannon. The centralized States which were rising in the age of Renaissance were everywhere faced with a desperate financial situation. It sprang from the combination of modern administrative and military methods with medieval systems of finance. They entrusted to bureaucracies work which, if done at all, had formerly been done as an incident of tenure, or by boroughs and guilds; officials had to be paid. They were constantly at war; and the new technique of war, involving the use of masses of professional infantry and artillery—which Rabelais said was invented by the inspiration of the devil, as a counterpoise to the invention of printing inspired by God—was making it, as after 1870, a highly capitalized industry. Government after Government, undeterred, with rare exceptions, by the disasters of its neighbors, trod a familiar round of expedients, each of which was more disastrous than the last. They hoarded treasure, only to see the accumulations of a thrifty Henry VII or Frederick III dissipated by a Henry VIII or a Maximilian. They debased the currency and ruined trade. They sold offices, or established monopolies, and crushed the taxpayer beneath a load of indirect taxation. They plundered the Church, and spent gorgeously as income property which should have been treated as capital. They parted with Crown estates, and left an insoluble problem to their successors.

These agreeable devices had, however, obvious limits. What remained, when they were exhausted, was the money-market, and to the rulers of the money-market sooner or later all States came. Their dependence on the financier was that of an Ismail or an Abdul, and its results were not less disastrous. Naturally, the City interest was one of the great Powers of Europe. Publicists might write that the new Messiah was the Prince, and reformers that the Prince was Pope. But behind Prince and Pope alike, financing impartially Henry VII, Edward VI and Elizabeth, Francis, Charles and Philip, stood in the last resort a little German banker, with branches in every capital in Europe, who played in the world of finance the part of the *condottieri* in war, and represented in the economic sphere the morality typified in that of politics by Machiavelli's Prince. Compared with these financial dynasties, Hapsburgs, Valois and Tudors were puppets dancing on wires held by a money-power to which political struggles were irrelevant except as an opportunity for gain.

Adam Smith on the Principle of Mercantilism

That wealth consists in money, or in gold and silver, is a popular notion which naturally arises from the double function of money as the instrument of commerce, and as the measure of value. In consequence of its being the instrument of commerce, when we have money we can more readily obtain whatever else we have occasion for, than by means of any other commodity. The great affair, we always find, is to get money. When that is obtained, there is no difficulty in making any subsequent purchase. In consequence of its being the measure of value, we estimate that of all other commodities by the quantity of money which they will exchange for. We say of a rich man that he is worth a great deal, and of a poor man that he is worth very little money. A frugal man, or a man eager to be rich, is said to love money; and a careless, a generous, or a profuse man, is said to be indifferent about it. To grow rich is to get money; and wealth and money, in short, are, in common language, considered as in every respect synonymous.

It is not because wealth consist more essential in money than in goods, that the merchant finds it generally more easy to buy goods with money, than to buy money with goods; but because money is the known and established instrument of commerce, for which every thing is readily given in exchange, but which is not always with equal readiness to be got in exchange for every thing. The greater part of goods besides are more perishable than money, and he may frequently sustain a much greater loss by keeping them. When his goods are upon hand too, he is more liable to such demands for money as he may not be able to answer, than when he has got their price in his coffers. Over and above all this, his profit arises more directly from selling than from buying, and he is upon all these accounts generally much more anxious to exchange his goods for money, than his money for goods. But though a particular merchant, with abundance of goods in his warehouse, may sometimes be ruined by not being able to sell them in time, a nation or country is not liable to the same accident. The whole capital of a merchant frequently consists in perishable goods designed for purchasing money. But it is but a very small part of the annual produce of the land and labour of a country which can ever be destined for purchasing gold and silver from their neighbours. The far greater part is circulated and consumed among themselves; and even of the surplus which is sent abroad, the greater part is generally destined for the purchase of other foreign goods. Though gold and silver, therefore, could not be had in exchange for the goods destined to purchase them, the nation would not be ruined. It might, indeed, suffer some loss and inconveniency, and be forced upon some of those expedients which are necessary for supplying the place of money. The annual produce of its land and labour, however, would be the same, or very nearly the same, as usual, because the same, or very nearly the same consumable capital would be employed in maintaining it. And though goods do not always draw money so readily as money draws goods, in the long-run they draw it more necessarily than even it draws them. Goods can serve many other purposes besides purchasing money, but money can serve no other purpose besides purchasing goods. Money, therefore, necessarily runs after goods, but goods do not always or necessarily run after money. The man who buys, does not always mean to sell again, but frequently to use or to consume; whereas he who sells, always means to buy again. The one may frequently have done the whole, but the other can never have done more than the one-half of his business. It is not for its own sake that men desire money, but for the sake of what they can purchase with it.

Life in Sixteenth-Century England: As Described by Erasmus

. . . I am frequently astonished and grieved to think how it is that England has been now for so many years troubled by a continual pestilence, especially by a deadly sweat, which appears in a great measure to be peculiar to your country. I have read how a city was once delivered from a plague by a change in the houses, made at the suggestion of a philosopher. I am inclined to think that this, also, must be the deliverance for England.

First of all, Englishmen never consider the aspect of their doors or windows; next, their chambers are built in such a way as to admit of no ventilation. Then a great part of the walls of the house is occupied with glass casements, which admit light but exclude the air, and yet they let in the draught through holes and corners, which is often pestilential and stagnates there. The floors are, in general, laid with white clay, and are covered with rushes, occasionally renewed, but so imperfectly that the bottom layer is left undisturbed, sometimes for twenty years, harboring expectorations, vomitings, the leakage of dogs and men, ale droppings, scraps of fish, and other abominations not fit to be mentioned. Whenever the weather changes a vapor is exhaled, which I consider very detrimental to health. I may add that England is not only everywhere surrounded by sea, but is, in many places, swampy and marshy, intersected by salt rivers, to say nothing of salt provisions, in which the common people take so much delight. I am confident the island would be much more salubrious if the use of rushes were abandoned, and if the rooms were built in such a way as to be exposed to the sky on two or three sides, and all the windows so built as to be opened or closed at once, and so completely closed as not to admit the foul air through chinks; for as it is beneficial to health to admit the air, so it is equally beneficial at times to exclude it. The common people laugh at you if you complain of a cloudy or foggy day. Thirty years ago, if ever I entered a room which had not been occupied for some months, I was sure to take a fever. More moderation in diet, and especially in the use of salt meats, might be of service; more particularly were public officers appointed to see the streets cleaned from mud and filth, and the suburbs kept in better order. . . .

From E. P. Cheyney, *Readings in English History*, New York: Ginn and Company, 1908, pp. 316–17. Reprinted by permission of the publisher.

ANALYSIS AND INTERPRETATION OF THE READINGS

1. Did Sir Thomas More conceive of the enclosure movement as an economic problem or a moral problem?
2. What did R. H. Tawney mean by saying "Mankind, it seems, hates nothing so much as its own prosperity"?
3. Do you think Tawney exaggerated when he accused the bankers of the sixteenth and seventeenth centuries of so great a responsibility for the growth of militarism?
4. According to Adam Smith, why is it that "money . . . necessarily runs after good, but goods do not always or necessarily run after money"?

CHAPTER 23 | The Age of Absolutism (1660–1789)

IDENTIFICATIONS

In the blank after each description, write the correct name selected from the list below:

James I	Frederick William I
Charles I	Frederick II
Charles II	Maria Theresa
James II	Joseph II
Louis XIV	Peter the Great
Louis XV	Catherine the Great
William of Orange	Robert Walpole
Jean Bodin	Emelyan Pugachev
Elector Frederick William	George III
Hugo Grotius	Thaddeus Kosciuszko

1. This Habsburg ruler's 1789 "Edict on Idle Institutions" closed thousands of monastic houses.

_____

2. He cut off the beards of his subjects, annihilated their self-government, published a book of manners, and carried his country to the shores of the Baltic, all in the name of its westernization.

_____

3. His violation of Parliamentary Acts dealing with Catholics and his unexpected son by his second wife helped bring on the Glorious Revolution and make him the last Stuart king.

_____

4. Whether he said it or not, the phrase *"L'état, c'est moi"* perfectly expressed this monarch's conception of his proper authority.

_____

5. This Dutch prince, in accepting the offer of the English throne, acknowledged the supremacy of Parliament.

_____

6. An "enlightened absolutist" who corresponded with French philosophers, this German-born empress helped westernize her country but did little to relieve the woes of its peasants.

_____

7. A cynical contemporary remarked of this ruler's reluctance to share in the dismemberment of Poland: "She weeps, but she takes her share."

_____

8. This political leader, called Britain's "first prime minister," was important in developing the cabinet system of parliamentary government.

_____

9. Self-declared "first servant of the state," this industrious despot built the most efficient bureaucracy in Europe and involved his country in a series of wars.

_____

10. Witty, sensuous, and dissembling, this monarch by his policies sowed the whirlwind his more stubborn brother reaped in 1688.

_____

11. Claiming to be Tsar Peter III, he led an unsuccessful peasant-serf revolt that stiffened the absolutist tendencies of the empress Catherine.

_____

12. His determination to "be king" involved him in struggles with Parliament and contributed to England's loss of its most valuable overseas colonies.

_____

13. He was a veteran of the American War of Independence, but his efforts to free Poland from foreign domination were crushed in 1794–1795.

_____

Select the letter most appropriate for completion of each of the following statements:

_____ Bishop Boussuet's *Politics Drawn from the Very Words of Scripture*: (a) proclaimed the doctrine of papal supremacy; (b) traced the origin of governments to a social contract; (c) asserted that kings ruled by divine right; (d) claimed that the king was answerable to no one, not even to God.

_____ The French Estates General: (a) had powers similar to those of the British Parliament; (b) were large estates owned by the royal family; (c) were abolished by Louis XIV; (d) did not meet between 1614 and 1789.

_____ By revoking the Edict of Nantes in 1685, Louis XIV: (a) established religious toleration in France; (b) removed the disabilities imposed on Catholics; (c) demonstrated a statesmanship that ensured the loyalty of all his subjects; (d) contributed to industrial progress in rival Protestant countries by driving large numbers of Huguenots out of France.

_____ To finance his projects, Tsar Peter the Great laid the heaviest exactions upon: (a) peasants; (b) the Church; (c) the nobles; (d) bankers and industrialists.

_____ The Eurocentric world view of Peter the Great is most evident in his: (a) democratic reforms; (b) abolition of serfdom; (c) pacific relations with his western neighbors; (d) military conquests.

_____ The Clarendon Code: (a) was broken by French cryptographers during the War of the Spanish Succession; (b) penalized English Catholics and Protestant dissenters; (c) prescribed the public behavior of the English aristocracy; (d) was abolished by King Charles I.

_____ John Locke, in his *Two Treatises of Civil Government*, declared that the right to life, liberty, and property was derived from: (a) the law of nature; (b) the Bible; (c) custom; (d) acts of the legislature.

_____ The "diplomatic revolution" of 1756: (a) brought a rapprochement between France and Austria; (b) overthrew the Habsburg monarchy; (c) created an international peace-keeping organization; (d) pitted Prussia against Great Britain.

You should be able to place in context or define each of the following:

"Sun King"	*streltsy*
intendants	*boyar*
taille	Tories
parlements	Whigs
Junkers	Bill of Rights (English)
Cossacks	*asiento*

STUDY QUESTIONS

1. For at least a century before the reign of Louis XIV, what trends in Europe had been preparing the way for monarchical absolutism?
2. Explain the relationship between the growth of absolutism and the "iron century" in Europe.
3. What factors, if any, limited the exercise of complete absolutism?
4. What elements within European states were most likely to oppose absolutism? What tactics did the rulers use in dealing with these elements?
5. Describe Louis XIV's use of theater to centralize state power in the royal person.
6. What did the Quietists and the Jansenists teach? Why did Louis XIV consider these groups a threat? How did he deal with that threat?
7. How did Colbert's policies as finance minister illustrate the objectives of mercantilism?
8. What aspect of Colbert's reform program was most successful? Why? Did his sovereign master help or hinder its success?
9. What were the difficulties that blocked the establishment of absolutism in Germany? Did these difficulties discourage the various princes from trying?
10. By what instruments did Frederick William, the "Great Elector," make Brandenburg-Prussia a strongly centralized state?
11. Which elements of society under absolutist regimes were best able to retain their privileges in succeeding eras?
12. How did the absolutism of Peter the Great (Tsar Peter I) differ from that of his western European counterparts?
13. Describe some of the outward displays of monarchical authority European rulers used to illustrate their ideas of royal authority.
14. Both Charles II and his brother James II favored absolute rule. Why did revolution come under James rather than under Charles?
15. How did the "Glorious Revolution" of 1688 and its aftermath ensure that the English monarchy would henceforth be limited?
16. What aspects or consequences of the Revolution of 1688 could be considered as less than "glorious"?

17. On what grounds did John Locke establish the right of revolution? Why were his theories particularly useful to the leaders of the English Revolution of 1688?

18. What is meant by the emergence of a "state system"? How did this differ from what preceded it?

19. The growth of foreign ministries and embassies in European capitals reflected a desire to achieve international stability. Why was diplomacy also "a weapon in the armory of the absolutist state"?

20. How was the character of warfare changing during this period?

21. What wars resulted from Louis XIV's threat to the European balance of power?

22. What were the stakes at issue in the War of the Spanish Succession?

23. Summarize the provisions of the Treaty of Utrecht of 1713. What particular advantages accrued to the British?

24. Explain the term "enlightened absolutism." How did it differ from its predecessor? To what extent did the absolutism of eighteenth-century rulers become enlightened?

25. Why did the Catholic rulers Maria Theresa and Joseph II enact measures restricting the liberties of the Church?

26. Why was Catherine the Great able to establish a more nearly total absolutism in Russia than were contemporary Habsburg rulers in Austria?

27. How did the role of the English gentry in local government differ from that of the Continental aristocracy? By what means did they maintain their preponderant influence in the central government of England during the eighteenth century?

28. What significant shift in the European balance of power occurred in the second half of the eighteenth century? What brought about this shift?

29. Summarize the provisions of the Treaty of Paris of 1763.

30. What is the significance of the Treaty of Paris signed by the British in 1783?

31. Although seemingly essential to the maintenance of a European balance of power, Poland was unable to retain its independent existence. Explain why.

PROBLEMS

1. A longing for stability after exhausting crises and conflicts helps explain popular support of, or tolerance for, absolutist rulers. Does the rise of totalitarian regimes in our own day offer a parallel? Develop this theme as concretely as you can, making reference both to historical precedents and contemporary affairs.

2. The year is 1689. You are twenty years old and live in London. How does the prospect before you differ from the one that would confront you if you were living in Moscow?

3. To what extent was the English Glorious Revolution a conservative revolution? To what extent is it appropriate to call it a "revolution" at all?

4. Make a critique of "enlightened absolutism" as exemplified by the personality, character, and rule of Frederick the Great.

5. Study the career of Catherine the Great and assess the effects of her rule.

AIDS TO AN UNDERSTANDING OF THE AGE OF ABSOLUTISM

THE THEORY OF DIVINE RIGHT: From *Politics Drawn From the Holy Scriptures*
Bishop Bossuet

There are four qualities essential to royal authority. First, the royal authority is sacred; second, it is paternal; third, it is absolute; fourth, it is submitted to reason. . . .

Thus, as we have seen, the royal throne is not the throne of a man, but the throne of God himself. "Jehovah hath chosen Solomon my son to sit upon the throne of the kingdom of Jehovah over Israel" (I Chronicles 28:5). . . .

It appears from all this that the person of kings is sacred, and that to make an attempt on their lives is a sacrilege.

God causes them to be anointed by his prophets with a sacred unction, in the same way that he causes pontiffs and his ministry to be anointed.

But even without the exterior application of this unction, they are sacred by their charge, being representatives of the divine majesty, deputed by his providence to the execution of his designs. . . .

St. Paul, after having said that the prince is the minister of God, concludes thus: "Wherefore ye must needs be in subjection, not only because of the wrath, but also for conscience' sake" (Romans 13:5). . . .

And again: "Servants, obey in all things your masters according to the flesh. . . . And whatsoever ye do, do it heartily, as to the Lord, and not unto men" (Colossians 3:22–3). . . .

If the apostle speaks thus of servitude, an unnatural state, what ought we to think of legitimate subjection to princes and magistrates who are the protectors of public liberty. . . .

Even when princes do not do their duty, we must respect their office and ministry. "Servants, be subject to your masters with all fear; not only to the good and gentle, but also to the froward" (I Peter 2:18).

There is then something religious in the respect we pay to the prince. The service of God and the respect for kings are one and the same thing; and St. Peter puts these two duties together: "Fear God. Honour the king" (I Peter 2:17). . . .

However, because their power comes from above, princes must not think that they are free to use it at their pleasure; rather must they use it with fear and discretion, as a thing which comes to them from God, and of which God will demand a strict account. . . .

Kings should therefore tremble while using their God-given power, and think what a horrible sacrilege it is to misuse it. . . .

The royal authority is absolute.

In order to render this term odious and insupportable, some people try to confuse absolute and arbitrary government. But there is nothing more different, as we shall see when we speak of justice.

The prince is accountable to no one for what he orders. . . .

We must obey princes as justice itself, without which there would be no order nor purpose in human affairs.

They are gods, and participate in the divine independence. . . .

Whoever becomes a sovereign prince, holds in his hands everything together, both the sovereign authority to judge, and all the forces of the state. . . .

The end of government is the good and conservation of the state. . . .

The good constitution of the body of the state consists in two things: in religion and justice: these are the interior and constitutive principles of states. By the one, we render to God what is due to him; and by the other, we render to men what belongs to them. . . .

The prince must employ his authority to destroy false religions in his state. . . .

He is the protector of the public peace which depends upon religion; and he must sustain his throne, of which it is the foundation, as we have seen. Those who would not suffer the prince to act strictly in matters of religion because religion ought to be free, are in impious error. Otherwise it would be necessary to suffer, among his subjects and in the whole state, idolatry, Mohammedanism, Judaism, every false religion, blasphemy, even atheism, and the greatest crimes, would go unpunished. . . .

From Franklin L. Baumer, *Main Currents of Western Thought*, 2nd ed., New York: Alfred A. Knopf Inc., 1964.

The Political Philosophy of a Russian Absolutist: The "Instructions" of Catherine the Great

6. Russia is a European State.

7. This is clearly demonstrated by the following Observations: The Alterations which *Peter the Great* undertook in Russia succeeded with the greater Ease, because the Manners, which prevailed at that Time, and had been introduced amongst us by a Mixture of different Nations, and the Conquest of foreign Territories, were quite unsuitable to the Climate. *Peter the First*, by introducing the Manners and Customs of Europe among the European People in his Dominions, found at that Time such Means as even he himself was not sanguine enough to expect. . . .

9. The Sovereign is absolute; for there is no other Authority but that which centers in his single Person, that can act with a Vigour proportionate to the Extent of such a vast Dominion.

10. The Extent of the Dominion requires an absolute Power to be vested in that Person who rules over it. It is expedient so to be, that the quick Dispatch of Affairs, sent from distant Parts, might make ample Amends for the Delay occasioned by the great Distance of the Places. . . .

13. What is the true End of Monarchy? Not to deprive People of their natural Liberty; but to correct their Actions, in order to attain the *supreme Good*.

14. The Form of Government, therefore, which best attains this End, and at the same Time sets less Bounds than others to natural Liberty, is that which coincides with the Views and Purposes of rational Creatures, and answers the End, upon which we ought to fix a steadfast Eye in the Regulations of civil Polity.

15. The Intention and the End of Monarchy, is the Glory of the Citizens, of the State, and of the Sovereign.

16. But, from this Glory, a Sense of Liberty arises in a people governed by a Monarch; which may produce in these States as much Energy in transacting the most important Affairs, and may contribute as much to the Happiness of the Subjects, as even Liberty itself. . . .

33. The Laws ought to be so framed, as to secure the Safety of every Citizen as much as possible.

34. The Equality of the Citizens consists in this; that they should all be subject to the same Laws.

35. This Equality requires Institutions so well adapted, as to prevent the Rich from oppressing those who are not so wealthy as themselves, and converting all the Charges and Employments intrusted to them as Magistrates only, to their own private Emolument.

36. General or political Liberty does not consist in that licentious Notion, *That a Man may do whatever he pleases.*

37. In a State or Assemblage of People that live together in a Community, where there are Laws, Liberty can only consist *in doing that which every One ought to do, and not to be constrained to do that which One ought not to do.*

38. A Man ought to form in his own Mind an exact and clear Idea of what Liberty is. *Liberty is the Right of doing whatsoever the Laws allow:* And if any one Citizen could do what the Laws forbid, there would be no more Liberty; because others would have an equal Power of doing the same. . . .

96. Good Laws keep strictly a just Medium: They do not always inflict pecuniary, nor always subject Malefactors to corporal, Punishment.

All Punishments, by which the human Body might be maimed, ought to be abolished. . . .

240. It is better to *prevent* Crimes, than to *punish* them.

241. To *prevent* Crimes is the *Intention,* and the *End* of every *good* Legislation; which is nothing more than the Art of

conducting People to the *greatest* Good, or to leave the least Evil possible amongst them, if it should prove impracticable to *exterminate* the whole. . . .

243. Would you *prevent* Crimes? order it *so*, That the laws might rather favour every *Individual*, than any particular Rank of Citizens, in the Community . . .

245. Would you prevent Crimes? order it so, that the *Light of Knowledge may be diffused* among the people. . . .

248. Finally, the *most sure*, but, at the same Time, the *most difficult* Expedient to mend the Morals of the People, is a perfect System of Education.

From W. F. Reddaway, *Documents of Catherine the Great*, Cambridge University Press, 1931. Reprinted by permission of the publisher.

THE LIBERAL POLITICAL THEORY OF JOHN LOCKE: From *Concerning Civil Government*

But though this be a state of liberty, yet it is not a state of licence; though man in that state have an uncontrollable liberty to dispose of his person or possessions, yet he has not liberty to destroy himself, or so much as any creature in his possession, but where some nobler use than its bare preservation calls for it. The state of Nature has a law of Nature to govern it, which obliges every one, and reason, which is that law, teaches all mankind who will but consult it, that being all equal and independent, no one ought to harm another in his life, health, liberty or possessions; for men being all the workmanship of one omnipotent and infinitely wise Maker; all the servants of one sovereign Master, sent into the world by His order and about his business; they are His property, whose workmanship they are made to last during His, not one another's pleasure. And, being furnished with like faculties, sharing all in one community of Nature, there cannot be supposed any such subordination among us that may authorise us to destroy one another, as if we were made for one another's uses, as the inferior ranks of creatures are for ours. Every one as he is bound to preserve himself, and not to quit his station wilfully, so by the like reason, when his own preservation comes not in competition, ought he as much as he can to preserve the rest of mankind, and not unless it be to do justice on an offender, take away or impair the life, or what tends to the preservation of the life, the liberty, health, limb, or goods of another.

And that all men may be restrained from invading others' rights, and from doing hurt to one another, and the law of Nature be observed, which willeth the peace and preservation of all mankind, the execution of the law of Nature is in that state put into every man's hands, whereby every one has a right to punish the transgressors of that law to such a degree as may hinder its violation. For the law of Nature would, as all other laws that concern men in this world, be in vain if there were nobody that in the state of Nature had a power to execute that law, and thereby preserve the innocent and restrain offenders; and if any one in the state of Nature may punish another for any evil he has done, every one may do so. For in that state of perfect equality, where naturally there is no superiority or jurisdiction of one over another, what any may do in prosecution of that law, every one must needs have a right to do.

• • •

Though the legislative, whether placed in one or more, whether it be always in being or only by intervals, though it be the supreme power in every commonwealth, yet, first, it is not, nor can possibly be, absolutely arbitrary over the lives and fortunes of the people. For it being but the joint power of every member of the society given up to that person or assembly which is legislator, it can be no more than those persons had in a state of Nature before they entered into society, and gave it up to the community. For nobody can transfer to another more power than he has in himself, and nobody has an absolute arbitrary power over himself, or over any other, to destroy his own life, or take away the life or property of another. A man, as has been proved, cannot subject himself to the arbitrary power of another; and having, in the state of Nature, no arbitrary power over the life, liberty, or possession of another, but only so much as the law of Nature gave him for the preservation of himself and the rest of mankind, this is all he doth, or can give up to the commonwealth, and by it to the legislative power, so that the legislative can have no more than this. Their power in the utmost bounds of it is limited to the public good of the society. It is a power that hath no other end but preservation, and therefore can never have a right to destroy, enslave, or designedly to impoverish the subjects; the obligations of the law of Nature cease not in society, but only in many cases are drawn closer, and have, by human laws, known penalties annexed to them to enforce their observation. Thus the law of Nature stands as an eternal rule of all men, legislators as well as others. The rules that they make for other men's actions must, as well as their own and other men's actions, be conformable to the law of Nature—*i.e.*, to the will of God, of which that is a declaration, and the fundamental law of Nature being the preservation of mankind, no human sanction can be good or valid against it.

From John Locke, *Two Treatises on Civil Government*.

EXTRACTS FROM THE ENGLISH BILL OF RIGHTS

1. That the pretended power of suspending of laws, or for the execution of laws, by regal authority, without consent of Parliament is illegal.

2. That the pretended power of dispensing with laws, or the execution of laws, by regal authority, as it hath been assumed and exercised of late, is illegal.

3. That the commission for erecting the late Court of Commissioners for Ecclesiastical Causes, and all other commissions and courts of like nature, are illegal and pernicious.

4. That levying money for or to the use of the Crown, by pretence of prerogative, without grant of Parliament, for longer time, or in other manner than the same is or shall be granted, is illegal.

5. That it is the right of the subjects to petition the King, and all commitments and prosecutions for such petitioning are illegal.

6. That the raising or keeping a standing army within the kingdom in time of peace, unless it be with consent of Parliament, is against law.

7. That the subjects which are Protestants may have arms for their defence, suitable to their conditions, and as allowed by law.

8. That election of Members of Parliament ought to be free.

9. That the freedom of speech, and debates or proceedings in Parliament, ought not to be impeached or questioned in any court or place out of Parliament.

10. That excessive bail ought not to be required, nor excessive fines imposed; nor cruel and unusual punishments inflicted.

11. That jurors ought to be duly impanelled and returned, and jurors which pass upon men in trials for high treason ought to be freeholders.

12. That all grants and promises of fines and forfeitures of particular persons before conviction, are illegal and void.

13. And that for redress of all grievances, and for the amending, strengthening, and preserving of the laws, Parliaments ought to be held frequently. . . .

From John Fairburn, ed., *Magna Charta, the Bill of Rights; with the Petition of Right* . . .

ANALYSIS AND INTERPRETATION OF THE READINGS

1. What restraints on royal power does Bossuet postulate? Would these restraints be very effective? Why or why not?

2. According to Bossuet, what are the proper relations between church and state?

3. According to Locke, in what ways is the law-making power limited in political society?

4. What are the implications of the Empress Catherine's definition of liberty?

5. Why has the English Bill of Rights come to be regarded as an essential part of the British Constitution?

6. Compare the English Bill of Rights with the American Bill of Rights.

The Scientific Revolution and Enlightenment

IDENTIFICATIONS

Gotthold Lessing
William Harvey
Marquis de Condorcet
Henry Fielding
Karl von Linné (Linnaeus)
Wolfgang Amadeus Mozart
Jean-Baptiste Molière
Claudio Monteverdi

Francis Bacon
Cesare Beccaria
Edward Gibbon
Alexander Pope
René Descartes
Antoine Lavoisier
Antoine Watteau

From the list above, write in the blanks the names of the persons associated with the following items:

"I think, therefore I am" _____

Novum Organum _____

Correct description of
   circulation of the blood _____

Essay on Man _____

*Outline of the Progress
   of the Human Mind* _____

*Decline and Fall
   of the Roman Empire* _____

Nathan the Wise _____

On Crimes and Punishment _____

Law of the conservation of mass _____

Classes, genera, species _____

Tartuffe _____

Rococo style of painting _____

Tom Jones _____

Early Italian opera _____

The Magic Flute _____

Select the appropriate letter for completion of each of the following:

_____ 1. Boyle's law: (a) explained the circulation of the blood in animals; (b) described the behavior of gases under pressure; (c) stated the principle of the conservation of energy; (d) was a significant penal reform.

_____ 2. The discoverer of the cellular structure of plants was: (a) Robert Boyle; (b) Marcello Malpighi; (c) Jan Swammerdam; (d) Robert Hooke.

_____ 3. In formulating his law of universal gravitation, Newton drew most heavily on the work of: (a) Aristotle and Ptolemy; (b) the late medieval scholastics; (c) Bacon and Descartes; (d) Copernicus, Kepler, and Galileo.

_____ 4. Enlightenment thinkers treasured the "scientific method" because they believed it would: (a) lead to the discovery of general laws applicable to all phenomena, including human nature and society; (b) make possible more accurate classification of organisms; (c) provide new products and new sources of energy; (d) free mankind from all religious beliefs.

_____ 5. In his *Spirit of Laws*, Montesquieu advocated: (a) replacing monarchies with republics; (b) keeping human law in conformity with divine law; (c) resistance to any change in established laws; (d) the separation of governmental powers.

_____ 6. The prime intent of the authors of the French *Encyclopedia* was: (a) to provide a useful reference work; (b) to enhance France's literary reputation; (c) to promote the advancement and the understanding of science; (d) to foster an attitude of cynicism.

_____ 7. The Enlightenment's most extreme exponent of the idea of progress was: (a) Francis Bacon; (b) Sir Isaac Newton; (c) Diderot; (d) Condorcet.

_____ 8. Among philosophers of the Enlightenment the outstanding skeptic was: (a) Hume; (b) Condorcet; (c) Voltaire; (d) Gibbon.

_____ 9. The writer most influential in reforming penal codes was: (a) Smith; (b) Diderot; (c) Moses Mendelssohn; (d) Beccaria.

_____ 10. An outstanding advance in the field of medicine in the eighteenth century was: (a) the discovery of penicillin; (b) the discovery of veins and arteries; (c) the introduction of inoculation and vaccination; (d) the abandonment of blood-letting as a remedy.

_____ 11. Alexander Pope: (a) rejected Newtonian physics; (b) epitomized the classicism of the Augustan school; (c) was the greatest English prose writer of his century; (d) invented the novel.

_____ 12. A significant difference between Bach and Handel as composers was: (a) one was Baroque, the other Classical; (b) they lived during different centuries; (c) Bach composed only instrumental music while Handel wrote also for voices; (d) Handel's works reached a wider audience during his lifetime.

You should be able to explain each of the following terms:

Cartesianism	general will
inductive method	*laissez-faire*
philosophes	Leyden jar
tabula rasa	phlogiston theory
empiricism	Palladian revival
Écrasez l'infâme	Augustans

STUDY QUESTIONS

1. What do the authors of the textbook mean by a change in the "climate of opinion" in Western Europe?

2. What three significant changes in the character or direction of European thought were evident before the close of the seventeenth century?

3. What was the relationship between the scientific revolution and the age of Enlightenment? What time periods are assigned to each?

4. How did the astronomical discoveries of Kepler and Galileo prepare the way for an intellectual revolution?

5. What assumptions were shared by Bacon the empiricist and Descartes the rationalist? How did the differences in their philosophies affect the subsequent development of science?

6. What dualism was inherent in Descartes's conception of reality?

7. What is the justification for considering Sir Isaac Newton "the greatest scientist of all time"?

8. Why would historians of science consider Newton's law of gravity to be "the most stupendous single achievement of the human mind"?

9. What were the three basic premises of the thought of the Enlightenment?

10. Describe the religious belief known as Deism. In what respects does it illustrate the Enlightenment's climate of opinion? Why was it attractive to so many Enlightenment thinkers?

11. Enlightenment thinkers inclined to the belief that the science of human nature could be "reduced to a few clear points." What prompted such optimism?

12. How did John Locke's theory of knowledge encourage belief in human perfectibility?

13. What aspects of Voltaire's career or teachings entitle him to be called "the personification of the Enlightenment"?

14. How does the story *Candide* differ in its message from the bulk of Voltaire's pronouncements? In what way is *Candide* atypical of the Enlightenment?

15. What basic concept did David Hume share with John Locke? Why did Hume's conclusions undermine all assurance that anything can be known for certain?

16. How did the objectives of Diderot's *Encyclopedia* differ from the objectives of most encyclopedias today?

17. What was Rousseau's contribution to political theory?

18. What "simple system of natural liberty" did Adam Smith espouse? What effects of his teachings are in evidence today?

19. What factors limited the impact of the Enlightenment on the common people? Why did the *philosophes* not make a greater effort to reach the masses?

20. Citing specific advances in science, demonstrate that the Enlightenment was not restricted to France and England.

21. Why did the science of chemistry not develop as early as mathematics and physics? What factors slowed the progress of medicine?

22. In what respects was Kant's philosophy typical of the Enlightenment, and in what respects did it diverge? Explain what he meant by the "categorical imperative."

23. What varying influences were evident in the art of England and the Netherlands during this period?

24. What characteristics of the society that produced it are reflected in the Rococo style of architecture and interior decoration?

25. Why did the modern novel begin its development in England rather than in France? What are the essential differences between the romance and the novel?

26. Explain this statement: "That a woman should emerge around 1800 as a greater writer of novels than most men was almost inevitable."

27. In what ways did Jane Austen surpass her male predecessors as a novelist?

28. Why, according to the authors of the text, was music the most innovative of all the arts during the Enlightenment?
29. What does the term "Classical" mean as applied to the composers Mozart and Haydn?
30. What new musical forms arose during the eighteenth-century Classical era?

PROBLEMS

1. The period of the Enlightenment witnessed "the most important mutation in all of European intellectual history between the Middle Ages and the present." Prove or disprove this assertion.
2. Defend or attack this proposition: "The *philosophes* were on the whole visionary idealists rather than practical reformers."
3. If man was so noble a work in their estimate, why did characteristic philosophers of the Enlightenment, such as Voltaire, so much despise the general run of men?
4. To what extent were such Americans as Benjamin Franklin and Thomas Jefferson good representatives of the Enlightenment?
5. What significant resemblances and differences can you discover between the scientific revolution of the seventeenth and eighteenth centuries and that of the Hellenistic Age?
6. In *Gulliver's Travels*, Jonathan Swift calls humans "the most pernicious race of little odious vermin." How could such a verdict come from the age of Enlightenment?
7. Read Thomas Paine's *Age of Reason* to see how teachings of the Enlightenment were utilized by a crusading pamphleteer.
8. John Locke and Jean-Jacques Rousseau both believed that civil society arose from a social contract. How did they differ in their interpretation of the contract and the character of the government instituted thereby?
9. Read a novel by Jane Austen (*Pride and Prejudice*, *Sense and Sensibility*, *Persuasion*) for a sense of the attitudes and manners of the English gentry.
10. Read Alexander Pope's *Essay on Man* as an example of Enlightenment classicism. What was Pope's conception of the functioning of the universe? What was the place of mankind in the universe? Why was it that Pope argued "the proper study of Mankind is Man"?
11. Study Carl Becker's critique of the skepticism of Hume and Diderot (Becker, *The Heavenly City of the Eighteenth-Century Philosophers*, Chapters 2 and 3).
12. Read the American Declaration of Independence and Constitution. How much influence from the Enlightenment can you find in these documents? What specific ideas—and from whom—did the authors of these documents borrow?

AIDS TO AN UNDERSTANDING OF THE SCIENTIFIC REVOLUTION AND ENLIGHTENMENT

JOHN LOCKE'S THEORY OF KNOWLEDGE: From *Essay Concerning Human Understanding*

It is an established opinion amongst some men, that there are in the understanding certain *innate principles*; some primary notions, characters, as it were stamped upon the mind of man; which the soul receives in its very first being, and brings into the world with it. It would be sufficient to convince unprejudiced readers of the falseness of this supposition, if I should only show (as I hope I shall in the following parts of the Discourse) how men, barely by the use of their natural faculties, may attain to all the knowledge they have, without the help of any innate impressions; and may arrive at certainty, without any such original notions or principles. . . . For I imagine any one will easily grant, that it would be impertinent to suppose, the ideas of colours innate in a creature to whom God hath given sight, and a power to receive them by the eyes, from external objects: and no less unreasonable would it be to attribute several truths to the impressions of nature, and innate characters, when we may observe in ourselves faculties, fit to attain as easy and certain knowledge of them, as if they were originally imprinted on the mind. . . .

Let us then suppose the mind to be, as we say, white paper, void of all characters, without any ideas:—How comes it to be furnished? Whence comes it by that vast store which the busy and boundless fancy of man has painted on it with an almost endless variety? Whence has it all the *materials* of reason and knowledge? To this I answer, in one word, from EXPERIENCE. In that all our knowledge is founded; and from that it ultimately derives itself. Our observation employed either, about external sensible objects, or about the internal operations of our minds perceived and reflected on by ourselves, is that which supplies our understandings with all the *materials* of thinking. These two are the fountains of knowledge, from whence all the ideas we have, do spring. . . .

Sense and intuition reach but a very little way. The greatest part of our knowledge depends upon deductions and intermediate ideas: and in those cases where we are fain to substitute assent instead of knowledge, and take propositions for true, without being certain they are so, we have need to find out, examine, and compare the grounds of their probability. In both these cases, the faculty which finds out the means, and rightly applies them, to discover certainty in the one, and probability in the other, is that which we call reason. For as reason perceives the necessary and indubitable connexion of all the ideas or proofs one to another, in each step of any demonstration that produces knowledge, so it likewise perceives the probable connexion of all the ideas or proofs one to another, in every step of a discourse, to which it will think assent due. This is the lowest degree of that which can truly be called reason. . . .

By what has been before said of reason, we may be able to make some guess at the distinction of things, into those that are according to, above, and contrary to reason. 1. *According to reason* are such propositions whose truth we can discover by examining and tracing those ideas we have from sensation and reflection; and by natural deduction find to be true or probable. 2. *Above reason* are such propositions whose truth or probability we cannot by reason derive from those principles. 3. *Contrary to reason* are such propositions as are inconsistent with or irreconcilable to our clear and distinct ideas. Thus the existence of one God is according to reason; the existence of more than one God, contrary to reason; the resurrection of the dead, above reason. . . .

———

From John Locke, *Essay Concerning Human Understanding.*

Voltaire, Personification of the Enlightenment

Natural religion has a thousand times prevented citizens from committing crimes. A well-trained mind has not the inclination for it; a tender one is alarmed at it, representing to itself a just and avenging God; but artificial religion encourages all cruelties which are exercised by troops—conspiracies, seditions, pillages, ambuscades, surprises of towns, robberies, and murder. Each marches gaily to crime, under the banner of his saint.

A certain number of orators are everywhere paid to celebrate these murderous days; some are dressed in a long black close coat, with a short cloak; others have a shirt above a gown; some wear two variegated stuff streamers over their shirts. All of them speak for a long time, and quote that which was done of old in Palestine, as applicable to a combat in Veteravia.

The rest of the year these people declaim against vices. They prove, in three points and by antitheses, that ladies who lay a little carmine upon their cheeks, will be the eternal objects of the eternal vengeances of the Eternal; that Polyeuctus and Athalia are works of the demon; that a man who, for two hundred crowns a day, causes his table to be furnished with fresh sea fish during Lent, infallibly works his salvation; and that a poor man who eats two sous and a half worth of mutton, will go forever to all the devils.

Of five or six thousand declamations of this kind, there are three or four at most, composed by a Gaul named Massillon, which an honest man may read without disgust; but in all these discourses, you will scarcely find two in which the orator dares to say a word against the scourge and crime of war, which contains all other scourges and crimes. The unfortunate orators speak incessantly against love, which is the only consolation of mankind, and the only mode of making amends for it; they say nothing of the abominable efforts which we make to destroy it.

You have made a very bad sermon on impurity—oh, Bourdaloue!—but none on these murders, varied in so many ways; on these rapines and robberies; on this universal rage which devours the world. All the united vices of all ages and places will never equal the evils produced by a single campaign.

Miserable physicians of souls! you exclaim, for five quarters of an hour, on some pricks of a pin, and say nothing on the malady which tears us into a thousand pieces! Philosophers! moralists! burn all your books. While the caprice of a few men makes that part of mankind consecrated to heroism, to murder loyally millions of our brethren, can there be anything more horrible throughout nature?

What becomes of, and what signifies to me, humanity, beneficence, modesty, temperance, mildness, wisdom, and piety, while half a pound of lead, sent from the distance of a hundred steps, pierces my body, and I die at twenty years of age, in inexpressible torments, in the midst of five or six thousand dying men, while my eyes which open for the last time, see the town in which I was born destroyed by fire and sword, and the last sounds which reach my ears are the cries of women and children expiring under the ruins, all for the pretended interests of a man whom I know not?

What is worse, war is an inevitable scourge. If we take notice, all men have worshipped Mars. Sabaoth, among the Jews, signifies the god of arms; but Minerva, in Homer, calls Mars a furious, mad, and infernal god.

The celebrated Montesquieu, who was called humane, has said, however, that it is just to bear fire and sword against our neighbors, when we fear that they are doing too well. If this is the spirit of laws, it is also that of Borgia and of Machiavelli. If unfortunately he says true, we must write against this truth, though it may be proved by facts.

This is what Montesquieu says: "Between societies, the right of natural defence sometimes induces the necessity of attacking, when one people sees that a longer peace puts another in a situation to destroy it, and that attack at the given moment is the only way of preventing this destruction."

How can attack in peace be the only means of preventing this destruction? You must be sure that this neighbor will destroy you, if he become powerful. To be sure of it, he must already have made preparations for your overthrow. In this case, it is he who commences the war; it is not you: your supposition is false and contradictory.

If ever war is evidently unjust, it is that which you propose: it is going to kill your neighbor, who does not attack you, lest he should ever be in a state to do so. To hazard the ruin of your country, in the hope of ruining without reason that of another, is assuredly neither honest nor useful; for we are never sure of success, as you well know.

If your neighbor becomes too powerful during peace, what prevents you from rendering yourself equally powerful? If he has made alliances, make them on your side. If, having fewer monks, he has more soldiers and manufacturers, imitate him in this wise economy. If he employs his sailors better, employ yours in the same manner: all that is very just.

———

From Voltaire, *Philosophical Dictionary, in Works, A Contemporary Edition,* Vol. VII.

DEISM, THE RELIGION OF THE ENLIGHTENMENT: From *The Age of Reason*
Thomas Paine

I believe in one God, and no more; and I hope for happiness beyond this life.

I believe in the equality of man; and I believe that religious duties consist in doing justice, loving mercy, and endeavouring to make our fellow creatures happy.

But, lest it should be supposed that I believe many other things in addition to these, I shall, in the progress of this work, declare the things I do not believe, and my reasons for not believing them.

I do not believe in the creed professed by the Jewish church, by the Roman church, by the Greek church, by the Turkish church, by the Protestant church, nor by any church that I know of. My own mind is my own church.

All national institutions of churches, whether Jewish, Christian, or Turkish, appear to me no other than human inventions, set up to terrify and enslave mankind, and monopolize power and profit.

I do not mean by this declaration to condemn those who believe otherwise; they have the same right to their belief as I have to mine. But it is necessary to the happiness of man, that he be mentally faithful to himself. Infidelity does not consist in believing, or in disbelieving; it consists in professing to believe what he does not believe. . . .

Every national church or religion has established itself by pretending some special mission from God, communicated to certain individuals. The Jews have their Moses; the Christians their Jesus Christ, their apostles, and saints; and the Turks their Mahomet, as if the way to God was not open to every man alike.

Each of those churches show certain books, which they call *revelation*, or the word of God. The Jews say, that their word of God was given by God to Moses, face to face; the Christians say, that their word of God came by divine inspiration; and the Turks say, that their word of God (the Koran) was brought by an angel from Heaven. Each of those churches accuse the other of unbelief; and, for my own part, I disbelieve them all.

From Thomas Paine, *The Age Reason.*

MAN AS THE REFERENCE POINT FOR ALL STUDY: *The Encyclopedia*

One consideration especially which we ought not to lose sight of, is that if we banish man, the thinking and contemplative being, from the surface of the earth, this pathetic and sublime spectacle of nature becomes a scene melancholy and dumb. Silence and night take possession of the universe. Everything is transformed into a vast solitude in which unobserved phenomena move in an obscure and secret manner. It is the presence of man that makes the existence of beings interesting. Can we propose anything better in the history of these beings than to submit ourselves to this consideration? Why should we not introduce man into our work, as he is placed in the universe? Why should we not make him a common center? . . .

This is what has determined us to find in the principal faculties of man the general division to which we have subordinated our work. . . . Man is the unique point to which we must refer everything, if we wish to interest and please amongst considerations the most arid and details the most dry. Abstract from my existence and the happiness of my fellow human beings, and the rest of nature is of no consequence.

From Franklin L. Baumer, *Main Currents of Western Thought*, 2nd ed. New York: Alfred A. Knopf Inc., 1964.

A CONFIDENT VISION OF THE FUTURE: From *The Progress of the Human Mind*
Marquis de Condorcet

The result of [my work] will be to show, from reasoning and from facts, that no bounds have been fixed to the improvement of the human faculties; that the perfectibility of man is absolutely indefinite; that the progress of this perfectibility, henceforth above the control of every power that would impede it, has no other limit than the duration of the globe upon which nature has placed us. The course of this progress may doubtless be more or less rapid, but it can never be retrograde; at least while the earth retains its situation in the system of the universe, and the laws of this system shall neither effect upon the globe a general overthrow, nor introduce such changes as would no longer permit the human race to preserve and exercise therein the same faculties, and find the same resources. . . .

Every thing tells us that we are approaching the era of one of the grand revolutions of the human race. . . .

If man can predict, almost with certainty, those appearances of which he understands the laws; if, even when the laws are unknown to him, experience of the past enables him to foresee, with considerable probability, future appearances; why should we suppose it a chimerical undertaking to delineate, with some degree of truth, the picture of the future destiny of mankind from the results of its history? The only foundation of faith in the natural sciences is the principle, that the general laws, known or unknown, which regulate the phenomena of the universe, are regular and constant; and why should this principle, applicable to the other operations of nature, be less true when applied to the development of the intellectual and moral faculties of man? In short, as opinions formed from experience, relative to the same class of objects, are the only rule by which men of soundest understanding are governed in their conduct, why should the philosopher be proscribed from supporting his conjectures upon a similar basis, provided he attribute to them no greater certainty than the number, the consistency, and the accuracy of actual observations shall authorise?

Our hopes, as to the future condition of the human species, may be reduced to three points: the destruction of inequality between different nations; the progress of equality in one and the same nation; and lastly, the real improvement of man.

Will not every nation one day arrive at the state of civilization attained by those people who are most enlightened, most free, most exempt from prejudices, as the French, for instance, and the Anglo-Americans? Will not the slavery of countries subjected to kings, the barbarity of African tribes, and the ignorance of savages gradually vanish? Is there upon the face of the globe a single spot the inhabitants of which are condemned by nature never to enjoy liberty, never to exercise their reason?

• • •

The people being more enlightened, and having resumed the right of disposing for themselves of their blood and their treasure, will learn by degrees to regard war as the most dreadful of all calamities, the most terrible of all crimes. The first wars that will be superseded, will be those into which the usurpers of sovereignty have hitherto drawn their subjects for the maintenance of rights pretendedly hereditary.

Nations will know, that they cannot become conquerors without losing their freedom; that perpetual confederations are the only means of maintaining their independence; that their object should be security, and not power. By degrees commercial prejudices will die away; a false mercantile interest will lose the terrible power of imbuing the earth with blood, and of ruining nations under the idea of enriching them. As the people of different countries will at last be drawn into closer intimacy, by the principles of politics and morality, as each, for its own advantage, will invite foreigners to an equal participation of the benefits which it may have derived either from nation or its own industry, all the causes which produce, envenom, and perpetuate national animosities, will one by one disappear, and will no more furnish to warlike insanity either fuel or pretext.

Institutions, better combined than those projects of perpetual peace which have occupied the leisure and consoled the heart of certain philosophers, will accelerate the progress of this fraternity of nations; and wars, like assassinations, will be ranked in the number of those daring atrocities, humiliating and loathsome to nature; and which fix upon the country or the age whose annals are stained with them, an indelible opprobrium.

From Franklin L. Baumer, *Main Currents of Western Thought*, 2nd ed. New York: Alfred A. Knopf Inc., 1964.

ROUSSEAU'S CONCEPTION OF TOTAL DEMOCRACY: *The Social Contract*

If, therefore, we take from the social compact every thing that is not essential to it, we shall find it reduced to the following terms: "We, the contracting parties, do jointly and severally submit our persons and abilities, to the supreme direction of the general will of all, and, in a collective body, receive each member into that body, as an indivisible part of the whole."

This act of association accordingly converts the several individual contracting parties into one moral collective body, composed of as many members also from the same act its unity and existence. This public personage, which is thus formed by the union of all its members, used formerly to be denominated a CITY, and, at present, takes the name of a *republic*, or *body politic*. It is also called, by its several members, a *state*, when it is passive; the *sovereign*, when it is active; and simply a *power*, when it is compared with other bodies of the same nature. With regard to the associates themselves, they take collectively the name of the *people*, and are separately called *citizens*, as partaking of the sovereign authority, and *subjects*, as subjected to the laws of the state. These terms, indeed, are frequently confounded, and mistaken one for the other; it is sufficient, however, to be able to distinguish them, when they are to be used with precision.

• • •

To the end, therefore, that the social compact should not prove an empty form, it tacitly includes this engagement, which only can enforce the rest, viz. that whosoever refuses to pay obedience to the general will, shall be liable to be compelled to it by the force of the whole body. And this is in effect nothing more, than that they may be compelled to be free; for such is the condition which, in uniting every citizen to the state, secured him from all personal dependence; a condition, which forms the whole artifice and play of the political machine: it is this alone that renders all social engagements just and equitable which, without it, would be absurd, tyrannical, and subject to the most enormous abuses.

• • •

It is agreed, that what an individual alienates of his power, his possession, or his liberty, by the social compact, is only such parts of them whose use is of importance to the community; but it must be confessed also, that the sovereign is the only proper judge of this importance.

From Jean Jacques Rousseau, *A Treatise on the Social Compact*, T. Becket edn.

ANALYSIS AND INTERPRETATION OF THE READINGS

1. Locke rejects "innate principles" in favor of "experience" as the foundation for knowledge. What does he mean by "experience"?
2. Why did Voltaire call upon philosophers and moralists to burn all their books?
3. What basic assumptions of the Enlightenment are reflected in the brief selection from *The Encyclopedia*?
4. By what reasoning does Condorcet support his belief in the inevitable progress of mankind?
5. To what extent are Voltaire and Condorcet in agreement?
6. What does Rousseau mean by the Sovereign? Why is the power of the Sovereign absolute?
7. What does Rousseau mean by "compelling men to be free"?

Overseas Exploration in the 15th and 16th Centuries

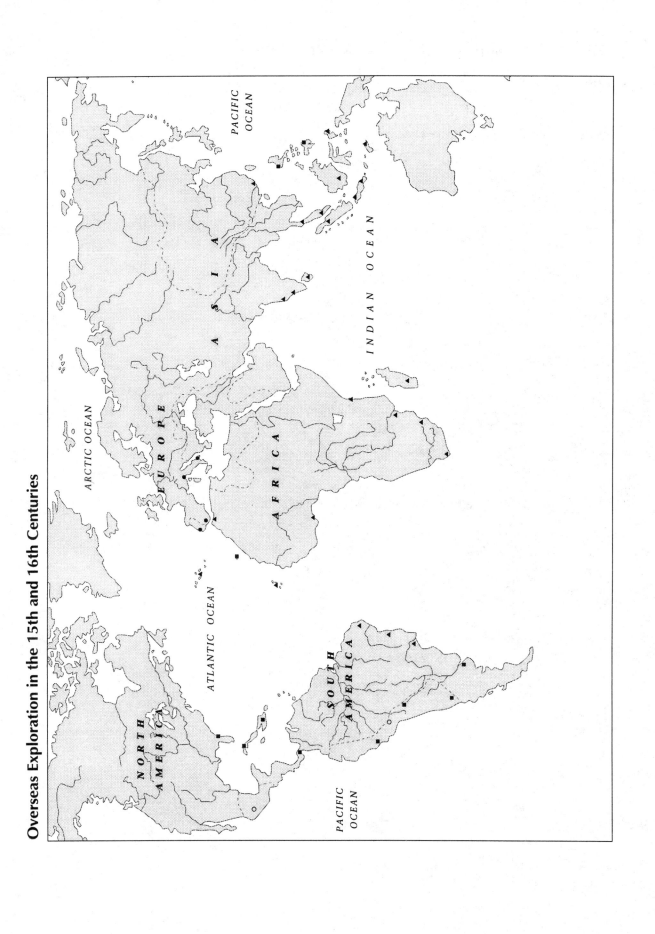

Europe in 1560

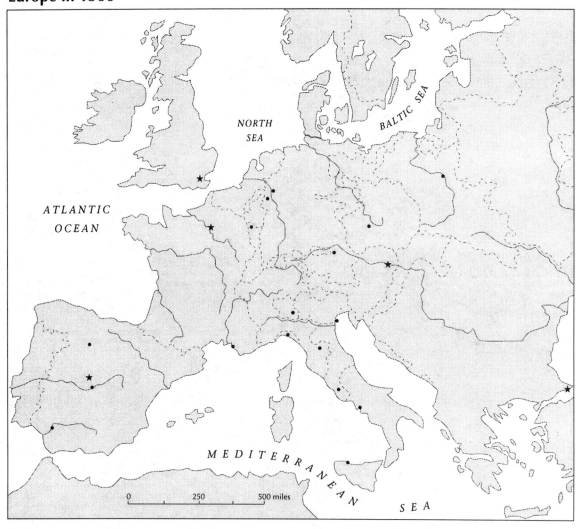

Overseas Exploration in the 15th and 16th Centuries and Europe in 1560

OVERSEAS EXPLORATION IN THE 15TH AND 16TH CENTURIES

1. On the "Exploration" map (see page 25), show the approximate routes followed by these explorers:

Christopher Columbus (first voyage; later voyages)
Bartholomew Diaz
Ferdinand Magellan (and Magellan's ship after his death)
Vasco Da Gama

2. Locate the areas of the Inca, Aztec, Ottoman, *and* Chinese *empires.*

3. Mark the following locations:

Labrador	Gold Coast
Hispaniola	Cape of Good Hope
Philippines	Malay Peninsula
East Indies	West Indies
Canary Islands	Madagascar

4. Label the following locations. Indicate with an S those that were controlled by the Spanish, and with a P those that were controlled by the Portuguese:

Havana	St. Augustine
Lima	Rio de Janeiro
Santiago	Buenos Aires
Panama	Goa
Calicut	Malacca
Macao	Ceuta

EUROPE IN 1560

1. On the "Europe in 1560" map (see page 26 opposite), outline the approximate boundary of the Holy Roman Empire *in the sixteenth century. Indicate the location of* France, Spain, Portugal, England, Poland, Austria, Denmark, *and the* Papal States.

2. Mark the following locations:

Genoa	Venice
Florence	Rome
Madrid	Seville
Bologna	Constantinople
Augsburg	Palermo
Vienna	Prague
Aachen	Worms
London	Geneva

3. Indicate with different shading or colors the areas of strongest influence of the following Christian religions: Anglican, Roman Catholic, Lutheran, Calvinist, Eastern Orthodox.

CHAPTER 25 | The French Revolution

CHRONOLOGY

Many of the specific dates of the French Revolution have an almost mystical significance to French citizens and other devotees of that great upheaval. Thus, one speaks of "the twentieth of June," "the fourteenth of July," and so on. Although there is no special virtue in learning a long list of such dates, for the student of world history a knowledge of a few of them is useful in pinning down the main outline of events. In the blank after each of the dates below, write the name of the event associated with it.

June 20, 1789

_____

July 14, 1789

_____

"October Days," 1789

_____

April 20, 1792

_____

September 21, 1792

_____

November 9, 1799

_____

June 18, 1815

_____

IDENTIFICATIONS

You should be able to define or describe each of the following:

third estate
nobles of the sword
nobles of the robe
parlements
banalités
gabelle
corvée
physiocrats
Estates-General
cahiers de doléances
National Assembly
sans-culottes

Constitution of 1791
Paris Commune
Declaration of Pillnitz
Jacobins
Girondins
National Convention
Committee of Public Safety
Directory
Code Napoleon
emigrés
Treaty of Campo Formio
"Continental System'

Declaration of the Rights of Man and of the Citizen

In the blanks, write the name that fits each description:

1. A prime mover of the Tennis Court Oath, this priest, when asked what he had done of note during the Terror, replied, "I lived."

_____

2. A fanatical believer in the philosophy of Rousseau, this zealous lawyer became the virtual dictator of France during the bloodiest period of the Terror.

_____

3. An intransigent defender of the common people, this distinguished physician was finally stabbed by Charlotte Corday, a Girondist zealot.

_____

4. An influential member of the physiocrats, this royal minister was dismissed from office when he advocated economic reform.

_____

5. This maverick aristocrat, an advocate of constitutional monarchy, was leader of the National Assembly at the time of his death in 1791.

_____

6. This organizer of the Terror, who in April 1794 became one of its victims, said in mounting the scaffold, "Show my head to the people."

_____

7. This Austrian statesman made "legitimacy" the catchword of the Congress of Vienna.

_____

STUDY QUESTIONS

1. Aside from the incompetence of the royal court, what characteristics of the French government in the eighteenth century prepared the way for revolution?
2. In what ways was tension among French upper and middle classes a contributing factor in the social breakdown that produced revolution?
3. Why is it problematic to speak of "class consciousness" when referring to the French bourgeoisie prior to the revolution?
4. How did the grievances of the peasants differ from those of the middle class in prerevolutionary France?
5. What were the causes of the deepening financial crisis in eighteenth-century France?
6. Describe taxation in France prior to the revolution. What were the most glaring defects in the tax system?
7. In what ways did Louis XVI try to be an "enlightened" monarch? Why did he fail?
8. In what ways were political and economic factors interrelated as causes of the French Revolution?
9. What do you regard as the immediate cause of the Revolution?
10. In the first weeks of the meeting of the Estates General in 1789 how did the third estate make its strength felt?
11. What was the "Great Fear"? What role did it play in the revolution?
12. Summarize the changes produced by the French National Assembly and Legislative Assembly.
13. In what way did the Civil Constitution of the Clergy alter the French church?
14. What were the chief features of the Constitution of 1791? Did it establish a democratic government?
15. Who were the "winners" of the first stage of the French Revolution? What is the evidence for this?
16. What factors account for the shift of the French Revolution in 1792 from moderate reform to radicalism?
17. How did the Jacobins differ from the Girondists in membership and program?
18. How and why did European reactions to the French Revolution change during its course?
19. What were the achievements of the second stage of the French Revolution?
20. In what sense did the rule of the Committee of Public Safety represent a "second" revolution? What were the causes of the Committee's eventual downfall?
21. Show how the Constitution of 1795 was a conservative document.
22. Compare and contrast the first and second stages of the revolution from the standpoints of leadership, basic objectives, and permanent effects.
23. Describe the government under Napoleon's Constitution of 1799. What democratic devices did it employ?
24. What were Napoleon's chief nonmilitary achievements?
25. How did the Code Napoleon reflect uniformity? How did it reflect individualism?
26. What was the significance of the Concordat of 1801?
27. What were the major parts (including dependencies) of Napoleon's empire at its peak?
28. What were the causes of Napoleon's downfall?
29. What were the chief objectives of the diplomats at the Congress of Vienna?
30. Which provisions of the Vienna settlement of 1815 upheld the principle of legitimacy? Which agreements violated this principle?

PROBLEMS

1. Compare and contrast, in as many ways as possible, the French Revolution with the Puritan Revolution and the Glorious Revolution in England, and with the American Revolution.
2. "In its origins and initial objectives the French Revolution was essentially a middle-class movement." Defend or refute this statement.
3. Why did the French Revolution involve conflicts between France and other countries?
4. Examine the role of women in the French Revolution.
5. "The French Revolution made the career of Napoleon inevitable." Defend or refute this statement.
6. Trace the specific applications of the concepts "Liberty, Equality, Fraternity" during the course of the French Revolution.

7. Examine, in as many ways as you can, the interplay between ideas and experience in the French Revolution.

8. Compare the causes, course, immediate results, and long-term effects of the French and American Revolutions.

9. To what extent was Napoleon a true "Son of the Revolution"?

10. Compare the objectives and accomplishments of the Congress of Vienna with the theory and practice of a "balance of power" in our own recent history and today.

AIDS TO AN UNDERSTANDING OF THE FRENCH REVOLUTION

THE FRENCH DECLARATION OF THE RIGHTS OF MAN AND OF THE CITIZEN

1. The aim of society is the common welfare. Government is established to guarantee to man the enjoyment of his natural and inalienable rights.

2. These rights are equality, liberty, security, and property.

3. All men are equal by nature and before law.

4. Law is the free and solemn expression of the general will. It is the same for all, whether it protects or whether it punishes; it may command only that which is just and useful to society; it may prohibit only that which is harmful to it.

5. All citizens are equally eligible for public office. Free people recognize no other basis of preference in their elections than virtue and talent.

6. Liberty is the power belonging to man to do anything which does not infringe upon the rights of others. It has for its principle, nature; for its rule, justice; for its safeguard, law. Its moral limit is expressed by this maxim: *do not that to any other which you wish not done to yourself.*

7. The right of manifesting one's thoughts and opinions, either by the voice of the press or by any other means, the right of peaceable assembly, the right of free worship, may not be forbidden.

8. Security consists in the protection that society accords each one of its members for the protection of his person, his rights, and his property.

9. The law must protect both public and individual liberty against the oppression of those who govern.

10. No one must be accused, arrested, or detained except in cases determined by law and in accordance with the forms which it prescribes. Any citizen summoned or seized by the authority of the law must obey immediately; he renders himself culpable by resistance.

11. Every act directed against a person outside the cases and forms determined by law is arbitrary and tyrannical; the person against whom one attempts to execute such an act by violence has the right of forcible resistance.

12. Those who incite, expedite, sign, execute, or cause to be executed, arbitrary acts are guilty and must be punished.

13. All men being presumed innocent until proved guilty, when it becomes necessary that a person be arrested, all severity beyond that necessary to secure his person must be strictly curbed by law.

14. No one must be judged and sentenced until after a legal summons and hearing, and by virtue of a law made public before the crime. Any law that punished crimes committed before its enactment would be tyrannical; the retroactive effect given to such a law would be criminal.

15. The law must impose only penalties which are strictly and obviously necessary; the penalties must be proportionate to the crime, and in themselves useful to society.

16. The right of property is the right which belongs to every citizen to enjoy, and at will to dispose of, his goods, his revenues, and the fruit of his labor and industry.

17. No form of labor, tillage, or commerce may be forbidden to the industry of the citizens.

18. Every man may lease his servants and his time, but he may not sell himself nor be sold; his person is not a transferable property. The law does not recognize servitude; the only bond which may exist between the laborer and the man who hires him is that based on protection and gratitude.

19. No one may be deprived of the least part of his property without his consent, except when a legally certified public necessity requires it, and then only on condition of a just, prearranged indemnity.

Raymond W. Short and Robert DeMaria trans. From *The Constitution* of 1793.

THE BRAVE NEW WORLD ENVISIONED BY A FRENCH RADICAL: The Republican Institutions of Saint-Just

I challenge you to establish liberty so long as it remains possible to arouse the unfortunate classes against the new order of things, and I defy you to do away with poverty altogether unless each one has his own land. . . . Where you find large landowners you find many poor people. Nothing can be done in a country where agriculture is carried on on a large scale. Man was not made for the workshop, the hospital, or the poorhouse. All that is horrible. Men must live in independence, each with his own wife and his robust and healthy children. We must have neither rich nor poor.

The poor man is superior to government and the powers of the world; he should address them as a master. We must have a system which puts all these principles in practice and assures comfort to the entire people. Opulence is a crime: it consists in supporting fewer children, whether one's own or adopted, than one has thousands of francs of income. . . .

Children shall belong to their mother, provided she has suckled them herself, until they are five years old; after that they shall belong to the republic until death. The mother who does not suckle her children ceases to be a mother in the eyes of the country. Child and citizen belong to the country, and a common instruction is essential. Children shall be brought up in the love of silence and scorn for fine talkers. They shall be trained in laconic speech. Games shall be prohibited in which they declaim, and they shall be habituated to simple truth.

The boys shall be educated, from the age of five to sixteen, by the country; from five to ten they shall learn to read, write, and swim. No one shall strike or caress a child. They shall be taught what is good and left to nature. He who strikes a child shall be banished. The children shall eat together and shall live on roots, fruit, vegetables, milk, cheese, bread, and water. The teachers of children from five to ten years old shall not be less than sixty years of age. . . . The education of children from ten to sixteen shall be military and agricultural. . . .

Every year on the first day of Floréal the people of each commune shall select, from among the inhabitants of the commune, and in the temple, a young man rich and virtuous and without deformity, at least twenty-one years of age and not over thirty, who shall in turn select and marry a poor maiden, in everlasting memory of human equality.

From J. H. Robinson, *Readings in European History*, Vol. II, New York: Ginn and Company, 1906, pp 452–54. Reprinted by permission of the publisher.

THE RETREAT FROM RUSSIA
Philippe-Paul de Ségur

Nevertheless, despite starvation, cold, and the most complete destitution, a considerable number of the wounded had been kept alive in this foul place of refuge by a shred of hope and the splendid devotion of the surgeons. When these poor creatures saw the army passing in a homeward direction and realized that they were going to be abandoned, that there was no longer anything to hope for, the strongest dragged themselves to the doors and lined the streets, holding out imploring hands toward us.

The Emperor ordered that one of those poor wretches should be placed on every available kind of wagon, while the weakest were to be left, as at Moscow, in the care of the wounded Russian officers who had recovered their strength under our treatment. Napoleon halted long enough to supervise the execution of this order, while he and most of his staff warmed themselves at fires fed by the wood of abandoned artillery wagons. Since early morning frequent explosions had been informing us of the great number of such sacrifices we were already forced to make.

During this halt an atrocious thing occurred. Several of the wounded had been put on the sutlers' carts. These scoundrels grumbled about the additional weight their carts, already overloaded with plunder from Moscow, would have to carry. However, they were compelled to obey, and said no more. But they had scarcely got under way when they slowed down and let the rest of the column go by. Then, taking advantage of a moment when they were alone, they threw their unfortunate charges into the ditch by the roadside. Only one of the victims, a general, lived long enough to be picked up by the first wagon of the next division that came along. Through him we learned of the crime. A shudder of horror ran through the column and finally reached the Emperor; for our suffering had not yet become keen and widespread enough to stifle all sense of pity.

In the evening of that long day, as the imperial column was approaching Czhatsk, we were surprised to find a number of dead Russians, still warm, on the road in front of us. We noticed that their heads had all been shattered in the same manner, and that their brains were scattered about. We knew that two thousand Russian prisoners had gone before us under the escort of Spanish, Portuguese, and Polish troops. Some of our generals greeted this with indifference, others with indignation, still others with approval. In the Emperor's presence no one expressed an opinion. Caulaincourt could no longer contain himself, and burst out, "It's an atrocity! This, then, is the civilization we are bringing to Russia! What effect will such inhumanity have on our enemies? Aren't we leaving our wounded in their care, as well as thousands of prisoners? Will they lack provocation for horrible reprisals?"

Napoleon maintained a gloomy silence; but the next day those murders had stopped. After that we simply let our unfortunate prisoners die of hunger in the enclosures where we penned them up for the night, like cattle. This was doubtless an atrocity; but what were we to do? Exchange them? The enemy refused to consider it. Set them free? They would have spread the news of our destitute condition far and wide, and soon would have joined up with others and returned to dog our steps. In this war to the death we should have sacrificed ourselves in letting them live. We were cruel by necessity. The evil lay in the fact that we had got ourselves in a position where we were faced with such a terrible alternative.

Besides, our own prisoners were certainly not treated more humanely by the Russians in their march toward the interior, though they had not the excuse of absolute necessity.

From Philippe-Paul de Ségur, *Napoleon's Russian Campaign*, J. David Townsend ed. and trans., Houghton Mifflin Company, 1958. Reprinted by permission of the publisher.

ANALYSIS AND INTERPRETATION OF THE READINGS

1. Compare the French *Declaration of the Rights of Man and of the Citizen* with the English Bill of Rights and the American Bill of Rights.
2. Comment on the practicality of the Republican Institutions of Saint-Just.

CHAPTER 26 | The Industrial Revolution

IDENTIFICATIONS

Below are lists of men and innovations significant for the Industrial Revolution. Write in each blank the name of the person associated with the invention or achievement.

Samuel Crompton   Eli Whitney
James Watt   Thomas Brassey
Thomas Newcomen   James Hargreaves
George Stephenson   Richard Arkwright

steam railway _____

spinning jenny_____

cotton gin _____

water frame _____

dual-chamber steam engine_____

spinning mule _____

STUDY QUESTIONS

1. What conditions in eighteenth-century Europe made it uniquely suitable as a site for the Industrial Revolution?
2. How had commercial developments during the preceding two centuries paved the way for a revolution in industry?
3. Describe what each of the following factors contributed to England's leadership in the early Industrial Revolution: (a) geographical position; (b) natural resources; (c) social structure and traditions; (d) the government's economic policy.
4. Explain why English cotton manufacture expanded so dynamically during the first half of the nineteenth century.
5. How did the expansion of textile manufacture stimulate the development of other industries?
6. What were the advantages of using coal instead of wood as a fuel in the heating of molten metal? Can you think of any disadvantages?
7. If the expansion and mechanization of industry was spread gradually over several generations, why did it nevertheless constitute a revolution?
8. What physical and what political or social factors delayed the progress of the Industrial Revolution on the European continent?
9. To what extent did the French Revolution inhibit, and to what extent did it promote, industrialization?
10. What major change in the population of Europe occurred in the nineteenth century, and how did this affect the process of industrialization?
11. Explain why government played a more active role in industrial development on the continent of Europe than in England.
12. What two motives were uppermost in the rapid growth of railroads in the 1840s? To what extent did railroad construction promote, and to what extent did it slow, the pace of industrialization in Europe?
13. Who were the "navvies"? What was their role in the process of industrialization?
14. In which branches of industry did Britain retain a commanding lead in 1870? In which branches did pressure from competitors become most intense? Who were the major competitors?
15. Why was the process of industrialization slowest in southern and eastern Europe?

PROBLEMS

1. Investigate further any of the following:
   a. James Watt and the steam engine

b. Early revolutionary inventions in the cotton cloth industry
c. George Stephenson and the Stockton-Darlington railway
d. The Prussian *Zollverein*
2. Compare developments in industry and transportation in England with those in France during the nineteenth century.
3. Examine the effects of European wars of the eighteenth century on changes in commerce and industry.

4. Read *Robinson Crusoe* and analyze Defoe's views on industrial enterprise.
5. "Europe used its economic and, when necessary, its military strength to ensure that the world remained divided between the producers of manufactured goods—Europe itself—and suppliers of the necessary raw materials and buyers of finished goods—everyone else." Examine the long-term consequences (political, economic, cultural) of this arrangement.

AIDS TO AN UNDERSTANDING OF THE INDUSTRIAL REVOLUTION

THE FACTORY APPRENTICE
T. S. Ashton

When Arkwright's water-frame thrust its way into a trade organized on a household basis [the cotton industry] there was much hasty improvisation. Early attempts to obtain adult labour proved futile. It had been the practice of many Poor Law authorities to assemble paupers in houses of industry and set them to spinning and other simple tasks; hence it was not unnatural that the new factories should be thought of as workhouses and given wide berth by the independent labourer. The geographical situation of the mills was such that, in any case, only a small fraction of the labour could be drawn from local sources. It was unthinkable that the male weaver would leave his loom and take to work of less skill as a spinner, and it was equally unthinkable that his wife and children would leave their home for the country factory. But there was, especially in London and the South, a large supply of unskilled, unemployed people who were a charge on the parishes, and in many places the growing burden of the rates led the overseers to offer to transfer batches of children, or whole families, to factories in the North. It was by such means that the cotton masters obtained a large part of their labour.

The story of the factory "apprentices" is a depressing one. The children, many of them only seven years of age, had to work twelve, or even fifteen, hours a day, for six days a week. As Mr. and Mrs. Hammond have said, "their young lives were spent, at best in monotonous toil, at worst in a hell of human cruelty." Employers who took their responsibilities seriously—the Arkwrights, the Gregs, Samuel Oldknow and, above all, Robert Owen—provided not only board in pleasant and well-designed prentice houses (such as can still be seen at Styal and Mellor) but also the rudiments of an education. The children were able to play in the fields, and some had little gardens of their own. Care was taken to keep the sexes apart (a visitor to the Cressbrook factory in Millers Dale was told that instruction in singing was given to the boys, but not to the girls, though "as the girls' rooms were immediately above the boys', the sweet sounds would ascend and the girls participate in the harmony"). Several of the boys at the Gregs' factory at Styal rose

to managerial posts, and as least half a dozen of Oldknow's apprentices afterwards set up as spinners on their own account. But at many other places, as at Backbarrow, the tale is one of neglect, promiscuity, and degradation.

When, in 1816, the first Sir Robert Peel was asked about apprentice labour he said: ". . . At the time when Arkwright's machinery had first an existence, steam power was but little known, and . . . those who wished to carry on their business, and benefit by these improvements, resorted to country places where there were great waterfalls, and consequently could not have any other than apprentice labour; and I was in that situation, for I had no other." A modern might have retorted that he had the alternative of refusing to adopt the new technique at all. But the modern would be passing judgement according to the code of an age which (because of the industrial revolution) has a standard of life immeasurably higher than that of Peel's day, and which (partly because children are now in short supply) sets a different value on child life. The conduct of the factory masters must be judged in the light of their own age and of that which preceded it. It was not very long since Jonas Hanway had remarked that "few parish children live to be apprenticed." Those who did live had been put out to tradesmen and others, and many had suffered miseries certainly no less than those of the factory children. It must be remembered, also, that the employers were, like their forbears, essentially merchants. David Dale (we have it on the authority of Robert Owen) did not visit his factory more than once in two or three months; and the vagueness of the answers that other cotton masters gave to questions put to them by committees of inquiry arose less, perhaps, from a consciousness that there was something to hide, than from sheer ignorance of conditions in their own works. The superintendents they appointed to their factories were largely technicians concerned with the running of the plant, and the administration of labour was lax. Not until the industrial revolution was well on its way did there arise a body of men capable of performing some at least of the functions of the labour manager of today.

From T. S. Ashton, *The Industrial Revolution 1760–1830*, New York, Oxford University Press, 1964. Reprinted by permission of the publisher.

A Vigorous Defense of Mechanization
J. R. McCulloch

Various bad consequences have been supposed to result from the continued extension and improvement of machinery. But a presumption arises at the outset, that they must be in a great degree fallacious, inasmuch as they would equally follow from the continued improvement of the skill and industry of the labourer. If the construction of a machine that would manufacture two pairs of stockings for the same expense that was previously required to manufacture one pair, be in any respect injurious, the injury would obviously be equal were the same thing accomplished by increased dexterity and skill on the part of the knitters; were the females, for example, who knitted two or three pairs in the week, able in future to knit four or six pairs. There is really no difference in the cases. And supposing the demand for stockings were already supplied, M. Sismondi could not, consistently with the principles he has advanced, [in "Nouveaux Principes"] hesitate about condemning such an improvement as a very great evil—as a means of throwing *half* the people engaged in the stocking manufacture out of employment. The question respecting the improvement of machinery is, therefore, at bottom, the same with the question respecting the improvement of the skill and industry of the labourer. The principles which regulate our decision in the one case, must regulate it in the other. If it be advantageous that the manual dexterity of the labourer should be indefinitely extended—that he should be able to produce greater quantities of commodities with the same, or a less quantity of labour, it surely must be advantageous that he should avail himself of such aids as may be most effectual in enabling him to bring about that result.

From J. R. McCulloch, *The Principles of Political Economy.*

Britain and Europe at Mid-Century
David S. Landes

At mid-century, then, continental Europe was still about a generation behind Britain in industrial development. The relative disparity showed clearly in the population figures. Where in 1851 about half of the people of England and Wales lived in towns, in France and Germany the proportion was about a quarter; not until the last years of the century did urban population pass rural in Germany, and in France the even point did not come until after the First World War. The occupational distribution tells a similar story. At mid-century, only a quarter of the British male working force (twenty years and older) was engaged in agriculture. For Belgium, the most industrialized nation on the Continent, the figure was about 50 per cent. Germany took another twenty-five years to reach this point; indeed, as later as 1895, there were more people engaged in agriculture than in industry. And in France industry was outnumbered until the Second World War and the economic recovery that followed.

By the same token, the continental proletariat was very different from the British. The concentration of large numbers of workers in huge factories was only just beginning, and then more in heavy industry than in textiles. There was nothing yet like the new slums of Manchester and Leeds, filled with pallid mill hands crowding into a smokestack jungle. Continental slums were different. They were usually the run-down older quarters, comparable to the wynds of Edinburgh, and were inhabited primarily by artisans and domestic workers—handloom weavers in the damp cellars of Lille or the tenements of Liège; woodworkers in the Faubourg Saint-Antoine. Here and there were new mill towns on the British pattern; but Roubaix, Mulhouse, and the cities of the Wuppertal were so much smaller than their counterparts in Lancashire and the West Riding that they were really a different species.

Much more than in Britain, industry was dispersed through the countryside. The continued reliance on water power was one factor; the greater place of metallurgy and mining, which were bound to locate at the sources of raw materials, was another. As late as 1858, 19 of 49 spinning mills, 49 of 57 blast furnaces, 75 of 152 wire mills, 158 of 167 steel plants, and 15 of 28 machine factories in Westphalia were *auf dem platten Lande.* To be sure, this was a legalistic definition, and many of these plants were in fact situated in communities that deserved to be called urban. Many, however, were located in what were in effect swollen villages, essentially rural in character. There was, as in Lancashire in the eighteenth century, a thickening of the countryside; it had not yet thickened enough, however, to form a continuous industrial conurbation.

There was, moreover, a great expansion of rural putting-out, a continuation of the trend of the eighteenth century, paradoxically accelerated by the mechanization of some—but not all—of the stages of manufacture. Thus the availability of cheaper semiprocessed materials—yarn, rough metal shapes, tanned leather—increased the demand for the corresponding finished goods and stimulated the trades that made them. Here differentiation of product was often pushed to the extreme, and the importance of skill or painstaking labour gave the shop and cottage an advantage over the factory. Even the march of the machine did not always favour power-driven, concentrated manufacture. When the embroidery loom was finally improved in Switzerland to the point of commercial effectiveness in the 1850's, it was installed at first in large weaving sheds; a device of this complexity was beyond the means of most home workers. But before long the manufacturers found that it paid to place these machines in cottages, as the stockingers of Nottingham had done with their frames two hundred years before; and in subsequent decades the loom found its way into the most isolated villages of the Voralberg.

The extension of putting-out on the Continent owed much to the pattern of land tenure. In Britain, the enclosures had promoted the absorption of small holdings into large, commercial exploitations. In east-Elbian Europe, the emancipation of the serfs had similar consequences: the debts imposed on the peasants as the price of their freedom and property so burdened them that many had no choice but to sell their land and either hire out as labourers or leave. Much of western Europe north of the Alps and Pyrenees, however, lay in the hands of independent proprietors; moreover, the prevalence of partible inheritance (written into the Code Civil in France) led to a progressive fragmentation of their already small holdings. The system held an ever larger population on the land, for the children of each generation tended to stay on to work their shares of a diminishing patrimony. On the other hand, even with improved techniques, these small plots were less and less adequate to nourish their occupants. Increasingly, the peasant had to eke out his income with earnings as a farm labourer or cottage worker. Poor soil and division of holdings were the parents of rural industry.

This persistence of the old social framework was a source of great satisfaction to many continental statesmen and writers. In France particularly, where the traditional structure was most tenacious and British industrial success least palatable, society was wont to congratulate itself on being spared the penalties of unbalanced and immoderate growth: the white slavery of the factories; the filth and misery of the cities; the godlessness and radicalism of a rootless proletariat.

In fact, the Continent had its poverty, as conscientious observers were quick to perceive, but much of it was dispersed and, as one investigator put it, latent. In societies where population was increasing more rapidly than the demand for factory labour, there was a heavy flow into cottage industry, depressing wages in the short run and creating in the long run huge pools of depressed humanity, barely subsisting until the day when even the wages of hunger would not be low enough. The same thing happened in Britain, but to a much smaller degree. For one thing, there was more alternative opportunity: industry drew people; people did not press into industry. The Irish handloom weaver was an exception, but, little as he earned, he was probably better off in Lancashire than in Mayo. At least he survived. For another, as we have already noted, it was the Continent that supplied much of the hand labour required to process the semi-finished manufactures of Britain. The weavers of Silesia, Saxony, and central France (the tulle trade of Tarare) were in one sense beneficiaries of British industrial progress; they were also its victims. In effect, they were taking part of the burden of adjustment to the new economic order from Britain's shoulders. The reckoning came in the 1840's, both for those processing British exports and those—in linen, for example—working up home materials. Technological advance, trade depression, and famine combined to produce misery and death on a scale that Britain never knew. Only in Ireland was there anything comparable to the tragedy of the Silesian woollen weavers or the flax spinners of Flanders.

The principal reason for the long survival of putting-out on the Continent was undoubtedly the low cost of rural labour. Linked to this, however, was the docility that normally accompanied dispersion: the entrepreneur found the cottage worker easier to deal with. Again and again, businessmen and officials note the dissipation and indiscipline of the urban proletariat, whether employed in mills or at home. The British hardly discuss the issue—and this in spite of the greater militancy and effectiveness of their labour movement.

The contrast is significant. It reflects, first of all, the difference in entrepreneurial response to factor costs. For the British employer, the best remedy for insubordination was technological unemployment. It hardly occurred to him to allow social considerations to modify the rational organization of his enterprise. Secondly, it reveals the insecurity of the continental bourgeoisie, the deep-rooted fear of another political and social upheaval like 1789. To be sure, England could have and did have her scares: witness Peterloo, or the emergency constabulary of 1848. But these passed, cured by good sense, humour, or both. Generally speaking, Britain took social order for granted. The industrialist had no illusions about the hostility of the working class or the possibility of violence; but he never doubted that the law would prevail. His French counterpart—and to a lesser extent, the German or Belgian manufacturer—was never sure when labour unrest or unemployment would turn into political revolution. Hence his readiness to equate working-class poverty and criminality—*les classes laborieuses* and *les classes dangereuses*.

Finally, the continental entrepreneur had a different conception of his role from the British. In societies with a strong feudal and manorial tradition, the successful factory owner tended to see himself as master as well as employer, with the duties as well as the privileges that such a position entails. He placed himself *in loco parentis*, treated his workers as minors in need of a firm tutorial hand, and felt a certain responsibility for their job security and welfare—always, of course, at the very modest level suitable to their station. This paternalistic sentiment varied considerably from person to person and place to place; just as Britain had her benevolent manufacturers, especially among the owners of the country mills, so the Continent had its 'exploiters'. On the whole, however, the continental industrialist never achieved that freedom of manœuvre and conscience that comes from looking on labour as just another factor of production, to be hired and fired as needed.

To be sure, even his paternalism was not entirely idealistic. Some of it was a response to the danger and inconvenience of losing a working force collected with difficulty and only too easily dispersed. This was one reason why, in contrast to what Marxist doctrine might lead us to expect, he often encouraged and assisted his men to become proprietors; or why he kept his working force on part time in moments of crisis, even at some sacrifice. Moreover, there was the pressure of public and official opinion. In these early decades of industrialization, both the traditional elites and the governments they dominated had serious qualms about the implications of a concentrated proletariat. There were many who felt that economic strength was not worth the price of social subversion. If many of these doubtful elements were won over in the long run to industrial capitalism, it was partly because they accepted the image of the paternalistic entrepreneur and saw in the maintenance of traditional personal bonds between employer and employed a powerful instrument of social control. And when the employer forgot his obligations, the state was prepared to remind him of them. In France, the government was sensitive to factory unemployment as to nothing else, keeping close watch on hiring and firing and utilizing political pressure when necessary to limit the number of jobless; even in—or rather, especially in—severe crises.

What we have, in short, is the usual phenomenon of legitimation by means of assumption of a role acceptable to the society as a whole. In the process, these attitudes, whatever their original motivation, tended to become an integral part of the entrepreneurial personality. The paternalistic manufacturer of the Continent believed that he was father to his men. And it was the very sincerity of this belief that often made him inflexible in his dealings with organized labour. For the British employer, a union may have been an adversary, a strike vexing and costly, the effort of labour to raise wages chimerical. He did not like these things, but he was prepared to face up to them. For the continental employer, however, a union was a conspiracy against public order and morals; a strike, an act of ingratitude; the effort of labour to raise wages, the indiscipline of an impatient son. All of this was evil. And there is no negotiating with evil.

Similarly with the efforts of the state to dictate hours or conditions of work: any such move was an intolerable intrusion that could only undermine the authority of the master. To the requirements of the factory act of 1841, the family enterprises of France, of northern France especially, opposed a deep, indignant immobility that discouraged examination and disarmed enforcement. The law called for voluntary inspectors from among the manufacturers themselves, active and retired. It was a fiasco: few volunteered and many of these soon resigned in despair or under pressure of friends and colleagues. There is no collaborating with evil.

From David S. Landes. *The Unbound Prometheus*, New York: Cambridge University Press, 1969. Reprinted by permission of the publisher.

PARLIAMENTARY INVESTIGATIONS INTO
CHILD LABOR IN THE FACTORIES OF INDUSTRIAL
ENGLAND: The Sadler Report

William Cooper, CALLED IN; AND EXAMINED.

What is your business?—I follow the cloth-dressing at present.

2. What is your age?—I was eight-and-twenty last February.

3. When did you first begin to work in mills or factories?—When I was about 10 years of age.

4. With whom did you first work?—At Mr. Benyon's flax mills, in Meadowlane, Leeds.

5. What were your usual hours of working?—We began at five, and gave over at nine; at five o'clock in the morning.

6. And you gave over at nine o'clock?—At nine at night.

7. At what distance might you have lived from the mill?—About a mile and a half.

8. At what time had you to get up in the morning to attend to your labour?—I had to be up soon after four o'clock.

9. Every morning?—Every morning.

10. What intermissions had you for meals?—When we began at five in the morning, we went on until noon, and then we had 40 minutes for dinner.

11. Had you no time for breakfast?—No, we got it as we could, while we were working.

12. Had you any time for an afternoon refreshment, or what is called in Yorkshire your "drinking?"—No; when we began at noon, we went on till night; there was only one stoppage, the 40 minutes for dinner.

13. Then as you had to get your breakfast, and what is called "drinking" in that manner, you had to put it on one side?—Yes, we had to put it on one side; and when we got our frames doffed, we ate two or three mouthfuls, and then put it by again.

14. Is there not considerable dust in a flax mill?—A flax mill is very dusty indeed.

15. Was not your food therefore frequently spoiled?—Yes, at times with the dust; sometimes we could not eat it, when it had got a lot of dust on.

16. What were you when you were ten years old?—What is called a bobbin-doffer; when the frames are quite full, we have to doff them.

17. Then as you lived so far from home, you took your dinner to the mill?—We took all our meals with us, living so far off.

18. During the 40 minutes which you were allowed for dinner, had you ever to employ that time in your turn in cleaning the machinery?—At times we had to stop to clean the machinery, and then we got our dinner as well as we could; they paid us for that.

19. At these times you had no resting at all?—No.

20. How much had you for cleaning the machinery?—I cannot exactly say what they gave us, as I never took any notice of it.

21. Did you ever work even later than the time you have mentioned?—I cannot say that I worked later there: I had a sister who worked up stairs, and she worked till 11 at night, in what they call the card-room.

22. At what time in the morning did she begin to work?—At the same time as myself.

23. And they kept her there till 11 at night?—Till 11 at night.

24. You say that your sister was in the card-room?—Yes.

25. Is not that a very dusty department?—Yes, very dusty indeed.

26. She had to be at the mill at five, and was kept at work till eleven at night?—Yes.

27. During the whole time she was there?—During the whole time; there was only 40 minutes allowed at dinner out of that.

28. To keep you at your work for such a length of time, and especially towards the termination of such a day's labour as that, what means were taken to keep you awake and attentive?—They strapped us at times, when we were not quite ready to be doffing the frame when it was full.

29. Were you frequently strapped?—At times we were frequently strapped.

30. What sort of a strap was it?—About this length [*describing it.*]

31. What was it made of?—Of leather.

32. Were you occasionally very considerably hurt with the strap?—Sometimes it hurt us very much, and sometimes they did not lay on so hard as they did at others.

33. Were the girls strapped in that sort of way?—They did not strap what they called the grown-up women.

34. Were any of the female children strapped?—Yes; they were strapped in the same way as the lesser boys.

35. What were your wages at 10 years old at Mr. Benyon's?—I think it was 4*s*. a week.

36. When you left Mr. Benyon, to what mill did you then go?—To Mr. Clayton's; that was a flax mill.

37. What age were you when you went there?—I was at Mr. Benyon's nearly a year and a half.

38. Then you were eleven years and a half old?—Yes.

39. What were your hours of work at Mr. Clayton's?—We started at five in the morning, and worked till ten minutes past eight at night.

40. That is 15 hours and 10 minutes?—Yes; and we had only 40 minutes out of that for dinner.

41. You assembled at five in the morning?—From five in the morning until ten minutes past eight at night.

42. Had you any time allowed for breakfast or drinking at that mill?—No, it was just the same as the other, with only 40 minutes for dinner.

43. So that, in point of fact, you had to be attending to your work on your legs for that length of time, with the short intermission of 40 minutes?—Yes, we had to get our meals as we could get them, all but our dinner.

44. Were your punishments the same in that mill as in the other?—Yes, they used the strap the same there.

45. How long did you work in that mill?—Five years.

46. And how did it agree with your health?—I was sometimes well, and sometimes not very well.

47. Did it affect your breathing at all?—Yes; sometimes we were stuffed.

48. When your hours were so long, you had not any time to attend to a day-school?—We had no time to go to a day-school, only to a Sunday-school; and then with working such long hours we wanted to have a bit of rest, so that I slept till the afternoon, sometimes till dinner, and sometimes after.

49. Did you attend a place of worship?—I should have gone to a place of worship many times, but I was in the habit of falling asleep, and that kept me away; I did not like to go for fear of being asleep.

50. Do you mean that you could not prevent yourself from falling asleep, in consequence of the fatigue of the preceding week?—Yes. . . .

William Osburn, Esq. called in; and Examined.

9854. WHERE do you reside?—At Leeds.

9855. Have you been an overseer of the town of Leeds?—I have; I was an overseer from Easter 1830 to Easter 1831, at which time the overseers are changed.

9856. Have you also been one of the trustees of the workhouse there?—Yes, I was a trustee of the workhouse at Leeds from May 1831 to last May.

9857. Then you, of course, are thoroughly conversant with the administration of the poor-rates in that great manufacturing town?—I attended the Board regularly, and a very great number of cases came under my observation; so that I became perfectly familiar with the mode of relieving them.

9858. Will you state upon what scale or rule you acted, in affording relief to families out of employment?—The scale of relief was 1 *s.* 6 *d.* per week for children under 10 years of age; no relief for the parents, nor any for the children above that age, except in case of sickness, or when they had been a very long time out of employment.

9859. Do you think that, generally speaking, the hours of labour in the mills and factories of Leeds and the neighbourhood are excessive, at least with respect to the capability of the children and young persons employed?—Very excessive in-

deed; a case came under my observation only the other day, of a girl who was labouring in Mr. Hogg's factory, at Holbeck, nineteen hours a day.

9860. What were the intervals for rest or refreshment during those nineteen hours?—I am not able exactly to speak of that; it came casually to my notice from a complaint of the mother.

9861. You made no particular inquiries with a view to this examination?—None whatever with that view.

9862. Supposing that the parents applying for relief for their children, refused to allow them to labour in mills or factories, in consequence of their believing and knowing that such labour would be prejudicial to their health, and probably destructive of their lives, would they, in the mean time, have had any relief from the workhouse Board, or from you, as overseer, merely on the ground that the children could not bear that labour?—Certainly not.

9863. So that you would not relieve those children unless the labour had actually destroyed their health?—They are only relieved in case of positive sickness, a report of which from one of the town's surgeons would be required, who, having visited the applicants, should state to the Board that they were absolutely ill, and incapable of working; if the persons applying are able to work in some degree, a mitigated relief is given to them, but still all paupers are expected to work to the extent of their capability of working.

9864. Would it be accepted as an excuse for not working, that they could not conform to those long hours of labour?—Certainly not.

9865. So that the children of the poor, and their parents, have no alternative in such cases, but submitting their children to this extravagant length of labour, or exposing them to absolute want and starvation, as the consequence of refusing so to to be employed?—None whatever.

9904. Do you coincide with the general impression, that this severe and long labour imposed upon the children in factories is very prejudicial to their health, to their morals, and to their future welfare?—Certainly; entirely so.

9905. You have already alluded to the fact of the appearance of weakly health that prevails among them, and also to the deformity that is so common, have you the same impression regarding the bad effects, in a moral point of view, produced upon the rising generation?—Certainly; I believe the moral effects of the system to be, if possible, worse than the physical ones; I will mention only one fact; vast numbers of girls who have wrought in factories are driven to prostitution when they are deprived of employment; girls not belonging to the parish of Leeds, probably to distant parishes, in some cases to no parish at all, have absolutely no other alternative but that of prostitution when trade is low and times are bad, so that they have no employment in mills; this was the universal complaint when I was at the workhouse Board.

9906. Have you not observed, that an excess of work at one period has been followed by a diminution of it at another, in consequence of the fluctuations and alternations in the market?—That is the observation, I may almost say, of every inhabitant of the town; it presses itself on the notice of every one.

9907. And is not the excessive labour of children, according to your opinion, accompanied by this pernicious effect, that the parents and the adults are in many instances thrown out of employment, either altogether or partially, by that practice?—That is exceedingly common; a great number of persons are now out of employment, and entirely supported by the labour of their children; some of them, I fear, have got to such a depth of degradation, that they are even willingly so.

9908. Is it not peculiarly distressing to those parents who are not so degraded in their minds, and so utterly debased in their feelings, that they have to subsist upon the labour of their children, themselves remaining idle?—Many of them have expressed that sentiment to me, and very forcibly. . . .

Mr. *Thomas Daniel*, CALLED IN; AND FURTHER EXAMINED.

9931. HAVE you been employed in any other business in mills and factories besides cotton?—In the silk mills I have been employed.

9932. Where both silk throwing and silk spinning have been conducted?—Yes.

9933. In what departments were you in any such mills?—I was a superintendent in throwing and spinning the silk.

9934. In both instances, therefore, you are competent to speak as to questions relating to that branch of business?—I am.

9935. Is a great proportion of children employed in that manufacture?—There is a great number.

9936. Does the proportion of boys or girls preponderate?—They are girls principally.

9937. Do you think that girls are as well capable of sustaining long-continued exertion as boys?—By no means.

9938. You have already mentioned that the labour of the children in the cotton factories has been considerably increased of late years?—It has been very considerably increased.

9939. Will you state whether that is the fact in regard to the labour of children in silk mills?—It is; their labour has been increased very much.

9940. Has the number of spindles that they have to attend been considerably increased by recent alterations in the machinery?—They have, more than one-half, I should think.

9941. Do you consider that those improvements or alterations in the machinery have materially lessened their labour with respect to the same number of spindles that children had previously to endure?—No, it has increased their labour very materially; they have as much labour again, thereabouts now, as they had to perform before.

———————

Parliamentary investigations into child labor in the factories of Industrial England: The Sadler Report. Taken from the Minutes of Evidence form the House of Commons, 8 August 1832. pp. 462–64, 467, 469.

ANALYSIS AND INTERPRETATION OF THE READINGS

1. According to Ashton, what was the principal reason for the employment of children in the factory?

2. What is the argument that J. R. McCulloch is attempting to refute?

| Consequences of Industrialization: Urbanization and Class Consciousness (1800–1850)

IDENTIFICATIONS

Samuel Smiles
Nassau Senior
Honoré Daumier
Honoré de Balzac
Jean-François Millet
Pierre Proudhon

Jeremy Bentham
Robert Owen
Auguste Comte
Dante Gabriel Rossetti
Thomas Malthus
David Ricardo

From the above list write the correct name in each of the blanks below:

_____ wrote *Essay on Population*

_____ wrote *The Principles of Morals and Legislation*

_____ wrote the popular *Self-Help*

_____ was a successful mill owner who denounced the profit system and established cooperative communities

_____ exposed middle-class greed and stupidity in *The Human Comedy*

_____ divided history into progressive stages and predicted a "positive" society

_____ claimed that all profit came only from the last hour of a business's daily operation

_____ satirized corruption and hypocrisy in his paintings

_____ led the pre-Raphaelite school of English painters

_____ devised a "law of rent" that supported middle-class interests

_____ taught that the price of an article should be determined by the amount of labor devoted to its production

STUDY QUESTIONS

1. Define "class consciousness." To what extent is it a useful concept for understanding Europe in the first half of the nineteenth century?
2. Why was there a decline in the standard of living in many rural areas of Europe in the first half of the nineteenth century?
3. Explain how changes in European agriculture in the early nineteenth century reflected the impact of a capitalist economy. What negative effects did improvements in communication have upon rural populations?
4. How did agricultural conditions in Russia contrast with those in England? In what ways was French agriculture different from the others?
5. What factors promoted the growth of cities between 1800 and 1850? Why was this growth "one of the most important facts in the social history of that period"?
6. What hazards to health and welfare resulted from the rapid urban growth that accompanied industrialization? Where might you find their parallel in the world today?
7. What elements of the nineteenth-century European population are included in the term "middle class"? In what sense did these diverse groups constitute a social class?
8. Why was mobility between the lower and middle classes low?
9. Describe Victorian middle-class family life. How do you account for its seeming peculiarities?
10. How do explain the differences between middle- and lower-class women in standards of sexual behavior? What contradictions do you see in the roles assigned to women?

11. How did the urban working class differ from that of preindustrial eras?
12. How did the factory system affect the conditions of labor?
13. What were the chief elements in the thought of the classical economists of the nineteenth century?
14. To what extent were the teachings of the classical economists compatible with the ideals of the Enlightenment? In what ways did they differ?
15. How did Ricardo's subsistence theory of wages comport with Malthus's theories of population?
16. How did the ideas of Malthus help "shift the responsibility for poverty from society to the individual"? Why did this shift appeal to the middle class?
17. How did Bentham's doctrine of utilitarianism enable the industrial middle class to "cut both ways" in pursuit of their objectives?
18. What contradictions developed within the middle-class creed of laissez-faire individualism?
19. How did John Stuart Mill depart from the teachings of the classical economists?
20. To what extent is middle-class ascendancy reflected in nineteenth-century art?
21. How did Louis Blanc's proposed reform program differ from the utopian projects of Robert Owen and Charles Fourier?

PROBLEMS

1. "Did the standard of living rise or fall in Europe during the first half-century of the Industrial Revolution?" Prepare a brief to support your argument in this ongoing debate.
2. Read a novel of Charles Dickens (*Oliver Twist*, *Dombey and Son*, or *David Copperfield*) and compare his description of lower-class conditions with available historical records.
3. Investigate some aspect of English mid-Victorian middle-class society, such as the status of women, sex mores, education of children, recreation, or relations with and attitude toward the lower classes.
4. Study John Stuart Mill's thought in relation to the ideas of the utilitarians, the classical economists, and the socialists.
5. Read Mill's essay *On Liberty* to determine to what extent it vindicated and to what extent it challenged the prevailing middle-class creed.
6. Investigate any of the following:
   a. Auguste Comte's positivism
   b. Charles Fourier's scheme of society
   c. Robert Owen's experiments with utopian communities
   d. the career of Louis Blanc

AIDS TO AN UNDERSTANDING OF THE CONSEQUENCES OF INDUSTRIALIZATION

A DEFENSE OF FREE ENTERPRISE
William Graham Sumner

Private property, also, which we have seen to be a feature of society organized in accordance with the natural conditions of the struggle for existence produces inequalities between men. The struggle for existence is aimed against nature. It is from her niggardly hand that we have to wrest the satisfactions for our needs, but our fellow-men are our competitors for the meager supply. Competition, therefore, is a law of nature. Nature is entirely neutral; she submits to him who most energetically and resolutely assails her. She grants her rewards to the fittest, therefore, without regard to other considerations of any kind. If, then, there be liberty, men get from her just in proportion to their works, and their having and enjoying are just in proportion to their being and their doing. Such is the system of nature. If we do not like it, and if we try to amend it, there is only one way in which we can do it. We can take from the better and give to the worse. We can deflect the penalties of those who have done ill and throw them on those who have done better. We can take the rewards from those who have done better and give them to those who have done worse. We shall thus lessen the inequalities. We shall favor the survival of the unfittest, and we shall accomplish this by destroying liberty. Let it be understood that we cannot go outside of this alternative: liberty, inequality, survival of the fittest; not-liberty, equality, survival of the unfittest. The former carries society forward and favors all its best members; the latter carries society downwards and favors all its worst members.

From William Graham Sumner, *The Challenge of Facts and Other Essays.*

THE BASES OF UTOPIAN SOCIALISM
Robert Owen

No one, it may be supposed, can now be so defective in knowledge as to imagine that it is a different human nature, which by its own power forms itself into a child of ignorance, of poverty, and of habits leading to crime and to punishment; or into a votary of fashion, claiming distinction from its folly and inconsistency; or to fancy that it is some undefined, blind, unconscious process of human nature itself, distinct from instruction, that forms the sentiments and habits of the men of commerce, of agriculture, the law, the church, the army, the navy, or of the private and illegal depredator on society. . . . No!

human nature, save the minute differences which are ever found in all the compounds of the creation, is one and the same in all; it is without exception universally plastic, and, by judicious training, THE INFANTS OF ANY ONE CLASS IN THE WORLD MAY BE READILY FORMED INTO MEN OF ANY OTHER CLASS; EVEN TO BELIEVE AND DECLARE THAT CONDUCT TO BE RIGHT AND VIRTUOUS, AND TO DIE IN ITS DEFENCE, WHICH THEIR PARENTS HAD BEEN TAUGHT TO BELIEVE AND SAY WAS WRONG AND VICIOUS, AND TO OPPOSE WHICH, THOSE PARENTS WOULD ALSO HAVE WILLINGLY SACRIFICED THEIR LIVES.

From Robert Owen, *A New View of Society.*

ON THE PRINCIPLE OF POPULATION
Thomas Malthus

I say that the power of population is indefinitely greater than the power in the earth to produce subsistence for man.

Population, when unchecked, increases in a geometrical ratio. Subsistence increases only in an arithmetical ratio. A slight acquaintance with numbers will shew the immensity of the first power in comparison of the second. By that law of our nature which makes food necessary to the life of man, the effects of these two unequal powers must be kept equal. This implies a strong and constantly operating check on population from the difficulty of subsistence. This difficulty must fall somewhere; and must necessarily be severely felt by a large portion of mankind.

Through the animal and vegetable kingdoms, nature has scattered the seeds of life abroad with the most profuse and liberal hand. She has been comparatively sparing in the room and the nourishment necessary to rear them. The germs of existence contained in this spot of earth, with ample food, and ample room to expand in, would fill millions of worlds in the course of a few thousand years. Necessity, that imperious all pervading law of nature, restrains them within the prescribed bounds. The race of plants and the race of animals shrink under this great restrictive law. And the race of man cannot, by any efforts of reason, escape from it. Among plants and animals its effects are waste of seed, sickness, and premature death. Among mankind, misery and vice. The former, misery, is an absolutely necessary consequence of it. Vice is a highly probable consequence, and we therefore see it abundantly prevail; but it ought not, perhaps, to be called an absolutely necessary consequence. The ordeal of virtue is to resist all temptation to evil.

This natural inequality of the two powers of population, and of production in the earth, and that great law of our nature which must constantly keep their effects equal, form the great difficulty that to me appears insurmountable in the way to the perfectibility of society. All other arguments are of slight and subordinate consideration in comparison of this. I see no way by which man can escape from the weight of this law which pervades all animated nature. No fancied equality, no agrarian regulations in their utmost extent, could remove the pressure of

it even for a single century. And it appears, therefore, to be decisive against the possible existence of a society, all the members of which should live in ease, happiness, and comparative leisure; and feel no anxiety about providing the means of subsistence for themselves and families.

Consequently, if the premises are just, the argument is conclusive against the perfectibility of the mass of mankind.

From Thomas S. Malthus, *Essay on a Theory of Population.*

THE LABOR THEORY OF VALUE
David Ricardo

Labour, like all other things which are purchased and sold, and which may be increased or diminished in quantity, has its natural and its market price. The natural price of labour is that price which is necessary to enable the labourers, one with another, to subsist and to perpetuate their race, without either increase or diminution. With a rise in the price of food and necessaries, the natural price of labour will rise; with the fall in their price, the natural price of labour will fall.

With the progress of society the natural price of labour has always a tendency to rise, because one of the principal commodities by which its natural price is regulated, has a tendency to become dearer, from the greater difficulty of producing it. As, however, the improvements in agriculture, the discovery of new markets, whence provisions may be imported, may for a time counteract the tendency to a rise in the price of necessaries, and may even occasion their natural price to fall, so will the same causes produce the correspondent effects on the natural price of labour.

The market price of labour is the price which is really paid for it, from the natural operation of the proportion of the supply to the demand; labour is dear when it is scarce, and cheap when it is plentiful. However much the market price of labour may deviate from its natural price, it has, like commodities, a tendency to conform to it.

It is when the market price of labour exceeds its natural price, that the condition of the labourer is flourishing and happy, that he has it in his power to command a great proportion of the necessaries and enjoyments of life, and therefore to rear a healthy and numerous family. When, however, by the encouragement which high wages give to the increase of population, the number of labourers is increased, wages again fall to their natural price, and indeed from a reaction sometimes fall below it.

When the market price of labour is below its natural price, the condition of the labourers is most wretched: then poverty deprives them of those comforts which custom renders absolute necessaries. It is only after their privations have reduced their number, or the demand for labour has increased, that the market price of labour will rise to its natural price, and that the labourer will have the moderate comforts which the natural rate of wages will afford.

Notwithstanding the tendency of wages to conform to their natural rate, their market rate may, in an improving society, for an indefinite period, be constantly above it; for no sooner may the impulse, which an increased capital gives to a new demand for labour be obeyed, than another increase of capital may produce the same effect; and thus, if the increase of capital be gradual and constant, the demand for labour may give a continued stimulus to an increase of people.

Thus, then, with every improvement of society, with every increase in its capital, the market wages of labour will rise; but the permanence of their rise will depend on the question, whether the natural price of labour has also risen; and this again will depend on the rise in the natural price of those necessaries on which the wages of labour are expended.

ANALYSIS AND INTERPRETATION OF THE READINGS

1. Do you agree with William Graham Sumner's arguments that unlimited competition is necessary to the preservation of liberty, and that liberty and inequality necessarily go together? Explain.

2. Why do you think that Robert Owen was so anxious to prove the plasticity of human nature?

3. What degree of importance does Malthus attach to "reason" in checking the growth of population?

4. According to David Ricardo, what conditions must prevail for the laborer to achieve a decent standard of living?

CHAPTER 28 | The Rise of Liberalism (1815–1870)

CHRONOLOGY

In the blanks write the correct dates from the list below:

1818	1833	1819
1834	1823	1846
1830	1848	1832
1852		

Repressive Six Acts of British Parliament _____

Beginning of Second French Empire _____

Defeat of the "People's Charter" in England _____

Formation of Quintuple Alliance _____

English Parliamentary Reform Bill _____

Repeal of Corn Laws _____

Suppression of Spanish liberals _____

Organization of Grand National Consolidated
Trades Union _____

Abolition of slave trade in British colonies _____

Liberal French revolution that served the
interests of the middle class _____

IDENTIFICATIONS

You should be able to identify or define each of the following terms:

Quadruple & Quintuple Alliances	"rotten" boroughs
Holy Alliance	Decembrists
Carbonari	Luddites
Constitutional Charter (France)	People's Charter
"Peterloo" Massacre	"June Days"
Corn Laws	*Crédit Mobilier*

In the blanks below write the appropriate names from the following list:

Alexander Ypsilanti	Charles X
Louis Blanc	Louis Napoleon
Tsar Alexander I	François Guizot
Louis Philippe	Benjamin Disraeli

_____ A socialist member of the provisional French government in 1848, he sponsored national workshops.

_____ A stubborn reactionary whose repressive policies led to a revolution which cost him his throne.

_____ A wily opportunist, he courted workers' support with his book *The Extinction of Pauperism.*

_____ An unsuccessful empire builder, he contributed to the movement for Greek independence.

_____ A Conservative English prime minister, he sponsored a major reform measure.

_____ Brought to the French throne by revolution, he was dethroned by another revolution eighteen years later.

_____ A hereditary autocrat whose flirtation with liberal principles worried other European monarchs.

_____ "Enrich yourselves!" he advised his critics during the reign of Louis Philippe.

STUDY QUESTIONS

1. Define "liberalism" in its nineteenth-century context.

2. What was the "Concert of Europe" intended to accomplish? Why did it largely disintegrate in the decade following 1815?

3. How did European rivalries help to vindicate the United States' Monroe Doctrine? Why was Britain willing to support such a statement?

4. What did Tsar Nicholas I mean by "orthodoxy, autocracy, and nationality"?

5. Why did revolutions in Spain's colonies succeed while liberalism was being suppressed in Spain?

6. During a period of general reaction, why did English conservative politicians support some reform measures? Why type of reform did they most stoutly oppose?

7. In what ways and to what extent was the English Parliament changed by the 1832 Reform Bill? Which class did the reforms benefit the most?

8. What were the objectives of the European revolutions of 1830? Where did they succeed? Why did the revolution fail in Poland?

9. What group benefited most from the Revolution of 1830 in France? How did they benefit?

10. How did English poor law reform reflect the beliefs and interests of the middle class?

11. How do both the new poor law and the repeal of the Corn Law illustrate the nineteenth-century philosophy of liberalism?

12. What were the aims of the Chartist movement in England? How did its objectives differ from those of the Trades Unions?

13. Contrast mid-nineteenth-century England and France with regard to (a) the progress of social and economic reform, and (b) the educational systems.

14. Why did Louis Philippe's regime, originally supported by French liberals, succumb to revolution?

15. How did the French February Revolution (1848) differ from the Revolution of 1830? Although the February Revolution succeeded in ending the monarchy, what problems did it pose for the future?

16. How did Louis Napoleon gain the support of various groups in his rise to power? By what means did he maintain power after making himself emperor?

17. How did the Reform Bill of 1867 modify the English electoral system?

18. Who were the group referred to as labor "aristocrats" in Britain? What kinds of changes did they advocate, and why?

19. During the later years of the nineteenth century there was apparent solidarity between the English middle class and working class in support of liberal programs. Why was this less the case in France during the same period?

PROBLEMS

1. Investigate further any of the following:
   a. The personality and policies of Tsar Alexander I
   b. The July (1830) Revolution in France
   c. The February (1848) Revolution in France
   d. The career of Louis Napoleon before his accession to power
   e. The Chartist movement in England
   f. The political career of Benjamin Disraeli

2. In the light of political developments in England and France, trace the evolution of the concept of liberalism during the nineteenth century in terms of the following considerations: (a) elements of the population supporting it; (b) typical exponents or leaders; (c) political programs; (d) economic objectives.

3. Demonstrate how events and movements of nineteenth-century Europe reflect the ascendancy of the middle class. Indicate the changes that took place in the composition of the middle-class during this period and the factors limiting the success of its program.

4. Read either *The Hunchback of Notre-Dame* or *Les Misérables* by Victor Hugo. (The latter in particular is very long. Ideally you should read the full text, but abridged versions are available.) What elements of social and political injustice during this period does Hugo criticize? Compare his fictional accounts with historical documents.

AIDS TO AN UNDERSTANDING OF THE RISE OF LIBERALISM

THE STRUGGLE FOR THE FIRST REFORM ACT
IN GREAT BRITAIN
Justin McCarthy

The new Parliament met on October 26, 1830. [During the interval between the Revolution in France and the assembling of Parliament there had been many symptoms in England of a widespread popular discontent, and a determination to have some change in the policy of the Government. Incendiary fires alarmed many parts of the country in September and October, great public meetings were held in various cities and towns, and tumultuous demands were made for the dismissal of the Tory Ministers.]

The actual work of the session began on November 2. On that day the King came to the House and delivered his speech in person. A debate arose in the House of Lords on the Address, and during this discussion the Duke of Wellington made his declaration with regard to parliamentary reform. Replying to a speech from Lord Grey, the Duke declared distinctly that he had never read or heard of any measure which could in any degree satisfy his mind "that the state of representation could be improved or be rendered more satisfactory to the country at large than at the present moment." "I am fully convinced," he said, "that the country possesses a legislature which answers all the good purposes of legislation, and this to a greater degree than any legislature has answered in any other country whatever." He went further. He declared that not only the legislature but the system of representation possessed deservedly the full and entire confidence of the country. He therefore declared plainly that he was not prepared to bring forward any measure of reform. Not only, he said, was he not prepared to bring forward any such measure, but: "I will at once declare that, as far as I am concerned, so long as I hold any station in the Government of the country, I shall always feel it my duty to resist such a measure when proposed by others."

• • •

The wild commotion that spread all over the country alarmed for a while even the stoutest opponents of reform. The Duke of Wellington himself may have felt his heart sink within him. Utter commotion prevailed in the palace. The King sent for Lord Lyndhurst and begged for his advice. Lord Lyndhurst recommended that the Duke of Wellington should be sent for. The King endeavoured to prevail on the Duke to take the leadership of a new administration. The Duke did not see his way, and recommended that Peel should be invited to form a Government. Peel knew well that he could not maintain a Ministry, and he naturally and properly declined. The Duke of Wellington was once more urged, and, out of sheer loyalty and devotion to his Sovereign, he actually made the vain attempt to get together an anti-reform administration. It was only an attempt. It came to nothing. Before the game was fairly started it had to be given up. Nothing was left but for the King to recall Lord Grey to power and consent to the measures necessary for the passing of the Reform Bill. Meantime the perplexed King was openly denounced all over the country. When his carriage was seen in London it was surrounded by hooting and shrieking crowds. The guards had to take the utmost care lest some personal attack should be made on him. Lord Grey and Lord Brougham insisted, as a condition of their returning to office, that the King should give his consent to the creation of a sufficient number of new peers. The King yielded at last and yielded in dissatisfied and angry mood, a mood which was intensified when Lord Brougham requested that the consent should be put into writing. At last William gave way, and handed a piece of paper to Lord Brougham, containing the statement that "the King grants permission to Earl Grey and to his Chancellor, Lord Brougham, to create such a number of peers as will be sufficient to insure the passing of the Reform Bill." When that consent had been given there was an end to the opposition. The Duke of Wellington withdrew, not only from any part in the debates on the Bill, but even from the House of Lords altogether until after the Bill had been passed. The Waverers of course gave way. It would be no further use to oppose the Bill. Lord Wharncliffe spoke bitterly against it because he evidently thought he had been outwitted, if not actually deceived, by the Ministry, but there was no further substantial opposition to the measure. The Bill passed through the Lords on June 4, and the Royal assent was give to the measure a few days later.

———

From Justin McCarthy, *The Epoch of Reform.*

THE AIMS OF THE CHARTISTS

To the honorable the Commons of Great Britain and Ireland, in parliament assembled, the petition of the undersigned their suffering countrymen.

Humbly showeth:

That we, your petitioners, dwell in a land whose merchants are noted for their enterprise, whose manufacturers are very skillful, and whose workmen are proverbial for their industry. The land itself is goodly, the soil rich, and the temperature wholesome. It is abundantly furnished with the materials of commerce and trade. It has numerous and convenient harbors. In facility of internal communication it exceeds all others. For three and twenty years we have enjoyed a profound peace. Yet with all the elements of national prosperity, and with every disposition and capacity to take advantage of them, we find ourselves overwhelmed with public and private suffering. We are bowed down under a load of taxes, which, notwithstanding, fall greatly short of the wants of our rulers. Our traders are trembling on the verge of bankruptcy; our workmen are starving. Capital brings no profit, and labor no remuneration. The home of the artificer is desolate, and the warehouse of the pawnbroker is full. The workhouse is crowded, and the manufactory is deserted. We have looked on every side; we have searched diligently in order to find out the causes of distress so sore and so long continued. We can discover none in nature or in Providence . . . The energies of a mighty kingdom have been wasted in building up the power of selfish and ignorant men, and its resources squandered for their aggrandisement. The few have governed for the interest of the few, while the interests of the many have been sottishly neglected, or insolently and tyrannously trampled upon. It was the fond expectation of the friends of the people that a remedy for the greater part, if not for the whole, of their grievances would be found in the Reform Act of 1832. They regarded that act as a wise means to a worthy end, as the machinery of an improved legislation, where the will of the masses would be at length potential. They have been bitterly and basely deceived. The fruit which looked so fair to the eye has turned to dust and ashes when gathered. The Reform Act has effected a transfer of power from one domineering faction to another, and left the people as helpless as before. Our slavery has been exchanged for an apprenticeship to liberty, which has aggravated the painful feelings of our social degradation by adding to them the sickening of still deferred hope. We come before your honorable house to tell you, with all humility, that this state of things must not be permitted to continue. That it cannot long continue, without very seriously endangering the stability of the throne, and the peace of the Kingdom, and that if, by God's help, and all lawful and constitutional appliances, an end can be put to it, we are fully resolved that it shall speedily come to an end.

Required, as we are universally, to support and obey the laws, nature and reason entitle us to demand that in the making of the laws the universal voice shall be implicitly listened to. We perform the duties of freemen; we must have the privileges of freemen. Therefore we demand universal suffrage. The suffrage, to be exempt from the corruption of the wealthy and the violence of the powerful, must be secret. The assertion of our right necessarily involves the power of its uncontrolled exercise. We ask for the reality of a good, not for its semblance; therefore we demand the ballot. The connection between the representatives and the people, to be beneficial, must be intimate. The legislative and constituent powers, for correction and for instruction, ought to be brought into frequent contact. Errors which are comparatively light when susceptible of a speedy popular remedy may produce the most disastrous effects when permitted to grow inveterate through years of compulsory endurance. To public safety, as well as public confidence, frequent elections are essential. Therefore we demand annual parliaments.

With power to choose, and freedom in choosing, the range of our choice must be unrestricted. We are compelled by the existing laws to take for our representatives men who are incapable of appreciating our difficulties, or have little sympathy with them; merchants who have retired from trade and no longer feel its harassings; proprietors of land who are alike ignorant of its evils and its cure; lawyers by whom the notoriety of the senate is courted only as a means of obtaining notice in the courts. The labors of a representative who is sedulous in the discharge of his duty are numerous and burdensome. It is neither just, nor reasonable, nor safe, that they should continue to be gratuitously rendered. We demand that in the future election of members of your honorable house, the approbation of the constituency shall be the sole qualification, and that to every representative so chosen shall be assigned out of the public taxes a fair and adequate remuneration for the time which he is called upon to devote to the public service.

From R. G. Gammage, *History of the Chartist Movement, 1837–1854.*

LIBERTY IN A SOCIAL CONTEXT: From *On Liberty* *John Stuart Mill*

The object of this essay is to assert one very simple principle, as entitled to govern absolutely the dealings of society with the individual in the way of compulsion and control, whether the means used be physical force in the form of legal penalties or the moral coercion of public opinion. That principle is that the sole end for which mankind are warranted, individually or collectively, in interfering with the liberty of action

of any of their number is self-protection. That the only purpose for which power can be rightfully exercised over any member of a civilized community, against his will, is to prevent harm to others. His own good, either physical or moral, is not a sufficient warrant. He cannot rightfully be compelled to do or forbear because it will be better for him to do so, because it will make him happier, because, in the opinions of others, to do so would be wise or even right. These are good reasons for remonstrating with him, or reasoning with him, or persuading him, or entreating him, but not for compelling him or visiting him with any evil in case he do otherwise. To justify that, the conduct from which it is desired to deter him must be calculated to produce evil to someone else. The only part of the conduct of anyone for which he is amenable to society is that which concerns others. In the part which merely concerns himself, his independence is, of right, absolute. Over himself, over his own body and mind, the individual is sovereign. . . .

The time, it is to be hoped, is gone by when any defense would be necessary of the "liberty of the press" as one of the securities against corrupt or tyrannical government. No argument, we may suppose, can now be needed against permitting a legislature or an executive, not identified in interest with the people, to prescribe opinions to them and determine what doctrines or what arguments they shall be allowed to hear. . . .

If all mankind minus one were of one opinion, mankind would be no more justified in silencing that one person than he, if he had the power, would be justified in silencing mankind. Were an opinion a personal possession of no value except to the owner, if to be obstructed in the enjoyment of it were simply a private injury, it would make some difference whether the injury was inflicted only on a few persons or on many. But the peculiar evil of silencing the expression of an opinion is that it is robbing the human race, posterity as well as the existing generation—those who dissent from the opinion, still more than those who hold it. If the opinion is right, they are deprived of the opportunity of exchanging error for truth; if wrong, they lose, what is almost as great a benefit, the clearer perception and livelier impression of truth produced by its collision with error. . . .

From John Stuart Mill, *On Liberty.*

ANALYSIS AND INTERPRETATION OF THE READINGS

1. What reluctant but important part did the king play in the passage of the First Reform Bill?
2. What did the Chartists mean by annual Parliaments?
3. What did Mill see as the only circumstance under which an individual's exercise of liberty could be justifiably curtailed?
4. How, in Mill's view, should societies deal with contrary opinions? How do you see this principle either honored or breached today?

CHAPTER 29

Nationalism and Nation-Building (1815–1870)

CHRONOLOGY

In the blanks provided, supply the correct date for each of the following:

Founding of the University of Berlin _____

Cavour's appointment as prime minister
of Sardinia_____

Crimean War _____

Bismarck's appointment as minister-president
of Prussia_____

Seven Weeks' War_____

Formation of Dominion of Canada_____

Completion of the Union Pacific Railroad _____

Proclamation of the German Empire _____

Republic of Colombia proclaimed _____

End of European rule in South America_____

Abolition of slavery in Brazil _____

War of the Reform (Mexico)_____

Beginning of Australian Commonwealth _____

IDENTIFICATIONS

Johann von Herder
Johann Wolfgang von Goethe
François René de Chateaubriand
J. G. Fichte
Eugène Delacroix
Porfirio Díaz
Juan Manuel de Rosas
Toussaint L'Ouverture

Friedrich List
Georg Wilhelm Hegel
Giuseppe Mazzini
Pedro II
Benito Juárez
Simón Bolívar
José San Martín

Choosing from the list above, write the correct names in the blanks below:

_____ His philosophy of history incorporated most fully the concept of the organic evolution of society and the state.

_____ A German economist, he rejected the theory of free trade.

_____ He regarded civilization not as an artificial creation but as an expression of the unique character of the people that produced it.

_____ His painting *Liberty Leading the People* expressed French nationalism and courage.

_____ His *Addresses to the German Nation* aroused a spirit of resistance against the Napoleonic occupation of Prussia.

_____ A nationalist and a republican, he founded the Young Italy society.

_____ His novel *The Sorrows of Young Werther* conveyed the restless emotionalism of the romantic movement.

_____ His *Genius of Christianity* romanticized the past and traditional religion.

_____ Acclaimed as "Liberator," at one time he headed a republic uniting the northern tier of South American states.

_____ A native of Argentina and a monarchist by conviction, he helped Peru become an independent republic.

_____ Born into slavery, he was the outstanding hero of the Haitian revolution but died in prison.

_____ A full-blooded Indian who has been called Mexico's "Abraham Lincoln," he overthrew the regime of Maximilian, puppet of Napoleon III.

_____ A gaucho leader who played upon sectional rivalry between the plains and the capital, he became dictator of Argentina.

_____ After ruling Brazil ably as a constitutional monarch for forty-nine years, he died in exile.

_____ Dictator for more than thirty years, he brought Mexico the appearance of prosperity but depressed the condition of the majority.

You should be able to identify or define the following:

Volksgeist	Law of Papal Guaranties
risorgimento	Upper and Lower Canada
Zollverein	Durham Report
Burschenschaften	creoles
German Confederation	*caudillo*
Pan-Slavism	
"Little Germans" vs. "Great Germans"	
Realpolitik	
"red shirts"	

STUDY QUESTIONS

1. Differentiate between the terms *nationalism* and *nation-building*. How can liberalism be tied to each?
2. Explain how romanticism aided the rise of nationalism. Why was this especially evident in Germany?
3. How did the romantics' interpretation of history differ from that favored by the thinkers of the Enlightenment?
4. How did Hegel apply his dialectic concept (thesis, antithesis, synthesis) to history in general and to German history in particular?
5. Although he seems the epitome of romanticism, Goethe departed from the romantic school in significant respects. Explain.
6. Summarize the administrative and political reforms of Stein and Hardenberg in Prussia.
7. How did the economic ideas of Friedrich List differ from those of Adam Smith? Why did List's ideas appeal to many nationalists?
8. What were the strengths and the weaknesses of Pan-Slavism as a cultural nationalist movement?
9. What were the obstacles to nationalist aspirations in the Austrian Empire? In Italy? In Ireland?
10. How did the force of nationalism both cause and ultimately frustrate the 1848 revolutions in the Austrian Empire?
11. What were the professed objectives of the Frankfurt Assembly of 1848? How did the conflict between liberalism and nationalism contribute to its failure? What conflicting nationalist goals were also evident?
12. How did Bismarck utilize each of the following in his program of German unification between 1862 and 1870: (a) the Danish war of 1864; (b) the Seven Weeks' War of 1866; (c) the Ems telegram; (d) the Franco-Prussian War of 1870–1871?
13. Identify the steps in the national unification of Italy between 1852 and 1870. Show how these steps were related to those leading to the unification of Germany.
14. What were the contributions of Mazzini, Cavour, and Garibaldi, respectively, to Italian reunification?
15. Compare Jeffersonian and Jacksonian democracy.
16. Why were European governments inclined to sympathize with the Confederacy during the American Civil War?
17. "Nation-building in Europe and the United States helped insure the continuing expansion of capitalism." Explain how.
18. How did "dominion nationality" differ from nation-building in Europe? What similarities did the two display?
19. How were the competing interests of French and British Canadians dealt with in this period?
20. Describe the effects of the discovery of gold in New South Wales and Victoria. What new policies resulted from the gold rush?
21. Why was there such a relatively high degree of government ownership of enterprises so early in Australia, as compared with Great Britain?
22. What part did the French Revolution and the Napoleonic Wars play in the revolutionary movements in Latin America?
23. How were the revolutions in Latin America related to the North American Revolution? In what important respects did they differ from the North American Revolution?
24. In what respects was Brazil's transition from colony to independent statehood unique?
25. Describe how the plantation system of land ownership contributed to economic and social inequality and political instability in Latin America.
26. What were the basic causes of instability in the newly formed Latin American republics?
27. What factors assisted progress toward stability in Uruguay and Chile?

PROBLEMS

1. Investigate further any of the following:
   a. Nationalistic elements in the operas of Wagner or Verdi
   b. Delacroix's paintings
   c. Hegel's dialectic philosophy
   d. The philosophy of Fichte

e. The Hungarian Revolution of 1848
f. Garibaldi and the One Thousand
g. The roles of Bismarck and Napoleon III, respectively, in the precipitation of the Franco-Prussian War

2. How was it possible for romanticism to include both conservatives and radicals?
3. Explore the historical roots of modern nationalism. Consider ways in which modern nationalism differs from nineteenth-century varieties.
4. Read Number 14 of *The Federalist*, written by James Madison, and discuss his views on majority rule versus minority rights.
5. Read the original unamended Constitution of the United States. What can you infer about the political philosophy of the men who wrote it?

6. Why did Jacksonian Democrats approve a strong executive?
7. Investigate the career and political philosophy of Simón Bolívar.
8. Compare the process of nation-building in Brazil with that in Mexico.
9. "Latin American movements for independence did not fulfill the high expectations of their protagonists." Explore further the reasons for this throughout Latin America.
10. Critique the value of the concept of nationalism for understanding the history of the nineteenth century. Point out both the strengths and the weaknesses of the concept.

AIDS TO AN UNDERSTANDING OF NATIONALISM AND NATION-BUILDING

BISMARCK CONTRIVES A WAR WITH FRANCE

All these considerations, conscious and unconscious, strengthened my opinion that war could only be avoided at the cost of the honor of Prussia and of the national confidence in her. Under this conviction I made use of the royal authorization communicated to me through Abeken to publish the contents of the telegram; and in the presence of my two guests [General Moltke and General Roon] I reduced the telegram by striking out words, but without adding or altering anything, to the following form:

"After the news of the renunciation of the hereditary prince of Hohenzollern had been officially communicated to the imperial government of France by the royal government of Spain, the French ambassador at Ems made the further demand of his Majesty the king that he should authorize him to telegraph to Paris that his Majesty the king bound himself for all future time never again to give his consent if the Hohenzollerns should renew their candidature. His Majesty the king thereupon decided not to receive the French ambassador again, and sent to tell him, through the aid-de-camp on duty, that his Majesty had nothing further to communicate to the ambassador."

The difference in the effect of the abbreviated text of the Ems telegram as compared with that produced by the original was not the result of stronger words, but of the form, which made this announcement appear decisive, while Abeken's version would only have been regarded as a fragment of a negotiation still pending and to be continued at Berlin.

After I had read out the concentrated edition to my two guests, Moltke remarked: "Now it has a different ring; in its original form it sounded like a parley; now it is like a flourish in answer to a challenge." I went on to explain: "If, in execution of his Majesty's order, I at once communicate this text, which contains no alteration in or addition to the telegram, not only to the newspapers, but also by telegraph to all our embassies, it will be known in Paris before midnight, and not only on account of its contents, but also on account of the manner of its distribution, will have the effect of a red rag upon the Gallic bull.

"Fight we must if we do not want to act the part of the vanquished without a battle. Success, however, depends essentially upon the impression which the origination of the war makes upon us and others; it is important that we should be the ones attacked, and the Gallic insolence and touchiness will bring about this result if we announce in the face of Europe, so far as we can without the speaking tube of the Reichstag, that we fearlessly meet the public threats of France."

From A. J. Butler ed. and trans., *Bismarck, the Man and the Statesman; Being the Reflections and Reminiscences of Otto, Prince von Bismarck.*

ADVANTAGES OF THE NEW CONSTITUTION: *The Federalist*, No. 10
James Madison

From this view of the subject it may be concluded that a pure democracy, by which I mean a society consisting of a small number of citizens, who assemble and administer the government in person, can admit of no cure for the mischiefs of faction. A common passion or interest will, in almost every case, be felt by a majority of the whole; a communication and concert result from the form of government itself; and there is nothing to check the inducements to sacrifice the weaker party or an obnoxious individual. Hence it is that such democracies have ever been spectacles of turbulence and contention; have ever been found incompatible with personal security or the rights of property; and have in general been as short in their lives as they have been violent in their deaths. Theoretic politicians, who have patronized this species of government, have erroneously supposed that by reducing mankind to a perfect equality in their political rights, they would, at the same time, be perfectly equalized and assimilated in their possessions, their opinions, and their passions.

A republic, by which I mean a government in which the scheme of representation takes place, opens a different prospect, and promises the cure for which we are seeking. Let us examine the points in which it varies from pure democracy, and we shall comprehend both the nature of the cure and the efficacy which it must derive from the Union.

The two great points of difference between a democracy and a republic are: first, the delegation of the government, in the latter, to a small number of citizens elected by the rest; secondly, the greater number of citizens, and greater sphere of country, over which the latter may be extended.

The effect of the first difference is, on the one hand, to refine and enlarge the public views, by passing them through the medium of a chosen body of citizens, whose wisdom may best discern the true interest of their country, and whose patriotism and love of justice will be least likely to sacrifice it to temporary or partial considerations. Under such a regulation, it may well happen that the public voice, pronounced by the representatives of the people, will be more consonant to the public good than if pronounced by the people themselves, convened for the purpose. On the other hand, the effect may be inverted. Men of factious tempers, of local prejudices, or of sinister designs, may, by intrigue, by corruption, or by other means, first obtain the suffrages, and then betray the interests, of the people. The question resulting is, whether small or extensive republics are more favorable to the election of proper guardians of the public weal; and it is clearly decided in favor of the latter by two obvious considerations:

In the first place, it is to be remarked that, however small the republic may be, the representatives must be raised to a certain number, in order to guard against the cabals of a few; and that, however large it may be, they must be limited to a certain number, in order to guard against the confusion of a multitude. Hence, the number of representatives in the two cases not being in proportion to that of the two constituents, and being proportionally greater in the small republic, it follows that, if the proportion of fit characters be not less in the large than in the small republic, the former will present a greater option, and consequently a greater probability of a fit choice.

In the next place, as each representative will be chosen by a greater number of citizens in the large than in the small republic, it will be more difficult for unworthy candidates to practise with success the vicious arts by which elections are too often carried; and the suffrages of the people being more free, will be more likely to center in men who possess the most attractive merit and the most diffusive and established characters.

• • •

The other point of difference is, the greater number of citizens and extent of territory which may be brought within the compass of republican than of democratic government; and it is this circumstance principally which renders factious combinations less to be dreaded in the former than in the latter. The smaller the society, the fewer probably will be the distinct parties and interests composing it; the fewer the distinct parties and interests, the more frequently will a majority be found of the same party; and the smaller the number of individuals composing a majority, and the smaller the compass within which they are placed, the more easily will they concert and execute their plans of oppression. Extend the sphere and you take in a greater variety of parties and interests; you make it less probable that a majority of the whole will have a common motive to invade the rights of other citizens; or if such a common motive exists, it will be more difficult for all who feel it to discover their own strength, and to act in unison with each other. Besides other impediments, it may be remarked that, where there is a consciousness of unjust or dishonorable purposes, communication is always checked by distrust in proportion to the number whose concurrence is necessary.

Hence, it clearly appears, that the same advantage which a republic has over a democracy, in controlling the effects of faction, is enjoyed by a large over a small republic,—is enjoyed by the Union over the States composing it. Does the advantage consist in the substitution of representatives whose enlightened views and virtuous sentiments render them superior to local prejudices and to schemes of injustice? It will not be denied that the representation of the Union will be most likely to possess these requisite endowments. Does it consist in the greater security afforded by a greater variety of parties, against the event of any one party being able to outnumber and oppress the rest? In an equal degree does the increased variety of parties comprised within the Union, increase this security. Does it, in fine, consist in the greater obstacles opposed to the concert and accomplishment of the secret wishes of an unjust and interested majority? Here, again, the extent of the Union gives it the most palpable advantage.

The influence of factious leaders may kindle a flame within their particular States, but will be unable to spread a general conflagration through the other States. A religious sect may degenerate into a political faction in a part of the Confederacy; but the variety of sects dispersed over the entire face of it must secure the national councils against any danger from that source. A rage for paper money, for an abolition of debts, for an equal division of property, or for any other improper or wicked project, will be less apt to pervade the whole body of the Union than a particular member of it; in the same proportion as such a malady is more likely to taint a particular county or district, than an entire State.

In the extent and proper structure of the Union, therefore, we behold a republican remedy for the diseases most incident to republican government. And according to the degree of pleasure and pride we feel in being republicans, ought to be our zeal in cherishing the spirit and supporting the character of Federalists.

———

From James Madison, *The Federalist*, No. 10, Paul Leicester Ford ed.

THE STRUGGLE FOR INDEPENDENCE: Simón Bolívar's Proposals for a Venezuelan Constitution (1819)

If a people, perverted by their training, succeed in achieving their liberty, they will soon lose it, for it would be of no avail to endeavor to explain to them that happiness consists in the practice of virtue; that the rule of law is more powerful than the rule of tyrants, because, as the laws are more inflexible, everyone should submit to their beneficent austerity; that proper morals, and not force, are the bases of law; and that to practice justice is to practice liberty. Therefore, Legislators, your work is so much the more arduous, inasmuch as you have to reëducate men who have been corrupted by erroneous illusions and false incentives. Liberty, says Rousseau, is a succulent morsel, but one difficult to digest. Our weak fellow-citizens will have to strengthen their spirit greatly before they can digest the wholesome nutriment of freedom. Their limbs benumbed by chains, their sight dimmed by the darkness of dungeons, and their strength sapped by the pestilence of servitude, are they capable of marching toward the august temple of Liberty without faltering? Can they come near enough to bask in its brilliant rays and to breathe freely the pure air which reigns therein?. . . .

The more I admire the excellence of the federal Constitution of Venezuela, the more I am convinced of the impossibility of its application to our state. And, to my way of thinking, it is a marvel that its prototype in North America endures so successfully and has not been overthrown at the first sign of adversity or danger. Although the people of North America are a singular model of political virtue and moral rectitude; although that nation was cradled in liberty, reared on freedom, and maintained by liberty alone; and—I must reveal everything—although those people, so lacking in many respects, are unique in the history of mankind, it is a marvel, I repeat, that so weak and complicated a government as the federal system has managed to govern them in the difficult and trying circumstances of their past. But, regardless of the effectiveness of this form of government with respect to North America, I must say that it has never for a moment entered my mind to compare the position and character of two states as dissimilar as the English-American and the Spanish-American. Would it not be most difficult to apply to Spain the English system of political, civil, and religious liberty? Hence, it would be even more difficult to adapt to Venezuela the laws of North America. Does not *L'Esprit des lois* state that laws should be suited to the people for whom they are made; that it would be a major coincidence if those of one nation could be adapted to another; that laws must take into account the physical conditions of the country, climate, character of the land, location, size, and mode of living of the people; that they should be in keeping with the degree of liberty that the Constitution can sanction respecting the religion of the inhabitants, their inclinations, resources, number, commerce, habits, and customs? This is the code we must consult, not the code of Washington! . . . .

Venezuela had, has, and should have a republican government. Its principles should be the sovereignty of the people, division of powers, civil liberty, proscription of slavery, and the abolition of monarchy and privileges. We need equality to recast, so to speak, into a unified nation, the classes of men, political opinions, and public customs. . . .

Among the ancient and modern nations, Rome and Great Britain are the most outstanding. Both were born to govern and to be free and both were built not on ostentatious forms of freedom, but upon solid institutions. Thus I recommend to you, Representatives, the study of the British Constitution, for that body of laws appears destined to bring about the greatest possible good for the peoples that adopt it; but, however perfect it may be, I am by no means proposing that you imitate it slavishly. When I speak of the British government, I only refer to its republican features; and, indeed, can a political system be labelled a monarchy when it recognizes popular sovereignty, division and balance of powers, civil liberty, freedom of conscience and of press, and all that is politically sublime? Can there be more liberty in any other type of republic? Can more be asked of any society? I commend this Constitution to you as that most worthy of serving as model for those who aspire to the enjoyment of the rights of man and who seek all the political happiness which is compatible with the frailty of human nature. . . .

The creation of a hereditary senate would in no way be a violation of political equality. I do not solicit the establishment of a nobility, for, as a celebrated republican has said, that would simultaneously destroy equality and liberty. What I propose is an office for which the candidates must prepare themselves, an office that demands great knowledge and the ability to acquire such knowledge. All should not be left to chance and the outcome of elections. . . .

It has rightly been said that the upper house in England is invaluable to that nation because it provides a bulwark of liberty; and I would add that the Senate of Venezuela would be not only a bulwark of liberty but a bastion of defense, rendering the Republic eternal. . . .

No matter how closely we study the composition of the English executive power, we can find nothing to prevent its being judged as the most perfect model for a kingdom, for an aristocracy, or for a democracy. Give Venezuela such an executive power in the person of a president chosen by the people or their representatives, and you will have taken a great step toward national happiness. . . .

Unless the executive has easy access to all the [administrative] resources, fixed by a just distribution of powers, he inevitably becomes a nonentity or abuses his authority. By this I mean that the result will be the death of the government, whose heirs are anarchy, usurpation, and tyranny. Some seek to check the executive authority by curbs and restrictions, and nothing is more just; but it must be remembered that the bonds we seek to preserve should, of course, be strengthened, but not tightened.

Therefore, let the entire system of government be strengthened, and let the balance of power be drawn up in such a manner that it will be permanent and incapable of decay because of its own tenuity. Precisely because no form of government is so weak as the democratic, its framework must be firmer, and its institutions must be studied to determine their degree of stability. Unless this is done, we must plan on the establishment of an experimental rather than a permanent system of government; and we will have to reckon with an ungovernable, tumultuous, and anarchic society, not with a social order where happiness, peace, and justice prevail.

From H. A. Bierck, Jr., ed., *Selected Writings of Bolívar*, Vol. I, Colonial Press, 1951.

COLONISTS AND MAORIS IN NEW ZEALAND
Keith Sinclair

No Delphic oracle was needed to prophesy the history of the first few years of regular settlement and government in New Zealand. Anyone in the Colonial Office, anyone who had read the history of colonization in America or Australia, could imagine something of the native and land troubles, the shortage of capital, the confusion in the Civil Service, the unpopularity of the governors, and the settlers' demands for self-government. Despite lofty talk of systematic colonization and British law and order, for some years after 1840 New Zealand exhibited a scene of anarchy more varied than before. Where cultures met or colonies were planted it was always so. What distinguished the situation in New Zealand from that in earlier days in Australia was the numerical supremacy of the Maoris, their proximity and their formidable fighting prowess. The European towns for a decade or more were mere encampments on the fringe of Polynesia; the settlers held their land on the doubtful tenure of Maori sufferance. Consequently a solution of the problems arising from the contact of the two cultures was a necessity upon which, for both races, all progress attended.

Almost all of the more serious difficulties of the settlers and their government were related to—if they did not derive from—the fundamental problem of racial relations. But, though they were dependent on the Maoris even for food, the New Zealand Company settlers were blind to this reality or reluctant to face it. For instance, when Governor Hobson decided, in 1840, to place his capital on the Waitemata Harbour and not at Port Nicholson, the Company settlers were indignant. They maintained that the site should be decided on geographical grounds alone and that a glance at the map was sufficient to reveal the superior claims of their own town. But Auckland was central in another sense. It lay between the two chief European settlements at Kororareka and Port Nicholson (where Wellington was to be built), and between the two areas with the densest Maori population, the Waikato and surrounding districts, and the country to the north of Auckland. It was a good choice for the site of a capital for the kind of New Zealand society which Hobson envisaged: a bi-racial community. This was the natural anticipation of such persons as Hobson and his successor, Robert FitzRoy, who had visited the country in the days before British sovereignty. In his book *Poenamo*, Dr Logan Campbell relates how, on his arrival in 1840 at the Waitemata Harbour (where Auckland was soon to be established), he realized that, since the Maoris would long be 'the dominant race', his fortunes rested with them. For a time he went to live with a neighbouring tribe, where he served his apprenticeship in the new land by helping to hollow out a canoe, and came to love his hosts. But

to the Company settlers, as to Edward Gibbon Wakefield, the man who inspired their migration, New Zealand's destiny was to provide a home for British migrants. There was no room, except perhaps on the periphery of their vision, for Maoris. It was many years before they would admit that the success of their settlements depended on their ability to live with the native New Zealanders.

Even the government finances were largely derived, in one way of another, from the Maoris. For many years the settlers were poor and could not be expected to pay much in taxation. The British Government, in the face of all its past experience of colonies, persisted in hoping that Wakefield was to be trusted at least in his promise that systematic colonization would pay for itself. The Treasury waited until the colony was bankrupt before giving grudging aid. At first Hobson was hopeful that the re-sale of Crown land, purchased from the Maoris, would provide a large revenue. When sales failed to come up to expectations he tried to rely on customs revenues, which largely fell on the Maoris; but it was impossible to stop smuggling; and the cost of collecting the duties on such a long coastline absorbed a large part of the paltry revenues gained. Eventually he had to discount bills drawn on the British Treasury, at exorbitant interest, with an Australian bank; and the Treasury had reluctantly to pay them. When he died in 1842, worn out by his task, his successor, Robert FitzRoy, against instructions, issued government debentures which he declared legal tender. Needless to say this bad paper currency drove out good sovereigns.

From Keith Sinclair, *A History of New Zealand*. London: Allen Lane, 1980. pp. 73–75.

ANALYSIS AND INTERPRETATION OF THE READINGS

1. What was Bismarck's real purpose in distorting the Ems dispatch?
2. Why did James Madison consider a republic greatly superior to a pure democracy?
3. Was Madison opposed to democracy as the term is now understood?
4. Why did Bolívar recommend the British rather than the United States Constitution as a model for his country?
5. Did Bolívar foresee with accuracy any of the difficulties of the emerging Latin American states?
6. Why does Keith Sinclair argue that race relations were fundamental to all other matters in the early European settlement of New Zealand?

Toward the Unification of Germany, 1740–1871

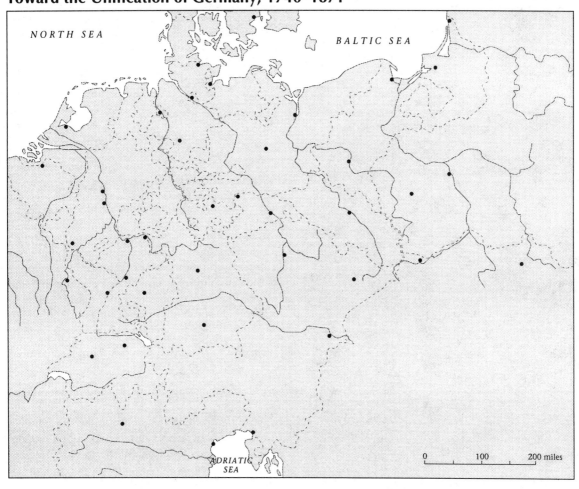

Latin America on the Eve of Independence c. 1800

ATLANTIC
OCEAN

GULF OF
MEXICO

CARIBBEAN SEA

PACIFIC
OCEAN

0   1000   2000 miles

Toward the Unification of Germany (1740–1871) and Latin America on the Eve of Independence (c.1800)

TOWARD THE UNIFICATION OF GERMANY (1740–1871)

1. On the "German Unification" map (see page 55), indicate the regions of the Austrian Empire *and* Prussia *following the Congress of Vienna (1815), and also the approximate boundary of the* German Confederation.

2. Outline the approximate boundaries of Germany in 1871.

3. Mark the location of the following cities:

Danzig	Amsterdam
Berlin	Antwerp
Munich	Prague
Copenhagen	Hamburg
Bonn	

4. Label the Danube and Rhine rivers.

LATIN AMERICA ON THE EVE OF INDEPENDENCE (c. 1800)

1. On the map of the Americas (see page 56 opposite), shade in the regions of Spanish and Portuguese control as of approximately 1800.

2. Label the islands of Jamaica *and* Cuba, *the* Amazon River, *the* Andes Mountains, *and* Cape Horn.

3. Identify Rio de Janeiro, Buenos Aires, Lima, *and* Mexico City.

CHAPTER 30 | The Progress of International Industrialization and Competition (1870–1914)

IDENTIFICATIONS

Alessandro Volta
Thomas Edison
Ram Mohan Roy
Ernest Solvay
Cecil Rhodes

Frederick W. Taylor
Leopold II
Louis Pasteur
Sayyid Ahmad Khan

From the above list write in the blanks below the names associated with each of the following:

_____ Perfection of a process of alkali manufacture

_____ Aggressive British imperialism in Africa

_____ Invention of chemical battery

_____ Invention of incandescent filament lamp

_____ Combining of scientific education with Islamic religious heritage

_____ The International Congo Association

_____ Location of source of bacteria

_____ Theory of scientific labor management

_____ Religion as a constructive social force

You should be able to define or explain each of the following:

piece rate
limited liability corporation
"finance" capital
cartel

"invisible" exports
"white man's burden"
Boers
"Great Mutiny"

STUDY QUESTIONS

1. What is the justification for speaking of a second industrial revolution following 1870?
2. Why was steel slow to replace iron as the key material in manufacturing? What were the advantages of steel over iron?
3. What did each of the following contribute to revolutionizing the production of steel in the later nineteenth century? Henry Bessemer, Pierre Martin, Sidney Gilchrist, and Sidney Gilchrist Thomas
4. What were the most important technological changes during the second period of industrial development?
5. What was the importance of the invention of the steam turbine? Of the internal combustion engine?
6. What factors caused a drastic population increase during the period 1870–1914? In what parts of Europe was the increase greatest?
7. How did the new industrial developments contribute to a rise in the standard of living?
8. "In all the countries of Europe, and in the United States, the pattern is one of expansion and consolidation." What factors promoted this trend? Why did it not entirely eliminate small workshops?
9. How did changes in the scale of industry and an increasing emphasis on efficiency lead to a change in wage scales?
10. What advantages and disadvantages for workers resulted from the increased scale of manufacturing? What were the advantages and disadvantages for employers?
11. Explain how the increase in scale and efficiency of production led to greater concentration of capital.
12. What is the difference between vertical combination and horizontal combination as forms of corporate growth? What is the objective of each type?

13. Why did monopolistic combinations develop more in Germany than in Great Britain?

14. Why, during a time of tariff increases throughout Europe, was Britain able to continue to espouse the doctrine of free trade?

15. How did economic trends in the later nineteenth century affect the relationship between government and business in western European countries?

16. In what areas of the world did the developed European markets look most avidly for new markets?

17. Compare J. A. Hobson's interpretation of imperialism with Lenin's interpretation.

18. In analyzing the causes of the "new" imperialism, what weight would you attach to economic, political, strategic, and psychological factors, respectively?

19. How did innovations in technology contribute to the advance of European imperialism in the late nineteenth century?

20. What important acquisitions in Africa were made by the British, the French, the Germans, and the Belgians, respectively? What reversals did the British suffer?

21. What "ground rules" for imperialism in Africa were formulated at the 1884–1885 Congress of Berlin?

22. Explain how British economic objectives in the Transvaal contributed to the outbreak of war in South Africa.

23. How did an initially small interest in India on the part of the British evolve into major economic and political involvement?

24. Trace the changes in the level of participation by the British East India Company in British involvement in India. How did the East India Company survive the Charter Act of 1834?

25. What were the important results of the "Great Mutiny" of 1857–1858? What policy changes followed?

26. Explain the theory behind British educational efforts in India, and the effects of those efforts.

27. What were the discernible effects of imperialism upon the non-Western peoples that were subjected to it?

28. To what extent did the United States become an imperial power in the late nineteenth and early twentieth centuries?

PROBLEMS

1. England's early leadership in the Industrial Revolution ultimately proved to be a disadvantage. Defend or attack this proposition.

2. Study the part played by any of the following in the development of late-nineteenth-century imperialism:
   a. Racist doctrines
   b. Technological and medical progress
   c. Intensified national sentiment
   d. Economic problems within European countries

3. Investigate any of the following:
   a. The evolution of steelmaking technology
   b. The development of the internal combustion engine
   c. Achievements in the field of industrial chemistry
   d. Anglo-Germanic industrial rivalry, 1870–1914
   e. The Boer War

4. Study in detail the history of the British East India Company in both India and China.

5. Compare American objectives and methods in pursuit of overseas interests with those of England, France, or Portugal. Note both similarities and differences (if you see any).

6. Explore further the paradox of democratic countries (England, the United States) engaging in undemocratic imperial enterprises. How did democratic countries justify imperialism?

7. Read William Leach's *Land of Desire*. What argument does Leach make regarding the promotion of consumption in the United States beginning in the late nineteenth century? What forces drove the increase in consumption, and whose interests did it serve? Do you accept Leach's argument?

AIDS TO AN UNDERSTANDING OF THE PROGRESS OF INTERNATIONAL INDUSTRIALIZATION AND COMPETITION

THE EVOLUTION OF MODERN CAPITALISM
John A. Hobson

There has arisen, therefore, in many quarters a new willingness to consider and to try bolder experiments, both in private and public enterprise, than have hitherto been possible. To realise the needed condition of higher productivity, more pacific relations between capital and labour, employer and employed, are essential. The peril of a situation in which falling wages and unemployment on an unprecedented scale are leading features drives the more active-minded employers to make considerable concessions from the old capitalist autocracy. From the employers' standpoint the problem is one of devising adequate and reliable stimuli to draw from the workers a larger and more regular output of productive energy, a greater willingness to adopt and apply new mechanical and business methods, and, in general, to cooperate more effectively with the other factors of production. But, in order thus to get labour to realise its community of interest with capital, that community itself must be established on a firmer footing. Labour must be given a more definite "interest" in the business and in its conduct, so far as matters directly affecting labour are involved. Hitherto, the business has "belonged to" the persons who owned the capital; it has been exclusively their property. The "interest" of any worker in it has been terminable by a week's notice, or less. Except so far as grudging concessions have been made to trade union pressure, the worker has had no voice in regulating the "conditions of labour" in the factory, mine, mill, or farm. Some more solid property in, and control of, the business must be secured for the workers in it. How to make that property and control consistent with the maintenance of the supremacy of the employer in the general conduct of the business, its organisation, as a technical instrument, the determination of the lines and methods of production, and the buying and selling processes, will be the great problem of business reconstruction. But closely related to it is the problem of securing to the workers a definite pecuniary interest in the success of the business as a whole. The wage system need not be displaced. The workers cannot be called upon to share fully in the risks and possible losses which the owners of the capital undertake. For no chances of participation in profits, however high, could secure the workers against the risks of periods of "working at a loss." But the wage system could be supplemented and strengthened by participation in the gains, applied so as to stimulate the greater efficiency of labour which should create gains. The evident defects which have caused the failure of most profit sharing schemes are being studied and remedies sought for them. For if capital and labour are to be brought into conscious harmony within the business, they must be got to realise that they stand to gain by effective cooperation. If the labourers, through their credited representatives, had some better understanding of the nature and methods of the business and of the factors contributing to success or failure, had some control over the conditions of working, and some definite interest in putting out the largest and best product compatible with reasonable consideration of their health and safety, the output of industry would undoubtedly be greatly increased, and its distribution would be more socially beneficial.

From John A. Hobson, *The Evolution of Modern Capitalism*, Allen & Unwin Ltd., 1926. Reprinted by permission of the publisher.

A CAPTAIN OF INDUSTRY
Alfred P. Sloan

[When I was vice-president of General Motors and Mr. Durant was president,] I was constantly amazed by his daring way of making decisions. My business experience had convinced me facts are precious things, to be eagerly sought and treated with respect. But Mr. Durant would proceed on a course of action guided solely, as far as I could tell, by some intuitive flash of brilliance. He never felt obliged to make an engineering hunt for facts. Yet at times he was astoundingly correct in his judgments.

One legend concerning him goes back to 1912, when a gathering of automobile manufacturers pooled guesses on the next year's production, each man dropping his slip of paper into a derby hat. That year 378,000 cars had been made. Mr. Durant guessed that in the next year they would manufacture half a million cars.

The others gasped. They said, "People can't buy that many cars. Our industry will be ruined by such overproduction before it really gets started."

Mr. Durant mildly rebuked them, saying, "Gentlemen, you don't realize the purchasing power of the American people. I look forward to the time we'll make and sell one million cars a year."

Those men thought he was being fantastic. Actually, his vision was clear. In 1929 the industry was to make, and sell, 5,621,000 automobiles. However, this example of Mr. Durant's vision does not alter the fact that many costly errors would have been avoided had his practice been to base decisions on a comprehensive analysis of all facts and circumstances. He was invariably optimistic. It was easy to be optimistic, though, if you had been in a position to observe the booming growth of Detroit, Flint, and other places where cars were being made; and Durant had seen all of it. . . .

Although I had important responsibilities under Mr. Durant, our methods of approaching operating problems were entirely different. But I liked him even when I disagreed with him. Durant's integrity? Unblemished Work? He was a prodigious worker. Devotion to General Motors? Why, it was his baby! He would have made any sacrifice for it, and he did make for it almost the ultimate sacrifice. But the question constantly in my mind was whether the potential industrial force under the General Motors emblem could be realized by the same boldness and daring that had been needed to enlist the units of that force. General Motors had become too big to be a one-man show. It was already far too complicated. The future required something more than an individual's genius. In any company I would be the first to say that William C. Durant was a genius. But General Motors justified the most competent executive group that could possibly be brought together.

In bringing General Motors into existence, Mr. Durant had operated as a dictator. But such an institution could not grow into a successful organization under a dictatorship. Dictatorship is the most effective way of administration, provided the dictator knows the complete answers to all questions. But he never does and never will. That is why dictatorships eventually fail. If General Motors were to capitalize its wonderful opportunity, it would have to be guided by an organization of intellects. A great industrial organization requires the best of many minds. . . .

After forty years of experience in American industry, I would say that my concept of the management scheme of a great industrial organization, simply expressed, is to divide it into as many parts as consistently can be done, place in charge of each part the most capable executive that can be found, develop a system of coordination so that each part may strengthen and support each other part; thus not only welding all parts together in the common interests of a joint enterprise, but importantly developing ability and initiative through the instrumentalities of responsibility and ambition—developing men and giving them an opportunity to exercise their talents, both in their own interests as well as in that of the business.

To formalize this scheme, I worked out what we speak of in industry as an organization chart. It shows how the business functions from the standpoint of the relationship of the different units, one to another, as well as the authority delegated to the executives, also in relation to one another. I grouped together those operations which had a common relationship, and I placed over each such group for coordinating purposes what I termed a Group Executive. These group executives were the only ones that reported to me. Then I developed a General Staff similar in name and purpose to what exists in the army. The general staff was on a functional basis, engineering, distribution, legal, financial affairs, and so on. Each of these functions was presided over by a vice-president, the purpose being twofold: first, to perform those functions that could be done more effectively by one activity in the interests of the whole; and second, to coordinate the functional activities of the different operating units as well as to promote their effectiveness. In the General Motors scheme, for instance, the vice-president in charge of sales is a coordinating executive. He has a staff at his command. His contribution is in developing better and more advanced policies of distribution technique through research and in other ways.

From Alfred P. Sloan, Jr., *Adventures of a White-Collar Worker*, in collaboration with Boyden Sparkes, Doubleday & Company, Inc., 1941. Reprinted by permission of the publisher.

The Voice of American Expansionism: Albert J. Beveridge in the United States Senate, January 9, 1900

Mr. President, the times call for candor. The Philippines are ours forever, "territory belonging to the United States," as the Constitution calls them. And just beyond the Philippines are China's illimitable markets. We will not retreat from either. We will not repudiate our duty in the archipelago. We will not abandon our opportunity in the Orient. We will not renounce our part in the mission of our race, trustee, under God, of the civilization of the world. And we will move forward to our work, not howling out regrets like slaves whipped to their burdens, but with gratitude for a task worthy of our strength, and thanksgiving to Almighty God that He has marked us as His chosen people, henceforth to lead in the regeneration of the world.

• • •

Mr. President, this question is deeper than any question of party politics; deeper than any question of the isolated policy of our country even; deeper even than any question of constitutional power. It is elemental. It is racial. God has not been preparing the English-speaking and Teutonic peoples for a thousand years for nothing but vain and idle self-contemplation and self-admiration. No! He has made us the master organizers of the world to establish system where chaos reigns. He has given us the spirit of progress to overwhelm the forces of reaction throughout the earth. He has made us adepts in government that we may administer government among savage and senile peoples. Were it not for such a force as this the world would relapse into barbarism and night. And of all our race. He has marked the American people as His chosen nation to finally lead in the regeneration of the world. This is the divine mission of America, and it holds for us all the profit, all the glory, all the happiness possible to man. We are trustees of the world's progress, guardians of its righteous peace. The judgment of the Master is upon us: "Ye have been faithful over a few things; I will make you ruler over many things."

From *Congressional Record* (56th Cong., 1st Sess.) Vol. XXXIII, pp. 705, 711.

The White Man's Burden
Rudyard Kipling

   Take up the White Man's Burden—
 Send forth the best ye breed—
Go bind your sons to exile
 To serve your captives' need;
To wait in heavy harness,
 On fluttered folk and wild—
Your new-caught, sullen peoples,
 Half-devil and half-child.

Take up the White Man's Burden—
 In patience to abide,
To veil the threat of terror
 And check the show of pride
By open speech and simple,
 An hundred times made plain.
To seek another's profit,
 And work another's gain.

Take up the White Man's Burden—
 The savage wars of peace—
Fill full the mouth of Famine
 And bid the sickness cease;
And when your goal is nearest
 The end for others sought,
Watch Sloth and heathen Folly
 Bring all your hope to nought.

Take up the White Man's Burden—
 No tawdry rule of kings,
But toil of serf and sweeper—
 The tale of common things.
The ports ye shall not enter,
 The roads ye shall not tread,
Go make them with your living,
 And mark them with your dead.

Take up the White Man's burden—
　　And reap his old reward:
The blame of those ye better,
　　The hate of those ye guard—
The cry of hosts ye humour
　　(Ah, slowly!) toward the light:—
"Why brought ye us from bondage,
　　"Our loved Egyptian night?"

Take up the White Man's burden—
　　Ye dare not stoop to less—
Nor call too loud on Freedom
　　To cloak your weariness;
By all ye cry or whisper,
　　By all ye leave or do,
The silent, sullen peoples
　　Shall weigh your Gods and you.

Take up the White Man's burden—
　　Have done with childish days—
The lightly proffered laurel,
　　The easy, ungrudged praise.
Comes now, to search your manhood
　　Through all the thankless years,
Cold, edged with dear-bought wisdom,
　　The judgment of your peers!

———

From Rudyard Kipling, "White Man's Burden." From *Rudyard Kipling's Verse.*

ANALYSIS AND INTERPRETATION
OF THE READINGS

1. What modification of the wage system does Hobson suggest?
2. How does Alfred Sloan's experience with General Motors illustrate both the pace of industrial expansion and the ensuing problems?
3. On what basis did Albert J. Beveridge justify American expansion? How widely was his opinion shared in the United States at the turn of the century?

| The Middle Class Challenged

CHRONOLOGY

1859	1880	1862
1889	1864	1895
1867	1898	1871
1900		

From the above list supply the correct date for each of the following:

Marx's *Capital* _____

Syllabus of Errors of Pope Pius IX_____

Darwin's *Origin of Species* _____

Paris Commune_____

International Workingmen's Association founded_____

Founding of the Second International_____

IDENTIFICATIONS

Mikhail Bakunin	Herbert Spencer
Eduard Bernstein	Sir James Frazer
Pius IX	Ivan Pavlov
George Bernard Shaw	Henrik Ibsen
Georges Sorel	Leo Tolstoy
Thomas Huxley	Paul Cézanne
Alexander Pushkin	Vincent van Gogh

From the above list write the correct name in each of the blanks below:

_____ Advocate of terrorism to overthrow the state, which he regarded as the supreme evil

_____ Vigorous defender of Darwin against religious critics

_____ Famous playwright, identified with a group of moderate socialists

_____ Dramatist in rebellion against the tyranny of conventional middle-class society

_____ Anthropologist who produced arguments to support cultural "relativism"

_____ Painter of *The Starry Night*

_____ Founder of expressionist movement in painting

_____ German parliamentarian who believed socialism could be achieved through gradual reform

_____ One of Russia's greatest novelists, champion of the simple life, and opponent of social and political evils

_____ English philosopher, exponent of extreme individualism and of evolutionary theory

_____ Author of *Reflections on Violence*, which expounded doctrine of the general strike

_____ Russian poet who shifted from romanticism to realism

_____ Discoverer of the conditioned reflex

You should be able to identify or define each of the following terms:

Communards	papal infallibility
natural selection	realists
mutation hypothesis	impressionism
agnosticism	expressionism
behaviorism	cubism
"social gospel"	symbolists

STUDY QUESTIONS

1. Explain each of the following in relation to Marx's analysis of capitalist economy: (a) the labor theory of value; (b) the proletariat; (c) the petty bourgeoisie.
2. How did Marx distinguish between socialism and communism in his theory of revolution?
3. In Marx's interpretation of history, what role was played by class struggle and by the dialectical view of conflict and resolution?
4. During what period was the International headed by Marx most successful? Why did it eventually expire?
5. How did Marx view the bloody conflict of 1871 in Paris? Did the facts substantiate his interpretation of the nature and objectives of the Commune?
6. Explain the appeal in the nineteenth century of Marx's long and complex work *Capital*.
7. Why did socialism gain ground more slowly on Europe's periphery than in its center?
8. What were the main differences between the "purist" and the "revisionist" socialists? Which group made more headway during the late nineteenth century?
9. Distinguish between anarchism and syndicalism. What ideas or objectives did each of them share with socialism?
10. Explain Darwin's idea of natural selection.
11. Compare Lamarck's and Darwin's theories of evolution.
12. How did Weismann and De Vries modify the Darwinian theory?
13. Why was the impact of Darwin's biological theory so disturbing to believers in an orderly universe?
14. What adaptation did the Social Darwinists make of Darwin's theory?
15. Explain Freud's theory of human motivation and behavior. Why were dreams important to Freudian psychoanalysis?
16. Although Nietzsche was a romantic poet more than a scientist, he employed a theory of evolution in his philosophy. Explain this statement.
17. How did both behaviorism and psychoanalysis encourage a deterministic outlook?
18. In what different ways did leading religious groups and individuals react to new scientific and philosophical challenges?
19. How did the scope and character of the reading public change in the later nineteenth century? How did writers and publishers react to this change?
20. What change in the artist's conception of the nature of art and of his own relationship to society had become evident by the end of the nineteenth century? What does it mean to say that "artists and public were ceasing to speak the same language"?
21. What different aspects of realism are seen in the works of Zola, Dickens, and Hardy, respectively?
22. Describe the development of painting from realism to cubism.

PROBLEMS

1. Investigate any of the following:
   a. Leo Tolstoy's social ideals
   b. Georges Sorel and syndicalism
   c. The activities and influence of the English Fabian socialists
   d. The Paris Commune of 1871
   e. The vicissitudes of the International Workingmen's Association
   f. Darwin and the voyage of the *Beagle*
   g. Pavlov and his experiments
   h. The impressionists
2. In what ways was Marx a product of the nineteenth century, and in what ways was he a rebel against it?
3. Explore the relationship between the decline of romanticism and such nineteenth-century phenomena as scientific discovery, industrial expansion, and middle-class ascendancy.
4. Read *Crime and Punishment* or *The Brothers Karamazov* by Dostoevsky. How did Dostoevsky use pain and anguish to explore the human condition? What would make his novels particularly appealing to the middle class and to workers?
5. Read any of the following literary works to discover what light it throws on nineteenth-century moods and anxieties: Tennyson, *In Memoriam*; Henry Adams, *The Education of Henry Adams*; Matthew Arnold, *Culture and Anarchy*.

AIDS TO AN UNDERSTANDING OF THE MIDDLE CLASS CHALLENGED

From *The Communist Manifesto*
Karl Marx and F. Engels

The history of all hitherto existing society is the history of class struggles.

Freeman and slave, patrician and plebeian, lord and serf, guild-master and journeyman, in a word, oppressor and oppressed, stood in constant opposition to one another, carried on an uninterrupted, now hidden, now open fight, a fight that each time ended, either in a revolutionary reconstitution of society at large, or in the common ruin of the contending classes.

In the earlier epochs of history, we find almost everywhere a complicated arrangement of society into various orders, a manifold gradation of social rank. In ancient Rome we have patricians, knights, plebeians, slaves; in the Middle Ages, feudal lords, vassals, guild-masters, journeymen, apprentices, serfs; in almost all of these classes, again, subordinate gradations.

The modern bourgeois society that has sprouted from the ruins of feudal society, has not done away with class antagonisms. It has but established new classes, new conditions of oppression, new forms of struggle in place of the old ones.

Our epoch, the epoch of the bourgeoisie, possesses, however, this distinctive feature: It has simplified the class antagonisms. Society as a whole is more and more splitting up into two great hostile camps, into two great classes directly facing each other—bourgeoisie and proletariat.

• • •

A similar movement is going on before our own eyes. Modern bourgeois society with its relations of production, of exchange and of property, a society that has conjured up such gigantic means of production and of exchange, is like the sorcerer who is no longer able to control the powers of the nether world whom he has called up by his spells. For many a decade past the history of industry and commerce is but the history of the revolt of modern productive forces against modern conditions of production, against the property relations that are the conditions for the existence of the bourgeoisie and of its rule. It is enough to mention the commercial crises that by their periodic return put the existence of the entire bourgeois society on trial, each time more threateningly. In these crises a great part not only of the existing products but also of the previously created productive forces, are periodically destroyed. In these crises there breaks out an epidemic that, in all earlier epochs, would have seemed an absurdity—the epidemic of over-production. Society suddenly finds itself put back into a state of momentary barbarism; it appears as if a famine, a universal war of devastation had cut off the supply of every means of subsistence; industry and commerce seem to be destroyed. And why? Because there is too much civilisation, too much means of subsistence, too much industry, too much commerce. The productive forces at the disposal of society no longer tend to further the development of the conditions of bourgeois property; on the contrary, they have become too powerful for these conditions, by which they are fettered, and no sooner do they overcome these fetters than they bring disorder into the whole of bourgeois society, endanger the existence of bourgeois property. The conditions of bourgeois society are too narrow to comprise the wealth created by them. And how does the bourgeoisie get over these crises? On the one hand by enforced destruction of a mass of productive forces; on the other, by the conquest of new markets, and by the more thorough exploitation of the old ones. That is to say, by paving the way for more extensive and more destructive crises, and by diminishing the means whereby crises are prevented.

The weapons with which the bourgeoisie felled feudalism to the ground are now turned against the bourgeoisie itself.

But not only has the bourgeoisie forged the weapons that bring death to itself; it has also called into existence the men who are to wield those weapons—the modern working class—the proletarians.

• • •

The Communists disdain to conceal their views and aims. They openly declare that their ends can be attained only by the forcible overthrow of all existing social conditions. Let the ruling classes tremble at a Communist revolution. The proletarians have nothing to lose but their chains. They have a world to win.

Workingmen of all countries, unite!

————

From Karl Marx and Friedrich Engels, *The Communist Manifesto.*

An Exposition of Darwinism by a Contemporary Naturalist
Alfred Russel Wallace

The point I wish especially to urge is this. Before Darwin's work appeared, the great majority of naturalists, and almost without exception the whole literary and scientific world, held firmly to the belief that species were realities, and had not been derived from other species by any process accessible to us; the different species of crow and of violet were believed to have been always as distinct and separate as they are now, and to have originated by some totally unknown process so far removed from ordinary reproduction that it was usually spoken of as "special creation." There was, then, no question of the origin of families, orders, and classes, because the very first step of all, the "origin of species," was believed to be an insoluble problem. But now this is all changed. The whole scientific and literary world, even the whole educated public, accepts, as a matter of common knowledge, the origin of species from other allied species by the ordinary process of natural birth. The idea of special creation or any altogether exceptional mode of production is absolutely extinct! Yet more: this is held also to apply to many higher groups as well as to the species of a genus, and not even Mr. Darwin's severest critics venture to suggest that the primeval bird, reptile, or fish must have been "specially created." And this vast, this totally unprecedented change in public opinion has been the result of the work of one man, and was brought about in the short space of twenty years! This is the answer to those who continue to maintain that the "origin of species" is not yet discovered; that there are still doubts and difficulties; that there are divergencies of structure so great that we cannot understand how they had their beginning. We may admit all this, just as we may admit that there are enormous difficulties in the way of a complete comprehension of the origin and nature of all the parts of the solar system and of the stellar universe. But we claim for Darwin that he is the Newton of natural history, and that, just so surely as that the discovery and demonstration by Newton of the law of gravitation established order in place of chaos and laid a sure foundation for all future study of the starry heavens, so surely has Darwin, by his discovery of the law of natural selection and his demonstration of the great principle of the preservation of useful variations in the struggle for life, not only thrown a flood of light on the process of development of the whole organic world, but also established a firm foundation for all future study of nature.

• • •

The theory of natural selection rests on two main classes of facts which apply to all organised beings without exception, and which thus take rank as fundamental principles or laws. The first is, the power of rapid multiplication in a geometrical progression; the second, that the offspring always vary slightly from the parents, though generally very closely resembling them. From the first fact or law there follows, necessarily, a constant struggle for existence; because, while the offspring always exceed the parents in number, generally to an enormous extent, yet the total number of living organisms in the world does not, and cannot, increase year by year. Consequently every year, on the average, as many die as are born, plants as well as animals; and the majority die premature deaths. They kill each other in a thousand different ways; they starve each other by some consuming the food that others want; they are destroyed largely by the powers of nature—by cold and heat, by rain and storm, by flood and fire. There is thus a perpetual struggle among them which shall live and which shall die; and this struggle is tremendously severe, because so few can possibly remain alive—one in five, one in ten, often only one in a hundred or even one in a thousand.

Then comes the question, Why do some live rather than others? If all the individuals of each species were exactly alike in every respect, we could only say it is a matter of chance. But they are not alike. We find that they vary in many different ways. Some are stronger, some swifter, some hardier in constitution, some more cunning. An obscure colour may render concealment more easy for some, keener sight may enable others to discover prey or escape from an enemy better than their fellows. Among plants the smallest differences may be useful or the reverse. The earliest and strongest shoots may escape the slug; their greater vigour may enable them to flower and seed earlier in a wet autumn; plants best armed with spines or hairs may escape being devoured; those whose flowers are most conspicuous may be soonest fertilised by insects. We cannot doubt that, on the whole, any beneficial variations will give the possessors of it a greater probability of living through the tremendous ordeal they have to undergo. There may be something left to chance, but on the whole *the fittest will survive.*

From Alfred Russel Wallace, *Darwinism: an Exposition of the Theory of Natural Selection with some of Its Applications.*

THE NEW PSYCHOLOGY: The Individual and Civilization
Sigmund Freud

When we look at the relation between the process of human civilization and the developmental or educative process of individual human beings, we shall conclude without much hesitation that the two are very similar in nature, if not the very same process applied to different kinds of object. The process of the civilization of the human species is, of course, an abstraction of a higher order than is the development of the individual and it is therefore harder to apprehend in concrete terms, nor should we pursue analogies to an obsessional extreme; but in view of the similarity between the aims of the two processes—in the one case the integration of a separate individual into a human group, and in the other case the creation of a unified group out of many individuals—we cannot be surprised at the similarity between the means employed and the resultant phenomena.

In view of its exceptional importance, we must not long postpone the mention of one feature which distinguishes between the two processes. In the developmental process of the individual, the programme of the pleasure principle, which consists in finding the satisfaction of happiness, is retained as the main aim. Integration in, or adaptation to, a human community appears as a scarcely avoidable condition which must be fulfilled before this aim of happiness can be achieved. If it could be done without that condition, it would perhaps be preferable. To put it in other words, the development of the individual seems to us to be a product of the interaction between two urges, the urge towards happiness, which we usually call "egoistic," and the urge towards union with others in the community, which we call "altruistic." Neither of these descriptions goes much below the surface. In the process of individual development, as we have said, the main accent falls mostly on the egoistic urge (or the urge towards happiness); while the other urge, which may be described as a "cultural" one, is usually content with the role of imposing restrictions. But in the process of civilization things are different. Here by far the most important thing is the aim of creating a unity out of the individual human beings. It is true that the aim of happiness is still there, but it is pushed into the background. It almost seems as if the creation of a great human community would be most successful if no attention had to be paid to the happiness of the individual. The developmental process of the individual can thus be expected to have special features of its own which are not reproduced in the process of human civilization. It is only in so far as the first of these processes has union with the community as its aim that it need coincide with the second process.

Just as a planet revolves around a central body as well as rotating on its own axis, so the human individual takes part in the course of development of mankind at the same time as he pursues his own path in life. But to our dull eyes the play of forces in the heavens seems fixed in a never-changing order; in the field of organic life we can still see how the forces contend with one another, and how the effects of the conflict are continually changing. So, also, the two urges, the one towards personal happiness and the other towards union with other human beings must struggle with each other in every individual; and so, also, the two processes of individual and of cultural development must stand in hostile opposition to each other and mutually dispute the ground.

From Sigmund Freud, *Civilization and Its Discontents.* Newly translated from the German and edited by James Strachey. Copyright © 1961 by James Strachey. First American Edition 1962 Reprinted by permission of W. W. Norton & Company, Inc., and the Hogarth Press Ltd.

ANALYSIS AND INTERPRETATION
OF THE READINGS

1. What did Marx and Engels mean by the conflict between modern "productive forces" and "modern property relations"? Why did they believe that bourgeois society had simplified class antagonisms?

2. Explain the fundamental difference between "special creation" and evolution.

3. What does Freud mean by "happiness"?

4. Does Freud believe that the demands of the individual and the demands of society are irreconcilable? Explain.

CHAPTER 32 | A Delicate Equilibrium (1870–1914)

IDENTIFICATIONS

You should be able to identify and summarize the importance of each of the following items or persons:

Bundesrat
Reichstag
Wilhelm Liebknecht
Marshal Marie-Edmé MacMahon
General Georges Boulanger
Alexandre Millerand
David Lloyd George
Herbert Asquith
Emmeline Pankhurst
"Cat and Mouse Act"
mir
zemstvos

Russification
Duma
Vladimir Ulanov
Bloody Sunday
October Manifesto
trasformismo
Young Turks
Eugene V. Debs
IWW
Triple Entente
drang nach osten
Francis Ferdinand

STUDY QUESTIONS

1. How did shifts in class structure in the late nineteenth century threaten the stability of European society?
2. How did the constitution established by Bismarck provide for Prussian domination of the German empire?
3. What democratic features did the constitution of the German Empire include?
4. Explain Bismarck's motives in his *Kulturkampf* against the Church. What was the outcome of this struggle?
5. How did Bismarck attempt to meet the threat posed by German socialists? To what extent was he successful?
6. To what extent and in what directions did Emperor William II modify Bismarck's policies?
7. How do you account for the increasing political strength of the German Social Democrats, as evidenced by their gains in the election of 1912? Why were they unable to enact a genuinely socialist program despite these gains?
8. What democratic features were incorporated in the constitution of the Third French Republic? In what ways did it copy the English parliamentary system of government? What factors made for unstable ministries?
9. How did the Dreyfus affair lead to an attack upon the Catholic Church? What was the outcome of this attack?
10. Explain the reasons why Germany had adopted such a large amount of social legislation by 1890.
11. Compare the labor policies of the French and German governments in the period under review.
12. What reform measures had brought Britain nearer to representative democracy by the 1880s?
13. Explain the nature and function of "ministerial responsibility" in the British political system.
14. What were the origins of the British Labour Party?
15. Why did the Liberal party budget of 1909 produce a constitutional crisis? How was the crisis resolved?
16. Summarize the program of social and economic reform in Britain during the Liberal era of the early twentieth century. Why did these reforms fail to satisfy the working class?
17. Summarize the reforms in the Russian judiciary under Tsar Alexander II.
18. Explain the importance of the populist movement in late-nineteenth-century Russia.
19. What policies were adopted by Alexander III and Nicholas II to stem the tide of reform?
20. Why was a working-class consciousness slow in developing in Russia?
21. What were the objectives of the Russian Social Revolutionaries and Social Democrats, respectively?

22. Explain the split between Mensheviks and Bolsheviks within the Social Democratic party. What was Lenin's program for the Bolsheviks?
23. What was the immediate cause of the Russian revolution of 1905? Did it achieve any degree of success? Why did it not accomplish the overthrow of autocracy?
24. Why did the introduction of universal male suffrage in the Austrian portion of the Dual Monarchy fail to satisfy the several national groups?
25. Indicate the stages in the dismemberment of the European portions of the Ottoman empire between 1829 and 1914.
26. Why was domestic turmoil in the United States less severe than in other major Western countries?
27. Describe the evolution of the rival alliance systems between 1872 and 1907. What factors led to the weakening of the Triple Alliance?
28. What arguments does Fritz Fischer advance in arguing for Germany's prime responsibility for the start of World War I? What are the objections to these arguments? Was Germany the only heavily militarized state in 1914?
29. Cite examples, in both large and small states, of nationalist ambitions threatening to European stability.
30. Point out the effects of the Moroccan crises, the Bosnian crisis of 1908, and the Balkan war of 1912 in heightening international tension.

PROBLEMS

1. Investigate further any of the following:
   a. The *Kulturkampf*
   b. The Dreyfus affair
   c. The Russian revolution of 1905
   d. The British campaign for women's suffrage
   e. The evolution of the Triple Entente
   f. The Progressive movement in the United States
   g. The early career of Lenin
   h. The rise of the British Labour party
2. Compare the English parliamentary system with the system of France under the Third Republic.
3. The outbreak of war in 1914 can be attributed, in part, to each of the following: the rival European alliance systems; the growth of militarism; social tensions and instability within the various countries. Which one do you consider most important? Substantiate your conclusions.

AIDS TO AN UNDERSTANDING OF A DELICATE EQUILIBRIUM (1870–1914)

THE BEGINNING OF THE DREYFUS AFFAIR:
Captain Dreyfus' Account

. . . Saturday, the 13th of October, 1894, I received a service-note directing me to go the following Monday, at nine o'clock in the morning, to the Ministry of War for the general inspection. . . .

On Monday morning I left my family. My son Pierre, who was then three and a half years old and was accustomed to accompany me to the door when I went out, came with me that morning as usual. That was one of my keenest remembrances through all my misfortunes. Very often in my nights of sorrow and despair I lived over the moment when I held my child in my arms for the last time. In this recollection I always found renewed strength of purpose.

The morning was bright and cool, the rising sun driving away the thin mist; everything foretold a beautiful day. As I was a little ahead of time, I walked back and forth before the Ministry Building for a few minutes, then went upstairs. On entering the office I was received by Commandant Picquart, who seemed to be waiting for me, and who took me at once into his room. I was somewhat surprised at finding none of my comrades, as officers are always called in groups to the general inspection. After a few minutes of commonplace conversation Commandant Picquart conducted me to the private office of the Chief of General Staff. I was greatly amazed to find myself received, not by the Chief of General Staff, but by Commandant du Paty de Clam, who was in uniform. Three persons in civilian dress, who were utterly unknown to me, were also there. These three persons were M. Cochefert, *Chef de la Sûreté* (the head of the secret police), his secretary, and the Keeper of the Records, M. Gribelin.

Commandant du Paty de Clam came directly toward me and said in a choking voice: "The General is coming. While waiting, I have a letter to write, and as my finger is sore, will you write it for me?" Strange as the request was under the circumstances, I at once complied. I sat down at a little table, while Commandant du Paty placed himself at my side and very near me, following my hand with his eye. After first requiring me to fill up an inspection form, he dictated to me a letter of which certain passages recalled the accusing letter that I knew afterward, and which was called the *bordereau*. In the course of his dictation the Commandant interrupted me sharply, saying: "You tremble." (I was not trembling. At the Court Martial of 1894, he explained his brusque interruption by saying that he had perceived I was not trembling under the dictation; believing therefore that he had to do with one who was simulating, he had tried in this way to shake my assurance.) This vehement remark surprised me greatly, as did the hostile attitude of Commandant du Paty. But as all suspicion was far from my mind, I thought only that he was displeased at my writing it badly. My fingers were cold, for the temperature outside was chilly, and I had been only a few minutes in the warm room. So I answered, "My fingers are cold."

As I continued writing without any sign of perturbation, Commandant du Paty tried a new interruption and said violently: "Pay attention; it is a grave matter." Whatever may have been my surprise at a procedure as rude as it was uncommon, I said nothing and simply applied myself to writing more carefully. Thereupon Commandant du Paty, as he explained to the Court Martial of 1894, concluded that, my self-possession being unshakable, it was useless to push the experiment further. The scene of the dictation had been prepared in every detail; but it had not answered the expectations of those who had arranged it.

As soon as the dictation was over, Commandant du Paty arose and, placing his hand on my shoulder, cried out in a loud voice: "In the name of the law, I arrest you; you are accused of the crime of high treason." A thunderbolt falling at my feet would not have produced in me a more violent emotion; I blurted out disconnected sentences, protesting against so infamous an accusation, which nothing in my life could have given rise to.

Next, M. Cochefert and his secretary threw themselves on me and searched me. I did not offer the slightest resistance, but cried to them: "Take my keys, open everything in my house; I am innocent." Then I added, "Show me at least the proofs of the infamous act you pretend I have committed." They answered that the accusations were overwhelming, but refused to state what they were or who had made them.

I was then taken to the military prison on the rue du Cherche-Midi by Commandant Henry, accompanied by one of the detectives. . . .

––––––

From Alfred Dreyfus, *Five Years of My Life.*

THE ENTENTE CORDIALE OF GREAT BRITAIN AND FRANCE, 1904

DECLARATION BETWEEN THE UNITED KINDOM AND FRANCE RESPECTING EGYPT AND MOROCCO. *Signed at London, April 8, 1904.*

ARTICLE I.

His Britannic Majesty's Government declare that they have no intention of altering the political status of Egypt.

The Government of the French Republic, for their part, declare that they will not obstruct the action of Great Britain in that country by asking that a limit of time be fixed for the British occupation or in any other manner, and that they give their assent to the draft Khedivial Decree annexed to the present Arrangement, containing the guarantees considered necessary for the protection of the interests of the Egyptian bondholders, on the condition that, after its promulgation, it cannot be modified in any way without the consent of the Powers Signatory of the Convention of London of 1885.

It is agreed that the post of Director-General of Antiquities in Egypt shall continue, as in the past, to be entrusted to a French savant.

The French schools in Egypt shall continue to enjoy the same liberty as in the past.

ARTICLE II.

The Government of the French Republic declare that they have no intention of altering the political status of Morocco.

His Britannic Majesty's Government, for their part, recognise that it appertains to France, more particularly as a Power whose dominions are conterminous for a great distance with those of Morocco, to preserve order in that country, and to provide assistance for the purpose of all administrative, economic, financial, and military reforms which it may require.

They declare that they will not obstruct the action taken by France for this purpose, provided that such action shall leave intact the rights which Great Britain, in virtue of Treaties, Conventions, and usage, enjoys in Morocco, including the right of coasting trade between the ports of Morocco, enjoyed by British vessels since 1901.

ARTICLE III.

His Britannic Majesty's Government, for their part, will respect the rights which France, in virtue of Treaties, Conventions, and usage, enjoys in Egypt, including the right of coasting trade between Egyptians ports accorded to French vessels.

ARTICLE IV.

The two Governments, being equally attached to the principle of commercial liberty both in Egypt and Morocco, declare that they will not, in those countries, countenance any inequality either in the imposition of customs duties or other taxes, or of railway transport charges.

The trade of both nations with Morocco and with Egypt shall enjoy the same treatment in transit through the French and British possessions in Africa. An Agreement between the two Governments shall settle the conditions of such transit and shall determine the points of entry.

This mutual engagement shall be binding for a period of thirty years. Unless this stipulation is expressly denounced at least one year in advance, the period shall be extended for five years at a time.

Nevertheless, the Government of the French Republic reserve to themselves in Morocco, and His Britannic Majesty's Government reserve to themselves in Egypt, the right to see that the concessions for roads railways, ports, &c., are only granted on such conditions as will maintain intact the authority of the State over these great undertakings of public interest.

ARTICLE V.

His Britannic Majesty's Government declare that they will use their influence in order that the French officials now in the Egyptian service may not be placed under conditions less advantageous than those applying to the British officials in the same service.

The Government of the French Republic, for their part, would make no objection to the application of analogous conditions to British officials now in the Moorish service.

ARTICLE VI.

In order to insure the free passage of the Suez Canal, His Britannic Majesty's Government declare that they adhere to the stipulations of the Treaty of the 29th October, 1888, and that they agree to their being put in force. The free passage of the Canal being thus guaranteed, the execution of the last sentence of paragraph 1 as well as of paragraph 2 of Article VIII of that Treaty will remain in abeyance.

From Great Britain, *Parliamentary Papers*, Treaty Series, 1911.

DAVID LLOYD GEORGE'S MANSION HOUSE SPEECH OF JULY, 1911

(during the third Moroccan Crisis)

Personally I am a sincere advocate of all means which would lead to the settlement of international disputes by methods such as those which civilization has so successfully set up for the adjustment of differences between individuals, and I rejoice in my heart at the prospect of a happy issue to Sir Edward Grey's negotiations with the United States of America for the settlement of disputes which may occur in future between ourselves and our kinsmen across the Atlantic by some more merciful, more rational, and by a more just arbitrament than that of the sword.

But I am also bound to say this—that I believe it is essential in the highest interests, not merely of this country, but of the world, that Britain should at all hazards maintain her place and her prestige amongst the Great Powers of the world. Her potent influence has many a time been in the past, and may yet be in the future, invaluable to the cause of human liberty. It has more than once in the past redeemed Continental nations, who are sometimes too apt to forget that service, from overwhelming disaster and even from national extinction. I would make great sacrifices to preserve peace. I conceive that nothing would justify a disturbance of international good will except questions of the greatest national moment. But if a situation were to be forced upon us in which peace could only be preserved by the surrender of the great and beneficent position Britain has won by centuries of heroism and achievement, by allowing Britain to be treated where her interests were vitally affected as if she were of no account in the Cabinet of nations, then I say emphatically that peace at that price would be a humiliation intolerable for a great country like ours to endure.

From *The Times*, London, July 22, 1911.

ANALYSIS AND INTERPRETATION OF THE READINGS

1. Why did the Entente Cordiale take the form of an agreement concerning Egypt and Morocco?
2. Why were the terms of the Entente Cordiale kept secret?
3. Why was Lloyd George's Mansion House Speech a significant declaration?

CHAPTER 33 | China, Japan, and Africa under the Impact of the West (1800–1914)

CHRONOLOGY

Number the items below in the order of their actual chronological sequence, and put the correct date (year or years) for each item in the parentheses following the description:

_____ Opium War (   )

_____ Outbreak of Taiping Rebellion (   )

_____ Russo-Japanese War (   )

_____ Promulgation of Japanese constitution (   )

_____ Boxer uprising (   )

_____ Harris Treaty (United States and Japan) (   )

_____ Beginning of extraterritoriality in China (   )

_____ End of extraterritoriality in Japan (   )

_____ Commodore Perry's mission to Tokyo (   )

_____ Abolition of the Shogunate (   )

_____ Establishment of French protectorate in Indonesia (   )

_____ Beginning of British control of Upper Burma (   )

_____ Collapse of Qing (Manchu) Dynasty (   )

_____ Founding of Sierra Leone (   )

_____ Opening of the Suez Canal (   )

_____ The Great Trek (   )

_____ Fall of the Zulu empire (   )

_____ Battle of Adowa (   )

_____ Denmark's abolition of the slave trade (   )

IDENTIFICATIONS

You should be able to identify each of the following and explain its importance:

Co-hong merchants
extraterritoriality
"unequal treaties"
treaty ports (China)
Arrow War
Hong Xiuquan
Zeng Guofan
Ci Xi
Kang Youwei
Hundred Days of Reform
Boxer Protocol of 1901
Sun Yat-sen
Yuan Shikai
Guomindang
International Settlement (Shanghai)

Liang Qichao
Yan Fu
Meiji era
Meiji Restoration
samurai revolt (1877)
Mitsui family
Anglo-Japanese Alliance
Eli Whitney
David Livingstone
Sayyid Said
kabaka
"Cape Colored"
Native Reserves
Candomblé

STUDY QUESTIONS

1. Explain why the opium traffic in China was increasing in the early nineteenth century. What effect did this traffic have on the balance of trade between the West and China, and on the Chinese economy generally?
2. Describe the conduct of foreign trade with China through Guangzhou prior to the Opium War.
3. Aside from the cession of Hong Kong to Britain in 1842, what limitations on its sovereignty did China suffer as a result of defeat in the Opium War?

4. What were the objectives of the leaders of the Taiping Rebellion? How did antidynastic and religious elements merge in the rebellion? Why and how was the rebellion suppressed? What were its consequences for China?

5. Outline the stages in the "Self-Strengthening Movement" in China. What was the role of Li Hongzhang in this movement? Why did the movement ultimately fail?

6. How did China's defeat in the Sino-Japanese War reflect broader problems of administration and planning? What change did this defeat bring in Western countries' stance toward China?

7. What motives are reflected in the terms that the Western powers imposed on China after suppressing the Boxer uprising?

8. Describe the official reform program undertaken in China in the first decade of the twentieth century. Why did it fail to preserve the dynasty or prevent revolution? How did it reflect the decentralization that had taken place in the administration of the empire?

9. Describe how the interplay of internal and external factors led to the downfall of China's last dynasty.

10. What appeal did Yuan Shikai have for various contenders for power in early-twentieth-century China? How did he end up becoming a virtual dictator?

11. Why, and in what ways, was the Chinese government's response to population growth in the nineteenth century inadequate?

12. What was the overall effect of foreign trade on China's handicraft industries in the Qing era?

13. Describe the connection between the women's movement in China and the foreign presence.

14. What Western ideas were introduced into China in the nineteenth century through the work of translators and popularizers? What was the appeal of these ideas? What was their impact?

15. Japan's response to pressure from the Western nations in the nineteenth century was radically different from China's. How do you account for this difference?

16. Explain how the break with Japan's policy of isolation led to the abolition of the Shogunate.

17. In what sense were the changes following the Meiji Restoration, which transformed Japan into a modern state, a "revolution from above"?

18. What important features of Western states were adopted or imitated in Japan during the Meiji era?

19. What were the origins of Japan's first political parties? What was their role in the development of representative government?

20. What were the peculiarities of Japan's economic development, and what social problems did they create or intensify?

21. Describe changes in educational policy during the Meiji era. What were the aims of these changes?

22. In what ways did traditional values and attitudes continue beyond the abolition of Japan's feudal political and economic system?

23. Describe the reasons for the rise of Japanese imperialism.

24. Why did Korea become the focus of Japanese imperialism? What conditions in Korea made the country susceptible to Japanese pressure?

25. What were the results of the Russo-Japanese War?

26. What factors contributed to the abolition of the slave trade? How long did the traffic continue after its formal abolition?

27. Why did slavery within Africa increase at a time when the overseas slave trade was being curtailed?

28. What was the rationale for the establishment of colonies for freed slaves in Sierra Leone, Liberia, and Libreville?

29. How were the African states affected by changes in European-African trading patterns in the mid-nineteenth century?

30. How did the European view of Africa change after 1875? What accounts for this change?

31. Trace the rivalry between British and Dutch settlers in South Africa.

32. Why was Ethiopia able to maintain its independence in spite of the advance of European imperialism?

33. What changes in African society took place during the century of European domination?

34. In what forms did native African religious beliefs and practices survive or reappear outside of Africa?

35. Explain the effects of Christian education on African society.

36. How did Christianity and Islam differ in their effects on African societies?

PROBLEMS

1. Attempt a critical evaluation of Western imperialism in China during the period 1800–1914. To what extent did it slow, and to what extent did it accelerate, China's national development? What permanent effects did it leave?

2. Make a study of the changing attitudes toward China and Japan on the part of Westerners during this period.

3. Compare the plantation system employed in Zanzibar by the Omani Arabs with that found in the southern United States.

4. Investigate further any of the following topics:
   a. The Opium War
   b. The Taiping Rebellion
   c. The career and ideas of Kang Youwei
   d. The Boxer movement
   e. The rise of political parties in Japan
   f. The Great Trek
   g. The abolition of the slave trade
   h. The industrialization of Japan

i. The Japanese press during the Meiji era
j. The career of Yuan Shikai
k. The personality, beliefs, and career of Hong Xiuquan
l. Commodore Perry's mission to Japan
m. Townsend Harris's contribution to the opening of Japan
n. The background and causes of the Russo-Japanese War
o. The social structure and economy of Liberia
p. The impact of the cotton gin on the slave trade
q. President Theodore Roosevelt's role in the Treaty of Portsmouth
r. The rise of the house of Mitsui
s. Exploration in mid-nineteenth-century Africa

5. Compare in more detail the responses of China and Japan to Western pressure in the nineteenth century.

Consider (but do not necessarily limit yourself to) the following factors: cultural differences, historical background, social structure, state structure, timing, objectives of Western countries.

6. Compare the Industrial Revolution in Japan with that in the West with regard to speed, social effects, involvement of the state, and dominant industries.

7. Read *Things Fall Apart*, by the Nigerian novelist Chinua Achebe. What does Achebe suggest about the strengths and weaknesses of traditional Ibo society? In what ways did the coming of Christian missionaries disrupt existing social and religious patterns? What is it that is threatening to "fall apart," and why?

AIDS TO AN UNDERSTANDING OF CHINA, JAPAN, AND AFRICA UNDER THE IMPACT OF THE WEST (1800–1914)

PRELUDE TO THE OPIUM WAR: A Confucian Official's Advice to the Queen of England
Lin Zexu, 1839

The kings of your honorable country by a tradition handed down from generation to generation have always been noted for their politeness and submissiveness. We have read your successive tributary memorials saying, "In general our countrymen who go to trade in China have always received His Majesty the Emperor's gracious treatment and equal justice," and so on. Privately we are delighted with the way in which the honorable rulers of your country deeply understand the grand principles and are grateful for the Celestial grace. For this reason the Celestial Court in soothing those from afar has redoubled its polite and kind treatment. The profit from trade has been enjoyed by them continuously for two hundred years. This is the source from which your country has become known for its wealth.

But after a long period of commercial intercourse, there appear among the crowd of barbarians both good persons and bad, unevenly. Consequently there are those who smuggle opium to seduce the Chinese people and so cause the spread of the poison to all provinces. Such persons who only care to profit themselves, and disregard their harm to others, are not tolerated by the laws of heaven and are unanimously hated by human beings. His Majesty the Emperor, upon hearing of this, is in a towering rage. He has especially sent me, his commissioner, to come to Kwangtung, and together with the governor-general and governor jointly to investigate and settle this matter.

All those people in China who sell opium or smoke opium should receive the death penalty. If we trace the crime of those barbarians who through the years have been selling opium, then the deep harm they have wrought and the great profit they have usurped should fundamentally justify their execution according to law. We take into consideration, however, the fact that the various barbarians have still known how to repent their crimes and re-

turn to their allegiance to us by taking the 20,183 chests of opium from their storeships and petitioning us, through their consular officer [superintendent of trade], Elliot, to receive it. It has been entirely destroyed and this has been faithfully reported to the Throne in several memorials by this commissioner and his colleagues....

We find that your country is sixty or seventy thousand *li* [three *li* make one mile, ordinarily] from China. Yet there are barbarian ships that strive to come here for trade for the purpose of making a great profit. The wealth of China is used to profit the barbarians. That is to say, the great profit made by barbarians is all taken from the rightful share of China. By what right do they then in return use the poisonous drug to injure the Chinese people? Even though the barbarians may not necessarily intend to do us harm, yet in coveting profit to an extreme, they have no regard for injuring others. Let us ask, where is your conscience? I have heard that the smoking of opium is very strictly forbidden by your country; that is because the harm caused by opium is clearly understood. Since it is not permitted to do harm to your own country, then even less should you let it be passed on to the harm of other countries—how much less to China! Of all that China exports to foreign countries, there is not a single thing which is not beneficial to people: they are of benefit when eaten, or of benefit when used, or of benefit when resold: all are beneficial. Is there a single article from China which has done any harm to foreign countries? Take tea and rhubarb, for example; the foreign countries cannot get along for a single day without them. If China cuts off these benefits with no sympathy for those who are to suffer, then what can the barbarians rely upon to keep themselves alive? Moreover the woolens, camlets, and longells [i.e., textiles] of foreign countries cannot be woven unless they obtain Chinese silk. If China, again, cuts off this beneficial export, what profit can the barbarians expect to make? As for other foodstuffs, beginning with candy, ginger, cinnamon, and so forth, and articles for use, beginning with silk, satin, chinaware, and so on, all the things that must be had by foreign countries are innumerable. On the other hand, articles coming from the outside to China can only be used as toys. We can take them or get along without them. Since they are not needed by China, what difficulty would there be if we closed the frontier and stopped the trade? Nevertheless our Celestial Court lets tea, silk, and other goods be shipped without limit and circulated everywhere without begrudging it in the slightest. This is for no other reason but to share the benefit with the people of the whole world.

The goods from China carried away by your country not only supply your own consumption and use, but also can be divided up and sold to other countries, producing a triple profit. Even if you do not sell opium, you still have this threefold profit. How can you bear to go further, selling products injurious to others in order to fulfill your insatiable desire?

Suppose there were people from another country who carried opium for sale to England and seduced your people into buying and smoking it; certainly your honorable ruler would deeply hate it and be bitterly aroused. We have heard heretofore that your honorable ruler is kind and benevolent. Naturally you would not wish to give unto others what you yourself do not want. We have also heard that the ships coming to Canton have all had regulations promulgated and given to them in which it is stated that it is not permitted to carry contraband goods. This indicates that the administrative orders of your honorable rule have been originally strict and clear. Only because the trading ships are numerous, heretofore perhaps they have not been examined with care. Now after this communication has been dispatched and you have clearly understood the strictness of the prohibitory laws of the Celestial Court, certainly you will not let your subjects dare again to violate the law. . . .

From Lin Zexu, a letter to Queen Victoria, reprinted in *China's Response to the West.* Ssu-yu Teng and John K. Fairbank, eds. Harvard University Press, 1979. pp. 24–26.

ADVOCATES OF REFORM IN CHINA: The Role of Nationalism
Liang Qichao

What concerns diplomatic affairs? Since the sixteenth century, about four hundred years ago, the reason for European development and world progress has been the stimulation and growth of extensive nationalist feeling everywhere. What does nationalism mean? It is that in all places people of the same race, the same language, the same religion, and the same customs regard each other as brothers and work for independence and self-government, and organize a more perfect government to work for the public welfare and to oppose the infringement of other races. When this idea had developed to an extreme at the end of the nineteenth century, it went further and became national imperialism within the last twenty or thirty years. What does national imperialism mean? It means that the industrial power of the citizens of a nation has been fully developed domestically and must flow to the outside, and thus they industriously seek to enlarge their powers in other (dependent) regions as appendages. The way of doing it is by military power, commerce, industry or religion, but they use a central policy to

direct and protect these activities. . . . Now, on the Asiatic continent there is located the largest country with the most fertile territory, the most corrupt government, and the most disorganized and weak people. As soon as the European race discovered our internal condition, they mobilized their national imperialism as swarms of ants attach themselves to what is rank and foul and as a myriad of arrows concentrate on a target. They were scattered but they concentrated in this corner, the Russians in Manchuria, the Germans in Shantung, the English in the Yangtze valley, the French in Kwangtung and Kwangsi, and the Japanese in Fukien. All are urged on by the tide of the new "ism" [national imperialism]. They cannot help doing this. . . .

If we wish to oppose the national imperialism of all the powers today and save China from great calamity and rescue our people, the only thing for us to do is to adopt the policy of promoting our own nationalism. If we wish to promote nationalism in China, there is no other means of doing it except through the renovation of the people.

Today, over the whole country, everybody is worrying about the foreign trouble. Nevertheless, if the foreigners can really cause us trouble, it cannot be ended just by worrying. The stubbornness and aggressiveness of national imperialism is very severe, and yet we are still discussing whether the foreigners can really cause us trouble or not. How foolish we are! I think the existence or non-existence of the trouble will not be decided by the foreigners, but by our domestic condition. In general, all nations are certainly using the same "ism." But why does Russia not apply it to England, and England not apply it to Germany, and Germany not apply it to America, and the various countries of Europe and America not apply it to Japan? It depends on whether there is a chance for doing so or not. . . . Thus, in consideration of present-day China, we must not depend upon a temporary wise emperor or minister to allay the disorder, nor expect a sudden rise of one or two heroes from the rural countryside to lead our struggle for success; it is necessary to have our people's virtue, people's wisdom, and people's power of the whole number of four hundred million all become equal to that of the foreigners—then they naturally cannot cause us trouble and we need not worry about them. . . .

All the phenomena in the world are governed by no more than two great principles: one is conservative and the other is aggressive. Those who are applying these two principles are inclined either to the one or to the other. Sometimes the two arise simultaneously and conflict with each other; and sometimes the two exist simultaneously and compromise with each other. No one can exist who is inclined only to one. Where there is conflict, there must be compromise, and conflict is the forerunner of compromise. He who is good at making compromises is a great citizen, such as you find among the Anglo-Saxon race. . . . Thus what I mean by "new people" are not those who are intoxicated with Western customs, despising the morals, academic learning, and customs of our several-thousand-year-old country in order to keep company with others; nor are they those who stick to old paper and say that merely embracing the several thousand years of our own morals, academic learning, and customs will be sufficient to enable us to stand up on the great earth.

From S. Y. Teng and J. K. Fairbank, *China's Response to the West*, Harvard University Press, 1954. Reprinted by permission of the publisher.

COMMENT ON THE JAPANESE CONSTITUTION OF 1889: By Its Drafter (the Ex-*Samurai* Ito Hirobumi)

If we look back into the history of the world to the origin of the representative body, we shall find that the principle has undergone an extraordinary degree of development. At the Restoration the institution, then well grown in Europe, was by an enlargement and extension of the scope of our national policy adopted in Japan. Now, by carefully adapting the principle to our national characteristics, manners, and customs, and by retaining what is excellent and discarding what is faulty, we are about to put into practice a system of constitutional politics that is without rival in the East. And this leads us not unnaturally to discuss briefly the English constitution, which in many quarters has been thought worthy of imitation. I shall, however, speak solely of the difference in the history and evolution of the two constitutions, and shall not attempt to define their relative merits. In England there is no codified constitution, and you must bear in mind how the English people obtained the so-called Great Charter. The nobles of England, as you no doubt are aware, not only form a large section of the population, but they were, and are still, powerful. The sovereign of that day, having engaged in unnecessary warfare with a foreign country, levied heavy burdens on the people, which policy led to much discontent. But the complaints were not confined to the mass of the people; the nobles were also angered by the monarch's actions and refused to obey his commands. Eventually they combined and required him to sign the Magna Carta; he at first refused but was at length compelled by force to comply. You will see then that while it is quite true that the king had oppressed the people, as a matter of fact this Magna Carta pledge was extorted from him by the nobles at the point of the sword. The case of Japan is totally different. The most cordial relations prevail between the Throne and the people while our Constitution is granted. The position of our court cannot be at all compared with that of England when the Magna Carta was granted, for we know that our Imperial House has a single aim—the welfare and happiness of the nation. Not only were there no such discontented barons in this country, but our feudal lords, great and small, joined in requesting the Crown to take back the military and political rights which for centuries they had enjoyed. Could any two things be more radically different than the origins of the English and Japanese Constitutions? If the English people felicitate themselves on the influence exercised in promoting and developing the national welfare and interest, by a Charter given under such ominous circumstances as was theirs, how much more should we congratulate ourselves on having received from our benevolent sovereign, under the most happy and peaceful auspices, the Constitution of the Japanese empire! . . .

The course which lies now before the Japanese empire is plain. Both ruler and ruled should apply their efforts smoothly and harmoniously to preserve tranquility; to elevate the status of the people; to secure the rights and promote the welfare of each individual; and finally, by manifesting abroad the dignity and power of Japan, to secure and maintain her integrity and independence.

From W. W. McLaren, "Japanese Government Documents," in *Translations of the Asiatic Society of Japan*, Series I, Vol. XLII.

A PERSONAL VIEW OF THE AFRICAN SLAVE TRADE
Samuel Ajayi Crowther

For some years, war had been carried on in my Oyo Country, which was always attended with much devastation and bloodshed; the women, such men as had surrendered or were caught, with the children, were taken captives. The enemies who carried on these wars were principally the Oyo Mahomedans, with whom my country abounds—with the Fulbe, and such foreign slaves as had escaped from their owners, joined together, making a formidable force of about 20,000, who annoyed the whole country. They had no other employment but selling slaves to the Spaniards and Fortuguese on the coast.

The morning in which my town, Osogun, shared the same fate which many others had experienced, was fair and delightful; and most of the inhabitants were engaged in their respective occupations. We were preparing breakfast without any apprehension; when, about 9 o'clock A.M., a rumour was spread in the town, that the enemies had approached with intentions of hostility. It was not long after when they had almost surrounded the town, to prevent any escape of the inhabitants; the town being rudely fortified with a wooden fence, about four miles in circumference, containing about 12,000 inhabitants, which would produce 3,000 fighting men. The inhabitants not being duly prepared, some not being at home; those who were, having about six gates to defend, as well as many weak places about the fence to guard against, and, to say in a few words, the men being surprised, and therefore confounded—the enemies entered the town after about three or four hours' resistance. Here a most sorrowful scene imaginable was to be witnessed!— women, some with three, four, or six children clinging to their arms, with the infants on their backs, and such baggage as they could carry on their heads, running as fast as they could through prickly shrubs, which, hooking their blies and other loads, drew them down from the heads of the bearers. While they found it impossible to go along with their loads, they endeavoured only to save themselves and their children: even this was impracticable with those who had many children to care for. While they were endeavouring to disentangle themselves from the ropy shrubs, they were overtaken and caught by the enemies with a noose of rope thrown over the neck of every individual, to be led in the manner of goats tied together, under the drove of one man. In many cases a family was violently divided between three or four enemies, who each led his away, to see one another no more. Your humble servant was thus caught—with his mother, two sisters, and a cousin—while endeavouring to escape in the manner above described. My load consisted in nothing else than my bow, and five arrows in the quiver; the bow I had lost in the shrub, while I was extricating myself, before I could think of making any use of it against my enemies. The last view I had of my father was when he came from the fight, to give us the signal to flee. Hence I never saw him more. I learned, some time afterward, that he was killed in another battle.

On the next morning, our cords being taken off our necks, we were brought to the Chief of our captors—for there were many other Chiefs—as trophies at his feet. In a little while, a separation took place, when my sister and I fell to the share of the Chief, and my mother and the infant to the victors. We dared not vent our grief by loud cries, but by very heavy sobs. My mother, with the infant, was led away. In a few hours after, it was soon agreed upon that I should be bartered for a horse in Iseyin, that very day. Thus was I separated from my mother and sister for the first time in my life; not to be seen more in this world. Thus, in the space of twenty-four hours, being deprived of liberty and all other comforts, I was made the property of three different persons.

[Some months later], an unhappy evening arrived, when I was sent with a man to get some money at a neighbouring house. I went; but with some fears, for which I could not account; and, to my great astonishment, in a few minutes I was added to the number of many other captives, enfettered, to be led to the market-town early the next morning. After a few days travel, we came to the market-town Ijaye. In a few days I was sold to a Mahomedan woman, with whom I travelled to many towns in our way to the Popo country, on the coast, much resorted to by the Portuguese, to buy slaves.

Now and then my mistress would speak with me and her son, that we should by-and-bye go to the Popo country, where we should buy tobacco, and other fine things, to sell at our return. Now, thought I, this was the signal of my being sold to the Portuguese; who, they often told me during our journey, were to be seen in that country. Being very thoughtful of this, my appetite forsook me, and in a few weeks I got the dysentery, which greatly preyed on me. I determined with myself that I would not go to the Popo country; but would make an end of myself, one way or another. In several nights I attempted strangling myself with my band; but had not courage enough to close the noose tight, so as to effect my purpose. May the Lord forgive me this sin! I determined, next, that I would leap out of the canoe into the river, when we should cross it in our way to that country. Thus was I thinking, when my owner, perceiving the great alteration which took place in me, sold me to some persons. Thus the Lord, while I knew Him not, led me not into temptation and delivered me from evil. After my price had been counted before my own eyes, I was delivered up to my new owners, with great grief and dejection of spirit, not knowing where I was now to be led. About the first cock-crowing, which was the usual time to set out with the slaves, to prevent their being much acquainted with the way, for fear an escape should be made, we set out for Ijebu, the third dialect from mine.

After having arrived at Ikereku-iwere, another town, we halted. In this place I renewed my attempt of strangling, several times at night; but could not effect my purpose. It was very singular, that no thought of making use of a knife ever entered my mind. However, it was not long before I was bartered, for tobacco, rum, and other articles. I remained here, in fetters, alone, for some time, before my owner could get as many slaves as he wanted. . . .

I had to remain alone, again, in another town in Ijebu, the name of which I do not now remember, for about two months. From hence I was brought, after a few days' walk, to a slave-market, called I'-ko-sy [Ikosi], on the coast, on the bank of a large river, which very probably was the Lagos on which we were afterwards captured. The sight of the river terrified me exceedingly, for I had never seen any thing like it in my life. The people on the opposite bank are called E'-ko. Before sun-set,

being bartered again for tobacco, I became another owner's. Nothing now terrified me more than the river, and the thought of going into another world. Crying was nothing now, to vent out my sorrow: my whole body became stiff. I was now bade to enter the river, to ford it to the canoe. Being fearful at my entering this extensive water, and being so cautious in every step I took, as if the next would bring me to the bottom, my motion was very awkward indeed. Night coming on, and the men having very little time to spare, soon carried me into the canoe, and placed me among the corn-bags, and supplied me with an abala for my dinner. Almost in the same position I was placed I remained, with my abala in my hand quite confused in my thoughts, waiting only every moment our arrival at Lagos; which we did not reach till about 4 o'clock in the morning.

In a few days after, I was made the eighth in number of the slaves of the Portuguese. Being a veteran in slavery, if I may be allowed the expression, and having no more hope of ever going to my country again, I patiently took whatever came; although it was not without a great fear and trembling that I received, for the first time, the touch of a White Man, who examined me whether I was sound or not. Men and boys were at first chained together, with a chain of about six fathoms in length, thrust through an iron fetter on the neck of every individual, and fastened at both ends with padlocks. In this situation the boys suffered the most: the men sometimes, getting angry, would draw the chain so violently that we were almost suffocated, or bruised to death. Thus we were for nearly the space of four months.

About this time, intelligence was given that the English were cruising the coast. This was another subject of sorrow with us—that there must be war also on the sea as well as on land— a thing never heard of before, or imagined practicable. This delayed our embarkation. . . .

After a few weeks' delay, we were embarked, at night in canoes, from Lagos to the beach; and on the following morning were put on board the vessel, which immediately sailed away. The crew being busy embarking us, 187 in number, had no time to give us either breakfast or supper; and we, being unaccustomed to the motion of the vessel, employed the whole of this day in sea-sickness, which rendered the greater part of us less fit to take any food whatever. On the very same evening, we were surprised by two English men-of-war; and on the next morning found ourselves in the hands of new conquerors, whom we at first very much dreaded, they being armed with long swords. In the morning, being called up from the hold, we were astonished to find ourselves among two very large men-of-war and several other brigs. . . .

Our owner was bound with his sailors; except the cook, who was preparing our breakfast. Hunger rendered us bold; and not being threatened at first attempts to get some fruits from the stern, we in a short time took the liberty of ranging about the vessel, in search of plunder of every kind. Now we began to entertain a good opinion of our conquerors. Very soon after breakfast, we were divided into several of the vessels around us. This was now cause of new fears, not knowing where our misery would end. Being now, as it were, one family, we began to take leave of those who were first transshipped, not knowing what would become of them and ourselves. About this time, six of us, friends in affliction, among whom was my Brother Joseph

Bartholomew, kept very close together, that we might be carried away at the same time. It was not long before we six were conveyed into the H.M.S. *Myrmidon*, in which we discovered not any trace of those who were transshipped before us. We soon came to a conclusion of what had become of them, when we saw parts of a hog hanging, the skin of which was white—a thing we never saw before; for a hog was always roasted on fire, to clear it of the hair, in my country; and a number of cannonshots were arranged along the deck. The former we supposed to be the flesh, and the latter the heads of the individuals who had been killed for meat. But we were soon undeceived, by a close examination of the flesh with cloven foot, which resembled that of a hog; and, by a cautious approach to the shot, that they were iron.

After nearly two months and a half cruising on the coast, we were landed at Sierra Leone, on the 17th of June 1822. The same day we were sent to Bathurst, formerly Leopold, under the care of Mr. [Thomas] Davey. Here we had the pleasure of meeting many of our country people, but none were known before. They assured us of our liberty and freedom; and we very soon believed them. But a few days after our arrival at Bathurst, we had the mortification of being sent for at Freetown, to testify against our Portuguese owner. It being hinted to us that we should be delivered up to him again, notwithstanding all the persuasion of Mr. Davey that we should return, we entirely refused to go ourselves, unless we were carried. I could not but think of my ill-conduct to our owner in the man-of-war. But as time was passing away, and our consent could not be got, we were compelled to go by being whipped; and it was not a small joy to us to return to Bathurst again, in the evening, to our friends.

From this period I have been under the care of the Church Missionary Society; and in about six months after my arrival at Sierra Leone, I was able to read the New Testament with some degree of freedom; and was made a Monitor, for which I was rewarded with seven-pence-halfpenny per month. The Lord was pleased to open my heart to hearken to those things which were spoken by His servants; and being convinced that I was a sinner, and desired to obtain pardon through Jesus Christ, I was baptized on the 11th of December, 1825, by the Rev. J. Raban.

———

From Philip D. Curtin, ed., *Africa Remembered: Narratives by West Africans from the Era of the Slave Trade*, University of Wisconsin Press, 1967. Reprinted by permission of the publisher.

ANALYSIS AND INTERPRETATION OF THE READINGS

1. Is Lin Zexu's argument against the opium trade based more on a moral foundation or a legal foundation? Which aspect of his appeal—the legal or the moral—do you find more persuasive?

2. How adequate is Liang Qichao's account of the role of nationalism and its relationship to "national imperialism"? What inferences does he draw for the problems of China?

3. What was the basis of Ito's claim that the Japanese Constitution should be even more successful than the British? Are there any flaws in his argument?

4. What aspects and effects of the slave trade does Crowther highlight as being most detrimental? How does Crowther perceive the Europeans he encountered?

CHAPTER 34 | The First World War

CHRONOLOGY

June 28, 1914	April 2, 1917
July 23, 1914	November 6, 1917
July 28, 1914	November 11, 1918
August 1, 1914	June 28, 1919
August 3, 1914	November 20, 1922

From the list above supply the correct date for each of the following events:

_____ Coup resulting in accession of Bolsheviks to power in Russia

_____ Assassination of Austrian heir to the throne

_____ Austrian ultimatum to Serbia

_____ German declaration of war against France

_____ Austrian declaration of war against Serbia

_____ Signing of the Treaty of Versailles

_____ Signing of the armistice by Germany

_____ Declaration of war by the United States

IDENTIFICATIONS

You should be able to identify and explain the importance of each of the following terms or persons:

Raymond Poincaré	"Peace, Bread, and Land"
Alfred von Schlieffen	Treaty of Brest-Litovsk
David Lloyd George	Easter Rebellion
Georges Clemenceau	Council of Three
U-boat	Mustapha Kemal
soviet	Alexander Kerensky

"war guilt" provision of Versailles treaty

STUDY QUESTIONS

1. It is generally held that the immediate cause of the First World War was the assassination of Archduke Francis Ferdinand. Explain the significance of the assassination in terms of: (a) Serbian nationalism; (b) Austro-Serbian relations; (c) the actions of the German imperial government.

2. Assess the importance of each of the following in the chain of events that precipitated the war: (a) Bethmann-Hollweg's "blank check" to the Austrian foreign minister; (b) Russian mobilization; (c) French support of Russia.

3. Why could the outbreak of war in 1914 be characterized as "a tragedy of miscalculation"?

4. What considerations led to Britain's entrance into the war?

5. Describe the competing propaganda efforts on the two sides during the war.

6. Why did Italy, a member of the Triple Alliance, finally enter the war on the side of the Triple Entente?

7. What changes in the technology of warfare were demonstrated in the First World War?

8. What were the reasons for the entrance of the United States into the war?

9. How did the war contribute to the outbreak of revolution in Russia?

10. How do you account for the failure of the Russian provisional government of 1917?

11. Why were peace proposals from the socialists and from the pope rejected by the belligerents?

12. Which of Wilson's Fourteen Points do you consider most important? What was the role of the Fourteen Points in bringing the war to an end? To what extent were the Fourteen Points embodied in the peace settlement?

13. Summarize the chief provisions of the peace settlement of 1919–1920. Why was the peace more like "a sentence from a court than a negotiated settlement"?

14. How was the professed principle of national self-determination violated in the peace settlements with Austria, Bulgaria, and Hungary?

15. Why did Turkey, in contrast to Germany and its other wartime allies, obtain a negotiated peace settlement?

16. What were the weaknesses of the League of Nations from its very inception?

17. In what ways did the First World War pave the way for the Second World War?

18. What was the overall effect of the war on national economies and international trade?

19. What did the war contribute to the emancipation of women?

PROBLEMS

1. Investigate any of the following:

a. The use of propaganda by belligerent governments
b. The first stage of the Russian Revolution
c. Peace offensives during the course of the war
d. The secret treaties among the Entente governments
e. The factors which led the United States into the war
f. The role of any one of the "Big Three" in the Paris peace conference
g. The rejection of the League of Nations by the United States Senate

2. Outline some policies which you think might have prevented the First World War, if they had been followed by the rulers of the chief European states between 1871 and 1914.

3. Defend or refute the proposition that if the peace settlement of 1919–1920 had been more wisely conceived, Hitler and the Nazis would never have triumphed in Germany.

AIDS TO AN UNDERSTANDING OF THE FIRST WORLD WAR

GERMANY'S WAR AIMS, SEPTEMBER 1914
Theobald von Bethmann-Hollweg

The general aim of the war is security for the German Reich in west and east for all imaginable time. For this purpose France must be so weakened as to make her revival as a great power impossible for all time. Russia must be thrust back as far as possible from Germany's eastern frontier and her domination over the non-Russian vassal peoples broken.

1. *France.* The military to decide whether we should demand cession of Belfort and western slopes of the Vosges, razing of fortresses and cession of coastal strip from Dunkirk to Boulogne.

The ore-field of Briey, which is necessary for the supply of ore for our industry, to be ceded in any case.

Further, a war indemnity, to be paid in installments; it must be high enough to prevent France from spending any considerable sums on armaments in the next 15–20 years.

Furthermore: a commercial treaty which makes France economically dependent on Germany, secures the French market for our exports and makes it possible to exclude British commerce from France. This treaty must secure for us financial and industrial freedom of movement in France in such fashion that German enterprises can no longer receive different treatment from French.

2. *Belgium.* Liége and Verviers to be attached to Prussia, a frontier strip of the province of Luxemburg to Luxemburg.

Question whether Antwerp, with a corridor to Liége, should also be annexed remains open.

At any rate Belgium, even if allowed to continue to exist as a state, must be reduced to a vassal state, must allow us to occupy any militarily important ports, must place her coast at our disposal in military respects, must become economically a German province. Given such a solution, which offers the advantages of annexation without its inescapable domestic political disadvantages, French Flanders with Dunkirk, Calais and Boulogne, where most of the population is Flemish, can without danger be attached to this unaltered Belgium. The competent quarters will have to judge the military value of this position against England.

3. *Luxemburg.* Will become a German federal state and will receive a strip of the present Belgian province of Luxemburg and perhaps the corner of Longwy.

4. We must create a *central European economic association* through common customs treaties, to include France, Belgium, Holland, Denmark, Austria-Hungary, Poland "sic", and perhaps Italy, Sweden and Norway. This association will not have any common constitutional supreme authority and all its members will be formally equal, but in practice will be under German leadership and must stabilise Germany's economic dominance over Mitteleuropa.

5. *The question of colonial acquisitions*, where the first aim is the creation of a continuous Central African colonial empire, will be considered later, as will that of the aims to be realised *vis-à-vis* Russia.

6. A short provisional formula suitable for a possible preliminary peace to be found for a basis for the economic agreements to be concluded with France and Belgium.

7. *Holland.* It will have to be considered by what means and methods Holland can be brought into closer relationship with the German Empire.

In view of the Dutch character, this closer relationship must leave them free of any feeling of compulsion, must alter nothing in the Dutch way of life, and must also subject them to no new military obligations. Holland, then, must be left independent in externals, but be made internally dependent on us. Possibly one might consider an offensive and defensive alliance, to cover the colonies; in any case a close customs association, perhaps the cession of Antwerp to Holland in return for the right to keep a German garrison in the fortress of Antwerp and at the mouth of the Scheldt.

From Fritz Fischer, *Germany's Aims in the First World War*, W. W. Norton & Company, Inc., 1967. Reprinted by permission.

THE UNITED STATES ENTERS THE WAR
Woodrow Wilson

We have no quarrel with the German people. We have no feeling towards them but one of sympathy and friendship. It was not upon their impulse that their government acted in entering this war. It was not with their previous knowledge or approval. It was a war determined upon as wars used to be determined upon in the old, unhappy days when peoples were nowhere consulted by their rulers and wars were provoked and waged in the interest of dynasties or of little groups of ambitious men who were accustomed to use their fellow men as pawns and tools. Self-governed nations do not fill their neighbour states with spies or set the course of intrigue to bring about some critical posture of affairs which will give them an opportunity to strike and make conquest. Such designs can be successfully worked out only under cover and where no one has the right to ask questions. Cunningly contrived plans of deception or aggression, carried, it may be, from generation to generation, can be worked out and kept from the light only within the privacy of courts or behind the carefully guarded confidences of a narrow and privileged class. They are happily impossible where public opinion commands and insists upon full information concerning all the nation's affairs.

A steadfast concert for peace can never be maintained except by a partnership of democratic nations. No autocratic government could be trusted to keep faith within it or obeserve its covenants. It must be a league of honour, a partnership of opinion. Intrigue would eat its vitals away; the plottings of inner circles who could plan what they would and render account to no one would be a corruption seated at its very heart. Only free peoples can hold their purpose and their honour steady to a common end and prefer the interests of mankind to any narrow interest of their own.

Just because we fight without rancor and without selfish object, seeking nothing for ourselves but what we shall wish to share with all free peoples, we shall, I feel confident, conduct our operations as belligerents without passion and ourselves observe with proud punctilio the principles of right and of fair play we profess to be fighting for.

We are now about to accept gauge of battle with this natural foe to liberty and shall, if necessary, spend the whole force of the nation to check and nullify its pretensions and its power. We are glad, now that we see the facts with no veil of false pretence about them, to fight thus for the ultimate peace of the world and for the liberation of its peoples, the German peoples included: for the rights of nations great and small and the privilege of men everywhere to choose their way of life and of obedience.

The world must be made safe for democracy. Its peace must be planted upon the tested foundations of political liberty. We have no selfish ends to serve. We desire no conquest, no dominion. We seek no indemnities for ourselves, no material compensation for the sacrifices we shall freely make. We are but one of the champions of the rights of mankind. We shall be satisfied when those rights have been made as secure as the faith and the freedom of nations can make them.

From President Wilson's War Message to Congress, April 2, 1917.

SPEECH ON THE FOURTEEN POINTS
Woodrow Wilson

It will be our wish and purpose that the processes of peace, when they are begun, shall be absolutely open and that they shall involve and permit henceforth no secret understandings of any kind. The day of conquest and aggrandizement is gone by; so is also the day of secret covenants entered into in the interest of particular governments and likely at some unlooked for moment to upset the peace of the world. It is this happy fact, now clear to the view of every public man whose thoughts do not still linger in an age that is dead and gone, which makes it possible for every nation whose purposes are consistent with justice and the peace of the world to avow now or at any other time the objects it has in view.

We entered this war because violations of right had occurred which touched us to the quick and made the life of our own people impossible unless they were corrected and the world secured once for all against their recurrence. What we demand in this war, therefore, is nothing peculiar to ourselves. It is that the world be made fit and safe to live in; and particularly that it be made safe for every peace-loving nation which, like our own, wishes to live its own life, determine its own institutions, be assured of justice and fair dealing by the other peoples of the world as against force and selfish aggression. All the peoples of the world are in effect partners in this interest, and for our own part we see very clearly that unless justice be done to others it will not be done to us. The programme of the world's peace, therefore, is our programme; and that programme, the only possible programme, as we see it, is this:

I. Open covenants of peace, openly arrived at, after which there shall be no private international understandings of any kind but diplomacy shall proceed always frankly and in the public view.

II. Absolute freedom of navigation upon the seas, outside territorial waters, alike in peace and in war, except as the seas may be closed in whole or in part by international action for the enforcement of international covenants.

III. The removal, so far as possible, of all economic barriers and the establishment of an equality of trade conditions among all the nations consenting to the peace and associating themselves for its maintenance.

IV. Adequate guarantees given and taken that national armaments will be reduced to the lowest point consistent with domestic safety.

V. A free, open-minded, and absolutely impartial adjustment of all colonial claims, based upon a strict observance of the principle that in determining all such questions of sovereignty the interests of the populations concerned must have equal weight with the equitable claims of the government whose title is to be determined.

VI. The evacuation of all Russian territory and such a settlement of all questions affecting Russia as will secure the best and freest cooperation of the other nations of the world in obtaining for her an unhampered and unembarrassed opportunity for the independent determination of her own political development and national policy and assure her of a sincere welcome into the society of free nations under institutions of her own choosing; and, more than a welcome, assistance also of every kind that she may need and may herself desire. The treatment accorded Russia by her sister nations in the months to come will be the acid test of their good will, of their comprehension of her needs as distinguished from their own interests, and of their intelligent and unselfish sympathy.

VII. Belgium, the whole world will agree, must be evacuated and restored, without any attempt to limit the sovereignty which she enjoys in common with all other free nations. No other single act will serve as this will serve to restore confidence among the nations in the laws which they have themselves set and determined for the government of their relations with one another. Without this healing act the whole structure and validity of international law is forever impaired.

VIII. All French territory should be freed and the invaded portions restored, and the wrong done to France by Prussia in 1871 in the matter of Alsace-Lorraine, which has unsettled the peace of the world for nearly fifty years, should be righted, in order that peace may once more be made secure in the interest of all.

IX. A readjustment of the frontiers of Italy should be effected along clearly recognizable lines of nationality.

X. The peoples of Austria-Hungary, whose place among the nations we wish to see safeguarded and assured, should be accorded the freest opportunity of autonomous development.

XI. Rumania, Serbia, and Montenegro should be evacuated; occupied territories restored; Serbia accorded free and secure access to the sea; and the relations of the several Balkan states to one another determined by friendly counsel along historically established lines of allegiance and nationality; and international guarantees of the political and economic independence and territorial integrity of the several Balkan states should be entered into.

XII. The Turkish portions of the present Ottoman Empire should be assured a secure sovereignty, but the other nationalities which are now under Turkish rule should be assured an undoubted security of life and an absolutely unmolested opportunity of autonomous development, and the Dardanelles should be permanently opened as a free passage to the ships and commerce of all nations under international guarantees.

XIII. An independent Polish state should be erected which should include the territories inhabited by indisputably Polish populations, which should be assured a free and secure access to the sea, and whose political and economic independence and territorial integrity should be guaranteed by international covenant.

XIV. A general association of nations must be formed under specific covenants for the purpose of affording mutual guaran-

tees of political independence and territorial integrity to great and small states alike.

From *Congressional Record*, vol. LVI, 1918. pp. 680–81.

Extracts from the Treaty of Versailles

Germany is forbidden to maintain or construct any fortifications either on the left bank of the Rhine or on the right bank to the west of a line drawn 50 kilometres to the East of the Rhine.

Article 45

As compensation for the destruction of the coal mines in the north of France and as part payment towards the total reparation due from Germany for the damage resulting from the war, Germany cedes to France in full and absolute possession, with exclusive rights of exploitation, unencumbered and free from all debts and charges of any kind, the coal mines situated in the Saar Basin as defined in Article 48 (which outlines boundaries).

Article 87

Germany, in conformity with the action already taken by the Allied and Associated Powers, recognises the complete independence of Poland. . . .

Article 89

Poland undertakes to accord freedom of transit to persons, goods, vessels, carriages, wagons and mails in transit between East Prussia and the rest of Germany over Polish territory, including territorial waters, and to treat them at least as favourably as the persons, goods, vessels, carriages, wagons and mails respectively of Polish or of any other more favoured nationality, origin, importation, starting-point, or ownership as regards facilities, restrictions and all other matters. . . .

Article 102

The principal Allied and Associated Powers undertake to establish the town of Danzig, together with the rest of the territory described in Article 100, as a Free City. It will be placed under the protection of the League of Nations. . . .

Article 116

Germany acknowledges and agrees to respect as permanent and inalienable the independence of all the territories which were part of the former Russian Empire on August 1, 1914.

In accordance with the provisions of Article 259 of Part IX (Financial Clauses) and Article 292 of Part X (Economic Clauses) Germany accepts definitely the abrogation of the Brest-Litovsk Treaties and of all other treaties, conventions and agreements entered into by her with the Maximalist Government in Russia.

The Allied and Associated Powers formally reserve the rights of Russia to obtain from Germany restitution and reparation based on the principles of the present Treaty.

ARTICLE 119

Germany renounces in favour of the Principal Allied and Associated Powers all her rights and titles over her oversea possessions. . . .

ARTICLE 159

The German military forces shall be demobilised and reduced as prescribed hereinafter.

ARTICLE 160

(1) By a date which must not be later than March 31, 1920, the German Army must not comprise more than seven divisions of infantry and three divisions of cavalry.

After that date the total number of effectives in the Army of the States constituting Germany must not exceed one hundred thousand men, including officers and establishments of depots. The Army shall be devoted exclusively to the maintenance of order within the territory and the control of the frontiers.

The total effective strength of officers, including the personnel of staffs, whatever their composition, must not exceed four thousand. . . .

ARTICLE 231

The Allied and Associated Governments affirm and Germany accepts the responsibility of Germany and her allies for causing all the loss and damage to which the Allied and Associated Governments and their nationals have been subjected as a consequence of the war imposed upon them by the aggression of Germany and her allies.

ARTICLE 232

The Allied and Associated Governments recognise that the resources of Germany are not adequate, after taking into account permanent diminution of such resources which will result from other provisions of the present Treaty, to make complete reparation for all such loss and damage.

The Allied and Associated Governments, however, require, and Germany undertakes, that she will make compensation for all damage done to the civilian population of the Allied and Associated Powers and to their property during the period of the belligerency of each as an Allied or Associated Power against Germany by such aggression by land, by sea and from the air, and in general all damage as defined in Annex I hereto. . . .

———

From *Treaty of Peace with Germany*, United States, 66th Congress, Senate Doc. No. 49, 1919.

ANALYSIS AND INTERPRETATION OF THE READINGS

1. Was President Wilson correct in assuming that democratic government and peaceful foreign policy go together?
2. How do you account for Articles 87, 89, and 102 of the Versailles Treaty?
3. Why, according to Woodrow Wilson, did the United States enter World War I? In what ways did Wilson's "Fourteen Points" address what he saw as the causes of that war?
4. What sort of economic future for Germany did the treaty-makers envision?

CHAPTER 35 | Turmoil Between the Wars

IDENTIFICATIONS

You should be able to explain the significance of the following items or terms:

Reds and Whites
NEP
Comintern
Council of the People's Commissars
Five-Year Plan
kulaks
"old" Bolsheviks
Il Popolo d'Italia

March on Rome
Spartacists
Dawes Plan
National Socialism
Third Reich
Schutzstaffel
Blut und Boden
Great Depression

And of the following individuals:

V. I. Lenin
Leon Trotsky
Joseph Stalin
Rosa Luxemburg
Benito Mussolini
Walter Rathenau
Hindenburg

Adolf Hitler
Heinrich Himmler
Edouard Herriot
J. Ramsay MacDonald
Léon Blum
Franklin D. Roosevelt

In the blank next to each item below, write the name of the person who was its author, creator, or exponent, selected from the following list:

Ludwig Wittgenstein
Max Weber
Oswald Spengler
Ernest Hemingway
T. S. Eliot
James Joyce

John Steinbeck
Jean-Paul Sartre
George Orwell
Salvador Dali
Igor Stravinsky
Frank Lloyd Wright

_____ *The Decline of the West*

_____ *1984*

_____ Logical Positivism

_____ *The Grapes of Wrath*

_____ *The Protestant Ethic and the Spirit of Capitalism*

_____ Functionalism in architecture

_____ Polytonality

_____ *The Sun Also Rises*

_____ Existentialism

_____ "Stream-of-consciousness" literature

_____ *The Waste Land*

STUDY QUESTIONS

1. What conditions following World War I promoted the decline rather than the rise of democracy?
2. Though it was based on Marxism, Bolshevism in fact had some significant differences from it. What were they?
3. How did the Bolsheviks survive the combination of foreign invasion and internal insurgency during the early years following the 1917 revolution?
4. What was the intention behind the founding of the USSR? What held the union together?
5. What were the causes of the struggle between Trotsky and Stalin? What major issues were involved?
6. What did Stalin mean by "socialism in one country"?
7. Explain why Stalin's collectivization of agriculture "represented a revolution far more immediate than that of 1917."

8. Explain the changes in Russia's foreign policy during the 1930s. How do you account for these changes? How do these changes represent a conservative trend in the Communist regime?

9. Describe the Russian constitution of 1936. How did it actually work?

10. What was the significance of Stalin's purges of the 1930s?

11. What were the principal accomplishments of the Soviet regime by 1939? What were its negative aspects?

12. How did the First World War contribute to revolution in Italy?

13. What were the chief elements of Fascist theory?

14. By what means did Mussolini enlist the support, and at the same time maintain control, of labor?

15. To what extent did fascism in Italy solve the problems that provided the fertile ground for its rise?

16. Describe the constitution of the Weimar Republic. What difficulties imperiled its survival?

17. What economic problems and policies of the 1920s contributed to the failure of a democratic regime in Germany?

18. Describe the circumstances under which Hitler came to power in Germany.

19. What was the place of anti-Semitism in the Nazi ideology and political program?

20. Compare German Nazism with Italian fascism.

21. What evidence supports the assertion that "fascism and Nazism were extreme expressions of tendencies prevalent in all industrialized countries"? Do you accept the assertion?

22. What is meant by deflation as an economic policy? Why did its application in France and Britain antagonize the working class?

23. Cite examples of policies by Western governments to deal with the Great Depression that might be termed "economic nationalism."

24. What were the economic reforms brought about in France by the Popular Front government of Léon Blum?

25. What were the objectives of the New Deal in the United States? In what area was it least successful?

26. Briefly describe the leading characteristics of twentieth-century Western philosophy.

27. Explain the meaning and appeal of Logical Positivism.

28. Existentialism postulates man's existence as a free individual. Why is it nevertheless basically pessimistic?

29. What was John Maynard Keynes's prescription for making capitalism work?

30. Compare the two schools of musical expressionism, atonality and polytonality.

31. In what directions and to what extent was art affected under totalitarian regimes?

PROBLEMS

1. Investigate any of the following:
   a. The rise of Hitler
   b. The Russian purges of 1936–1938
   c. Jean-Paul Sartre's existentialism
   d. The origins and achievements of the Popular Front in France
   e. The career of Mussolini
   f. The Soviet Five-Year Plans

2. Twentieth-century totalitarianism repudiated democracy. Yet in spite of their opposition to each other, these two ideologies shared certain common nineteenth-century roots. Explore these common roots, and how they diverged into such differing ideologies.

3. It is sometimes said that the nature of the Weimar Republic left Germany vulnerable to Nazi attack. Do you agree? Study the history of the Republic and the nature of its constitution in attempting to deal with this issue.

4. The term "Nazi" was derived from the German word *Nationalsozialistische*. Was the Nazi movement really "socialistic" in character?

5. Compare the actualities of the Bolshevik revolution in Russia with Marx's theory of revolution.

6. Study the conflict between Stalin and Trotsky. Try to determine to what extent it was ideological and to what extent personal.

7. Read one of the major examples of literature mentioned in the chapter. Analyze its philosophical implications, trying to determine what view it presents of human nature, human relations, and humanity's place in the universe.

8. Explore disillusionment as a theme in early-twentieth-century Western culture. Examine the extent to which it influenced writers and artists. You might wish to speculate on the impact of their works on popular attitudes, and the possible ways in which their works mirrored such attitudes.

AIDS TO AN UNDERSTANDING OF TURMOIL BETWEEN THE WARS

THE BASIC PHILOSOPHY OF FASCISM
Benito Mussolini

Thus Fascism could not be understood in many of its practical manifestations as a party organization, as a system of education, as a discipline, if it were not always looked at in the light of its whole way of conceiving life, a spiritualized way. The world seen through Fascism is not this material world which appears on the surface, in which man is an individual separated from all others and standing by himself, and in which he is governed by a natural law that makes him instinctively live a life of selfish and momentary pleasure. The man of Fascism is an individual who is nation and fatherland, which is a moral law, binding together individuals and the generations into a tradition and a mission, suppressing the instinct for a life enclosed within the brief round of pleasure in order to restore within duty a higher life free from the limits of time and space: a life in which the individual, through the denial of himself, through the sacrifice of his own private interests, through death itself, realizes that completely spiritual existence in which his value as a man lies.

Therefore it is a spiritualized conception, itself the result of the general reaction of modern times against the flabby materialistic positivism of the nineteenth century. Anti-positivistic, but positive: not sceptical, nor agnostic, nor pessimistic, nor passively optimistic, as are, in general, the doctrines (all negative) that put the centre of life outside man, who with his free will can and must create his own world. Fascism desires an active man, one engaged in activity with all his energies: it desires a man virilely conscious of the difficulties that exist in action and ready to face them. It conceives of life as a struggle, considering that it behoves man to conquer for himself that life truly worthy of him, creating first of all in himself the instrument (physical, moral, intellectual) in order to construct it. Thus for the single individual, thus for the nation, thus for humanity. Hence the high value of culture in all its forms (art, religion, science), and the enormous importance of education. Hence also the essential value of work, with which man conquers nature and creates the human world (economic, political, moral, intellectual).

• • •

Against individualism, the Fascist conception is for the State; and it is for the individual in so far as he coincides with the State, which is the conscience and universal will of man in his historical existence. It is opposed to classical Liberalism, which arose from the necessity of reacting against absolutism, and which brought its historical purpose to an end when the State was transformed into the conscience and will of the people. Liberalism denied the State in the interests of the particular individual; Fascism reaffirms the State as the true reality of the individual. And if liberty is to be the attribute of the real man, and not of that abstract puppet envisaged by individualistic Liberalism, Fascism is for liberty. And for the only liberty which can be a real thing, the liberty of the State and of the individual within the State. Therefore, for the Fascist, everything is in the State, and nothing human or spiritual exists, much less has value, outside the State. In this sense Fascism is totalitarian, and the Fascist State, the synthesis and unity of all values, interprets, develops and gives strength to the whole life of the people.

Outside the State there can be neither individuals nor groups (political parties, associations, syndicates, classes). Therefore Fascism is opposed to Socialism, which confines the movement of history within the class struggle and ignores the unity of classes established in one economic and moral reality in the State; and analogously it is opposed to class syndicalism. Fascism recognizes the real exigencies for which the socialist and syndicalist movement arose, but while recognizing them wishes to bring them under the control of the State and give them a purpose within the corporative system of interests reconciled within the unity of the State.

From Michael Oakeshott, *The Social and Political Doctrines of Contemporary Europe.* Cambridge University Press, 1942. Reprinted by permission of the publisher.

HITLER'S THEORIES OF RACE AND GERMAN EXPANSION

Just as little as Nature desires a mating between weaker individuals and stronger ones, far less she desires the mixing of a higher race with a lower one, as in this case her entire work of higher breeding, which has perhaps taken hundreds of thousands of years, would tumble at one blow.

Historical experience offers countless proofs of this. It shows with terrible clarity that with any mixing of the blood of the Aryan with lower races the result was the end of the culture-bearer. North America, the population of which consists for the greatest part of Germanic elements—which mix only very little with the lower, colored races—displays a humanity and a culture different from those of Central and South America, where chiefly the Romanic immigrants have sometimes mixed with the aborigines on a large scale. By this example alone one may clearly and distinctly recognize the influence of the race mixture. The Germanic of the North American continent, who has remained pure and less intermixed, has become the master of that continent, he will remain so until he, too, falls victim to the shame of blood-mixing.

The result of any crossing, in brief, is always the following:

(a) Lowering of the standard of the higher race,

(b) Physical and mental regression, and, with it, the beginning of a slowly but steadily progressive lingering illness.

To bring about such a development means nothing less than sinning against the will of the Eternal Creator.

• • •

Much as we all today recognize the necessity for a reckoning with France, it will remain largely ineffective if our foreign-policy aim is restricted thereto. It has and will retain significance if it provides the rear cover for an enlargement of our national domain of life in Europe. For we will find this question's solution not in colonial acquisitions, but exclusively in the winning of land for resettlement which increases the area of the motherland itself, and thereby not only keeps the new settlers in the most intimate community with the land of origin, but insures to the total area those advantages deriving from its united magnitude.

• • •

With this, we National Socialists consciously draw a line through the foreign-policy trend of our pre-War period. We take up at the halting place of six hundred years ago. We terminate the endless German drive to the south and west of Europe, and direct our gaze towards the lands in the east. We finally terminate the colonial and trade policy of the pre-War period, and proceed to the territorial policy of the future.

———

From Adolf Hitler, *Mein Kampf*, Reynal & Hitchcock, 1940. Reprinted by permission of Houghton Mifflin Company.

LENIN'S THEORY OF COMMUNIST MORALITY

But is there such a thing as Communist ethics? Is there such a thing as Communist morality? Of course there is. It is frequently asserted that we have no ethics, and very frequently the bourgeoisie makes the charge that we Communists deny all morality. That is one of their methods of confusing the issue, of throwing dust into the eyes of the workers and peasants.

In what sense do we deny ethics, morals?

In the sense in which they are preached by the bourgeoisie, a sense which deduces these morals from god's commandments. Of course, we say that we do not believe in god. We know perfectly well that the clergy, the landlords, and the bourgeoisie all claimed to speak in the name of god, in order to protect their own interests as exploiters. Or, instead of deducing their ethics from the commandments of morality, from the commandments of god, they deduced them from idealistic or semi-idealistic phrases which in substance were always very similar to divine commandments.

We deny all morality taken from superhuman or nonclass conceptions. We say that this is a deception, a swindle, a befogging of the minds of the workers and peasants in the interests of the landlords and capitalists.

We say that our morality is wholly subordinated to the interests of the class struggle of the proletariat. We deduce our morality from the facts and needs of the class struggle of the proletariat.

The old society was based on the oppression of all the workers and peasants by the landlords and capitalists. We had to destroy this society. We had to overthrow these landowners and capitalists. But to do this, organisation was necessary. God could not create such organisation.

———

From V. I. Lenin, *Religion*, International Publishers. Reprinted by permission of the publisher.

WHAT COMMUNISM REALLY MEANS
V. I. Lenin

Marx continues:

In a higher phase of Communist society, when the enslaving subordination of individuals in the division of labour has disappeared, and with it also the antagonism between mental and physical labour; when labour has become not only a means of living, but itself the first necessity of life; when, along with the all-around development of individuals, the productive forces too have grown, and all the springs of social wealth are flowing more freely—it is only at that stage that it will be possible to pass completely beyond the narrow horizon of bourgeois rights, and for society to inscribe on its banners: from each according to his ability; to each according to his needs!

Only now can we appreciate the full correctness of Engels' remarks in which he mercilessly ridiculed all the absurdity of combining the words "freedom" and "state." While the state exists there is no freedom. When there is freedom, there will be no state.

The economic basis for the complete withering away of the state is that high stage of development of Communism when the antagonism between mental and physical labour disappears, that is to say, when one of the principal sources of modern social inequality disappears—a source, moreover, which it is impossible to remove immediately by the mere conversion of the means of production into public property, by the mere expropriation of the capitalists.

This expropriation will make a gigantic development of the productive forces *possible*. And seeing how incredibly, even now, capitalism *retards* this development, how much progress could be made even on the basis of modern technique at the level it has reached, we have the right to say, with the fullest confidence, that the expropriation of the capitalists will inevitably result in a gigantic development of the productive forces of human society. But how rapidly this development will go forward, how soon it will reach the point of breaking away from the division of labour, of removing the antagonism between mental and physical labour, of transforming work into the "first necessity of life"—this we do not and cannot know.

Consequently, we have a right to speak solely of the inevitable withering away of the state, emphasising the protracted nature of this process and its dependence upon the rapidity of development of the *higher phase* of Communism; leaving quite open the question of lengths of time, or the concrete forms of withering away, since material for the solution of such questions is *not available*.

The state will be able to wither away completely when society has realised the rule: "From each according to his ability; to each according to his needs," i.e., when people have become accustomed to observe the fundamental rules of social life, and their labour is so productive that they voluntarily work *according to their ability*.

———

From V. I. Lenin. *The State and Revolution*, revised trans., International Publishers, 1922. Reprinted by permission of the publisher.

THE EXISTENTIALISM OF JEAN-PAUL SARTRE

What is meant here by saying that existence precedes essence? It means that, first of all, man exists, turns up, appears on the scene, and, only afterwards, defines himself. If man, as the existentialist conceives him, is indefinable, it is because at first he is nothing. Only afterward will he be something, and he himself will have made what he will be. Thus, there is no human nature, since there is no God to conceive it. Not only is man what he conceives himself to be, but he is also only what he wills himself to be after this thrust toward existence.

Man is nothing else but what he makes of himself. Such is the first principle of existentialism. It is also what is called subjectivity, the name we are labeled with when charges are brought against us. But what do we mean by this, if not that man has a greater dignity than a stone or table? For we mean that man first exists, that is, that man first of all is the being who hurls himself toward a future and who is conscious of imagining himself as being in the future. Man is at the start a plan which is aware of itself, rather than a patch of moss, a piece of garbage, or a cauliflower; nothing exists prior to this plan; there is nothing in heaven; man will be what he will have planned to be. Not what he will want to be. Because by the word "will" we generally mean a conscious decision, which is subsequent to what we have already made of ourselves. I may want to belong to a political patry, write a book, get married; but all that is only a manifestation of an earlier, more spontaneous choice that is called "will." But if existence really does precede essence, man is responsible for what he is. Thus, existentialism's first move is to make every man aware of what he is and to make the full responsibility of his existence rest on him. And when we say that a man is responsible for himself, we do not only mean that he is responsible for his own individuality, but that he is responsible for all men.

First, what is meant by anguish? The existentialists say at once that man is anguish. What that means is this: the man who involves himself and who realizes that he is not only the person he chooses to be, but also a law-maker who is, at the same time, choosing all mankind as well as himself, can not help escape the feeling of his total and deep responsibility. . . .

The existentialist, on the contrary, thinks it very distressing that God does not exist, because all possibility of finding values in a heaven of ideas disappears along with Him; there can no longer be an *a priori* Good, since there is no infinite and perfect consciousness to think it. Nowhere is it written that the Good exists, that we must be honest, that we must not lie; because the fact is we are on a plane where there are only men. Dostoievsky said, "If God didn't exist, everything would be possible." That is the very starting point of existentialism. Indeed, everything is permissible if God does not exist, and as a result man is forlorn, because neither within him nor without does he find anything to cling to. He can't start making excuses for himself.

If existence really does precede essence, there is no explaining things away by reference to a fixed and give human nature. In other words, there is no determinism man is free, man is freedom. On the other hand, if God does not exist, we find no values or commands to turn to which legitimize our conduct. So, in the bright realm of values, we have no excuse behind us, nor justification before us. We are alone, with no excuses.

That is the idea I shall try to convey when I say that man is condemned to be free. Condemned, because he did not create himself, yet, in other respects is free; because, once thrown into the world, he is responsible for everything he does. . . .

From Jean-Paul Sartre, *Existentialism*, Philosophical Library, 1947. Reprinted by permission of the publisher.

ANALYSIS AND INTERPRETATION OF THE READINGS

1. What is the meaning of the Italian Fascist doctrine that "Fascism reaffirms the State as the true reality of the individual"?
2. Criticize Hitler's racial explanation of the differences between North and South America.
3. Do Hitler's theories of expansion in *Mein Kampf* indicate that he was not a threat to Western Europe?
4. Was Lenin justified in affirming the existence of a Communist morality?
5. What did Lenin mean by "the highest phase of Communist society"?
6. Why did Lenin deny the possibility of freedom so long as the State exists?
7. Judging from the passage by Sartre, why is "existence" the essential starting point for the philosophy called "existentialism"?

CHAPTER 36 | The Second World War

IDENTIFICATIONS

You should be able to identify and give the significance of the following:

blitzkrieg	"phony war"
"Little Entente"	Vichy regime
Treaty of Rapallo	Battle of Britain
Locarno Agreements	Lend-Lease Act
Kellogg-Briand Pact	Rome-Berlin Axis
appeasement	D-Day
Spanish Civil War	Midway
"peace in our time"	Atlantic Charter
Nazi-Soviet non-aggression pact	
Economic and Social Council	

STUDY QUESTIONS

1. What were the similarities in causes and characteristics between the First and Second World Wars? What were the outstanding differences?
2. What were the chief causes of the breakdown of the peace of 1919–1920?
3. The European system of alliances was a factor leading to the First World War. To what extent was this system revived between the two world wars?
4. What attempts at disarmament were made between the two world wars, and why were they not more successful?
5. How did the Great Depression help to bring on the Second World War?
6. Show to what extent each of the following was a good example of appeasement as that term is used in this chapter: Japanese invasion of Manchuria; German remilitarization of the Rhineland; German and Italian intervention in the Spanish Civil War.
7. What were the consequences of the Munich Agreement of 1938? How do you account for the concessions made by Chamberlain and Daladier at Munich?
8. What events of 1942 and 1943 marked a turning point in the war?
9. What were some of the ways in which Resistance movements attempted to assist the Allies in their battle against the Axis powers?
10. How did the Second World War differ from all previous conflicts, including the First World War, in its effect on civilian populations? How do you account for its new level of inhumanity?
11. What were the basic difficulties in the way of planning a peace settlement?
12. What program was formulated at the Yalta Conference of 1945?
13. Why was the Potsdam Conference unable to resolve tensions among the wartime allies? What postwar European problems did the Conference foreshadow?
14. Summarize the provisions of the treaty with Japan immediately following the war.
15. Describe the structure and function of the United Nations Security Council. What is its great weakness?
16. In what fields has the United Nations been most successful? In what respects has it largely failed?

PROBLEMS

1. Investigate any of the following:
   a. The Spanish Civil War and the coming of the Second World War
   b. The genesis of the Munich Agreement of 1938
   c. The Battle of Britain
   d. The American defeat at Pearl Harbor

e. D-Day: June 6, 1944

f. The work of any of the specialized agencies of the U.N.: UNESCO, WHO, or FAO

2. Summarize the attempts to maintain peace between the two world wars. Suggest reasons why these attempts met with such limited success.

3. Attack or defend the proposition that the Great Depression was more responsible than the Versailles Treaty for the breakdown of world peace.

4. Write an essay on how you think the Second World War might have been avoided.

5. Compare the Charter of the United Nations with the Covenant of the League of Nations. In what ways, if any, is the U.N. an improvement over the League?

6. Study the arguments for and against the dropping of the atomic bomb on Japan. Try to determine the reasons for the decision to use the bomb.

AIDS TO AN UNDERSTANDING OF THE SECOND WORLD WAR

"PEACE IN OUR TIME": Speech in Defense of the Munich Agreement, 1938
Neville Chamberlain

The Prime Minister:

Before I come to describe the Agreement which was signed at Munich in the small hours of Friday morning last, I would like to remind the House of two things which I think it very essential not to forget when those terms are being considered. The first is this: We did not go there to decide whether the predominantly German areas in the Sudetenland should be passed over to the German Reich. That had been decided already. Czechoslovakia had accepted the Anglo-French proposals. What we had to consider was the method, the conditions and the time of the transfer of the territory. The second point to remember is that time was one of the essential factors. All the elements were present on the spot for the outbreak of a conflict which might have precipitated the catastrophe. We had populations inflamed to a high degree; we had extremists on both sides ready to work up and provoke incidents; we had considerable quantities of arms which were by no means confined to regularly organised forces. Therefore, it was essential that we should quickly reach a conclusion, so that this painful and difficult operation of transfer might be carried out at the earliest possible moment and concluded as soon as was consistent, with orderly procedure, in order that we might avoid the possibility of something that might have rendered all our attempts at peaceful solution useless. . . .

. . . To those who dislike an ultimatum, but who were anxious for a reasonable and orderly procedure, every one of [the] modifications [of the Godesberg Memorandum by the Munich Agreement] is a step in the right direction. It is no longer an ultimatum, but is a method which is carried out largely under the supervision of an international body.

Before giving a verdict upon this arrangement, we should do well to avoid describing it as a personal or a national triumph for anyone. The real triumph is that it has shown that representatives of four great Powers can find it possible to agree on a way of carrying out a difficult and delicate operation by discussion instead of by force of arms, and thereby they have averted a catastrophe which would have ended civilisation as we have known it. The relief that our escape from this great peril of war has, I think, everywhere been mingled in this country with a profound feeling of sympathy. [*Hon. Members:* Shame.] I have nothing to be ashamed of. Let those who have, hang their heads. We must feel profound sympathy for a small and gallant nation in the hour of their national grief and loss.

Mr. Bellenger:

It is an insult to say it.

The Prime Minister:

I say in the name of this House and of the people of this country that Czechoslovakia has earned our admiration and respect for her restraint, for her dignity, for her magnificent discipline in face of such a trial as few nations have ever been called upon to meet.

The army, whose courage no man has ever questioned, has obeyed the order of their President, as they would equally have obeyed him if he had told them to march into the trenches. It is my hope and my belief, that under the new system of guarantees, the new Czechoslovakia will find a greater security than she has ever enjoyed in the past. . . .

I pass from that subject, and I would like to say a few words in respect of the various other participants, besides ourselves, in the Munich Agreement. After everything that has been said about the German Chancellor today and in the past, I do feel that the House ought to recognise the difficulty for a man in that position to take back such emphatic declarations as he had already made amidst the enthusiastic cheers of his supporters, and to recognise that in consenting, even though it were only at the last moment, to discuss with the representatives of other Powers those things which he had declared he had already decided once for all, was a real and a substantial contribution on his part. With regard to Signor Mussolini, . . . I think that Europe and the world have reason to be grateful to the head of the Italian government for his work in contributing to a peaceful solution.

In my view the strongest force of all, one which grew and took fresh shapes and forms every day was the force not of any one individual, but was that unmistakable sense of unanimity among the peoples of the world that war must somehow be averted. The peoples of the British Empire were at one with those of Germany, of France and of Italy, and their anxiety, their intense desire for peace, pervaded the whole atmosphere of the conference, and I believe that that, and not threats, made possible the concessions that were made. I know the House will want to hear what I am sure it does not doubt, that throughout these discussions the Dominions, the Governments of the Dominions, have been kept in the closest touch with the march of events by telegraph and by personal contact, and I would like to say how greatly I was encouraged on each of the journeys I made to Germany by the knowledge that I went with the good wishes of the Governments of the Dominions. They shared all our anxieties and all our hopes. They rejoiced with us that peace was preserved, and with us they look forward to further efforts to consolidate what has been done.

Ever since I assumed my present office my main purpose has been to work for the pacification of Europe, for the removal of those suspicions and those animosities which have so long poisoned the air. The path which leads to appeasement is long and bristles with obstacles. The question of Czechoslovakia is the latest and perhaps the most dangerous. Now that we have got past it, I feel that it may be possible to make further progress along the road to sanity.

From Great Britain, *Parliamentary Debates*. Commons, Vol. 339 (October 3, 1938).

The Nazi-Soviet Pact of 1939: Defense by the Soviet Foreign Minister
V. Molotov

I shall now go on to the Soviet-German Non-Aggression Pact.

The decision to conclude a non-aggression pact between the U.S.S.R. and Germany was adopted after military negotiations with France and Great Britain had reached an impasse owing to the insuperable difficulties I have mentioned. As the negotiations had shown that the conclusion of a pact of mutual assistance could not be expected, we could not but explore other possibilities of ensuring peace and eliminating the danger of war between Germany and the U.S.S.R. If the British and French Governments refused to reckon with this, that is their affair. *It is our duty to think of the interests of the Soviet people, the interests of the Union of Soviet Socialist Republics*—all the more because we are firmly convinced that the interests of the U.S.S.R. coincide with the fundamental interests of the peoples of other countries.

But that is only one side of the matter. Another circumstance was required before the Soviet-German Non-Aggression Pact could come into existence. It was necessary that in her foreign policy Germany should make a turn towards good neighbourly relations with the Soviet Union. Only when this second condition was fulfilled, only when it became clear to us that the German Government desired to change its foreign policy so as to secure an improvement of relations with the U.S.S.R., was a basis found for the conclusion of the Soviet-German Non-Aggression Pact. Everybody knows that during the last six years, ever since the National-Socialists came into power, political relations between Germany and the U.S.S.R. have been strained. Everybody also knows that, despite the differences of outlook and political systems, the Soviet Government had endeavoured to maintain normal business and political relations with Germany. . . .

Since 1926 the political basis of our relations with Germany has been the Treaty of Neutrality which was prolonged by the present German Government in 1933. This Treaty of Neutrality remains in force to this day. The Soviet Government considered it desirable even before this to take a further step towards improving political relations with Germany, but circumstances have been such that this has become possible only now.

It is true that, in the present case, we are dealing *not with a pact of mutual assistance*, as in the case of the Anglo-French-Soviet negotiations, but *only with a non-aggression pact*. Nevertheless, conditions being what they are it is difficult to over-estimate the international importance of the Soviet-German pact. That is why we favoured the visit of the German Minister for Foreign Affairs, Herr von Ribbentrop, to Moscow.

August 23, 1939, the day the Soviet-German Non-Aggression Pact was signed, is to be regarded as a date of great historical importance. The non-aggression pact between the U.S.S.R. and Germany marks a turning point in the history of Europe, and not of Europe alone. Only yesterday German Fascists were pursuing a foreign policy hostile to us. Yes, only yesterday we were enemies in the sphere of foreign relations. Today, however, the situation has changed and we are enemies no longer.

The art of politics in the sphere of foreign relations does not consist in increasing the number of enemies for one's country. On the contrary, the art of politics in this sphere is to reduce the number of such enemies and make the enemies of yesterday good neighbours, maintaining peaceable relations one with the other. History has shown that enmity and wars between our country and Germany have been to the detriment of our countries, not to their benefit.

The countries which suffered most of all in the war of 1914–18 were Russia and Germany. Therefore, the interests of the peoples of the Soviet Union and Germany do not lie in mutual enmity. On the contrary, the peoples of the Soviet Union and Germany stand in need of peaceable relations. The Soviet-German Non-Aggression Pact puts an end to the enmity between Germany and the U.S.S.R. and this is in the interests of both countries. The fact that our outlooks and political systems differ must not and cannot be an obstacle to the establishment of good political relations between both States, just as like differences are no impediment to the good political relations which the U.S.S.R. maintains with other non-Soviet capitalist countries.

Only the enemies of Germany and the U.S.S.R. can strive to create and foment enmity between the peoples of these countries. We have always stood for amity between the peoples of the U.S.S.R. and Germany, and for the growth and development of friendship between the peoples of the Soviet Union and the German people.

The chief importance of the Soviet-German Non-Aggression Pact lies in the fact that the two largest States of Europe have agreed to put an end to enmity between them, to eliminate the menace of war and to live at peace one with the other, making narrower thereby the zone of possible military conflicts in Europe. . . .

From V. Molotov, *Soviet Foreign Policy, Four Speeches*, Oxford University Press. Reprinted by permission of the publisher.

PRIME MINISTER CHAMBERLAIN'S RADIO ADDRESS TO THE GERMAN PEOPLE, September 4, 1939

GERMAN PEOPLE—Your country and mine are at war. Your Government has bombed and invaded the free and independent State of Poland, which this country is in honour bound to defend. . . . God knows this country has done everything possible to prevent this calamity. But now that the invasion of Poland by Germany has taken place, it has become inevitable.

You were told by your Government that you are fighting because Poland rejected your Leader's offer and resorted to force. What are the facts? The so-called "offer" was made to the Polish Ambassador on Thursday evening, two hours before the announcement by your Government that it had been "rejected." So far from having been rejected, there had been no time even to consider it.

Your Government had previously demanded that a Polish representative should be sent to Berlin within twenty-four hours to conclude an agreement. The Polish representative was expected to arrive within a fixed time to sign an agreement which he had not even seen. This is not negotiation. This is a dictate. To such methods no self-respecting and powerful State could assent. Negotiations on a free and equal basis might well have settled the matter in dispute.

You may ask why Great Britain is concerned. We are concerned because we gave our word of honour to defend Poland against aggression. Why did we feel it necessary to pledge ourselves to defend this Eastern Power when our interests lie in the West? The answer is—and I regret to have to say it—that nobody in this country any longer places any trust in your Leader's word.

He gave his word that he would respect the Locarno Treaty; he broke it. He gave his word that he neither wished nor intended to annex Austria; he broke it. He declared that he would not incorporate the Czechs in the Reich; he did so. He gave his word after Munich that he had no further territorial demands in Europe; he broke it. He has sworn for years that he was the mortal enemy of Bolshevism; he is now its ally.

Can you wonder his word is, for us, not worth the paper it is written on?

The German-Soviet Pact was a cynical *volte-face*, designed to shatter the Peace Front against aggression. This gamble failed. The Peace Front stands firm. Your Leader is now sacrificing you, the German people, to the still more monstrous gamble of a war to extricate himself from the impossible position into which he has led himself and you.

In this war we are not fighting against you, the German people, for whom we have no bitter feeling, but against a tyrannous and forsworn régime which has betrayed not only its own people but the whole of Western civilisation and all that you and we hold dear.

May God defend the right!

From Great Britain, *Parliamentary Papers, 1938–39*.

THE DROPPING OF THE A-BOMB
Barton J. Bernstein

On July 16th, at Alamogordo, America tested the first A-bomb. It was a great success. On the basis of the test, Oppenheimer informed General Groves that the total energy released by the first bombs on Japan would be equivalent to between twelve thousand and twenty thousand tons of TNT, and the blast's power would be between eight thousand and fifteen thousand tons. Because the bombs would be exploded about a third of a mile in the air, "it is not expected that radioactive contamination will reach the ground," Oppenheimer wrote, though "lethal radiation will, of course, reach the ground from the bomb itself." The implication, tucked away in scientific, impersonal language, was that radiation would help kill residents of the city but not persist very long.

General Groves promptly informed Oppenheimer, "It is necessary to drop the first Little Boy [uranium gun weapon] and the first Fat Man [implosion plutonium weapon] and probably a second one in accordance with our original plans. It may be that as many as three of the latter [will be necessary]."

Truman was then at Potsdam for the conference with Prime Minister Winston Churchill and Premier Joseph Stalin, a meeting that the President had delayed a few weeks so that he would know the results of the Alamogordo test. On July 16th, Truman received the report on Alamogordo that he was anxiously awaiting. "Operated on this morning," the coded message announced. "Diagnosis not yet complete but results seem satisfactory and already exceed expectations." The next day, when more details arrived about the bomb's awesome power, Truman expressed his delight. "The President was evidently very greatly re-enforced over the message," Stimson happily recorded in his diary.

On the 21st, the President received a full report on the Alamogordo test. The blast was equivalent to at least fifteen to twenty thousand tons of TNT, evaporating a one-hundred-foot steel tower, leaving a crater with a diameter of 1,200 feet, knocking over at a half-mile a seventy-foot steel tower anchored in concrete, and knocking over observers at six miles. "The effects on the [seventy-foot] tower indicate," Groves reported, "that, at that distance, unshielded permanent steel and masonry buildings would have been destroyed. I no longer consider the Pentagon a safe shelter from such a bomb." The bomb would be more powerful than American experts had foreseen.

So impressed was Truman that he summarized the report in his private diary. Both Truman and Secretary of State Byrnes "were immensely pleased," Stimson noted in his own diary. "The President was tremendously pepped up by it and spoke to me of it again and again . . . He said it gave him an entirely new feeling of confidence." Churchill, when he saw the report, stated that he now understood why Truman had seemed suddenly emboldened at the negotiating table and pushed matters through with a new confidence and authority. The bomb made Truman tougher in negotiating with the Soviets, for, as he realized, its power might intimidate them.

When Stimson received from Groves the formal military order listing the target cities—Hiroshima, Kokura, Niigata, and Nagasaki (replacing Kyoto)—Truman easily approved the directive. He did not call in other advisers for consultation. Truman was simply implementing the shared assumption, recently confirmed by the Interim Committee, that the bomb would be used. He felt no need to discuss alternatives. "The weapon is to be used against Japan between now [July 25th] and August 10th," Truman recorded in his private diary.

"I have told . . . Stimson," Truman wrote in his diary, "to use it so that military objectives and soldiers and sailors are the target and not women and children. Even if the Japs are savages, ruthless, merciless, and fanatic, we as the leader for the common welfare cannot drop the terrible bomb on the old capital [Kyoto] or the new [Tokyo]. He and I are in accord. The target will be a purely military one. . . ."

None of the target cities was a purely military one, and in the case of Hiroshima the aiming point was not a military target but the center of the city itself. Indeed, as the recently declassified documents show, the cities were chosen partly because of their vulnerable civilian populations. The mass killing of civilians was a major goal.

Yet Truman had privately described the targets as "purely military." Why? Probably he was engaging in a necessary self-deception, for he could not admit to himself that the bomb would kill many thousands of civilians. The great power of the weapon and the earlier criteria for the choice of targets made the mass deaths inevitable.

"The attack [on Hiroshima]," according to the official Air Force history, "was directed against a densely built-up area, a mixture of residential, commercial, military, and small industrial buildings. . . . Planners, calculating on a 7,500-foot radius of destruction, thought that a bomb exploding [there] would wreck all important parts of the city except the dock areas. In this they were eminently correct."

World War II had transformed morality. The mass bombings of Dresden, Hamburg, and Tokyo had been designed to destroy morale and industry, and to kill workers and other civilians, all sinews of war, in what had become total war. Most of the citizens of the civilized world—in Germany, Britain, Russia, Japan, and ultimately America—had become inured to the intentional mass killing of civilians.

America had held out longer than Britain or Germany before following such tactics, but by 1945 all the civilized nations at war had adopted such tactics. Very few in America openly protested, and most Americans disregarded their arguments. War had come to justify virtually any weapons and tactics.

From Barton J. Bernstein, "The Dropping of the A-Bomb, *The Center Magazine*, March/April 1983, pp. 11–12. Copyright © by the Robert Maynard Hutchins Center for Study of Democratic Institutions.

ANALYSIS AND INTERPRETATION OF THE READINGS

1. Was Prime Minister Chamberlain naïve in assuming that Hitler and Mussolini accepted the Munich Agreement because of a sincere desire to avert war? Explain.

2. Was the Nazi-Soviet Pact of 1939 really a "turning point in the history of Europe"? Explain.

3. Why did Chamberlain, in his radio address to the German people, indict Hitler so severely for signing the Nazi-Soviet Pact?

China and Japan in the 19th Century

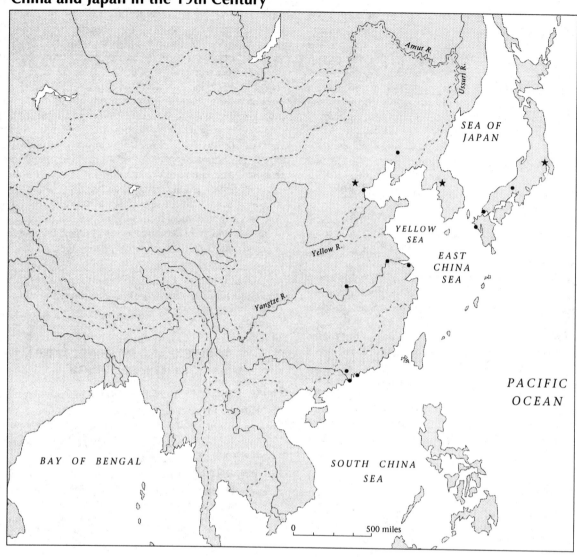

19th Century China and Japan;
Europe and Africa on the Eve of World War II

CHINA AND JAPAN IN THE 19TH CENTURY

1. On the "China/Japan" map (see page 100 opposite), outline the approximate extent of the Qing (Manchu) Empire.

2. Mark the locations of Korea, Japan, Formosa, Indo-China, *and* Mongolia.

3. Identify the following:

Hong Kong   Peking
Macao   Shanghai
Kyoto   Canton
Tokyo   Nanking
Seoul

4. Circle the major "spheres of influence" of the various European powers in China.

TERRITORIAL CHANGES RESULTING FROM
WORLD WAR I
AND EUROPE ON THE EVE OF WORLD WAR II

1. On the first map of Europe (see page 102), indicate the boundaries of the countries listed below for the year 1914, and then show changes by the year 1920. On the second map, indicate the boundaries of the same countries at the beginning of World War II.

Germany   Hungary
Italy   Rumania
Russia/USSR   Bulgaria
Finland   Serbia—Yugoslavia
Czechoslovakia   Poland
Austria   Greece

2. On one of the maps of Europe (see pages 102–103), indicate the following cities:

Moscow   Rome
Kiev   St. Petersburg
Sofia   Bucharest
Berlin   Belgrade
Prague   London
Vienna   The Hague
Madrid   Warsaw
Paris   Helsinki

IMPERIALISM IN AFRICA
TO THE EVE OF WORLD WAR II

1. On the "Imperialism in Africa" map (see page 104), using different colors or patterns, shade in on the map of Africa the areas controlled by Britain, France, Belgium, Portugal, and Italy at the high point of European imperialism in Africa.

2. Label the following:

Union of South Africa   Belgian Congo
Algeria   Kenya
Ethiopia   Egypt
Nigeria   Gold Coast

Territorial Changes Resulting from World War I

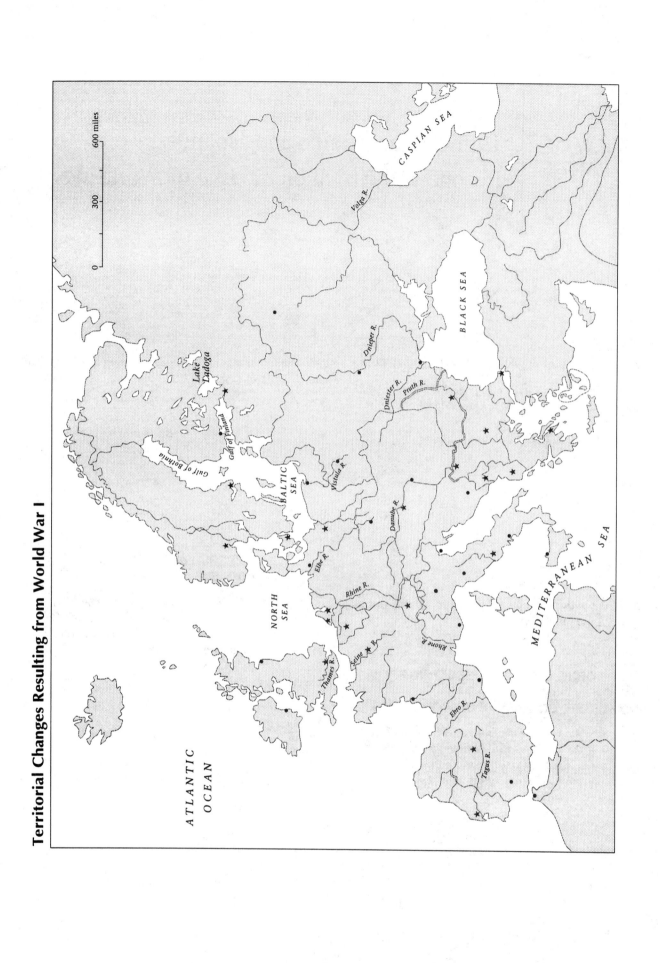

Europe on the Eve of World War II

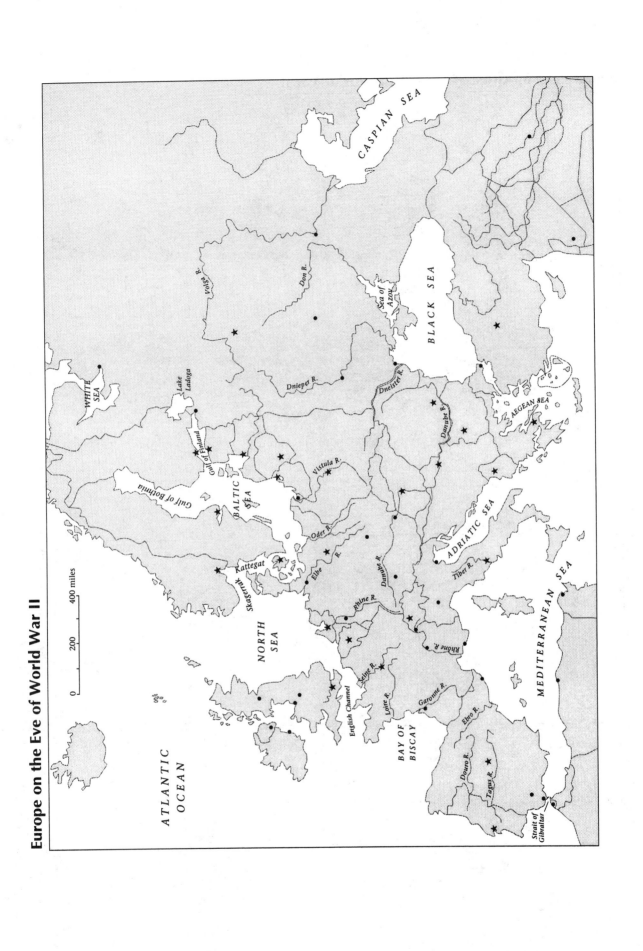

Imperialism in Africa to the Eve of World War II

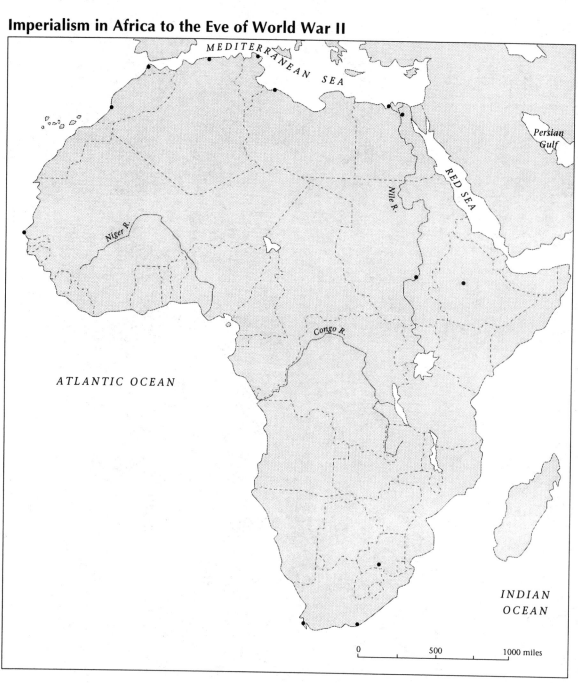

CHAPTER 37 | The Postwar Years: Rivalry and Recovery

IDENTIFICATIONS

You should be able to explain the meaning or substance of each of the following terms:

Truman Doctrine
Marshall Plan
NATO
Cominform
Warsaw Pact
German Democratic Republic
Federal Republic of Germany
Berlin crisis of 1948
"containment"

"peaceful coexistence"
Berlin Wall
Solidarity
Common Market
Viet Cong
NAFTA
Khmer Rouge
Kampuchea

You should also be able to identify each of the following individuals:

Andrei Zhdanov
John Foster Dulles
Nikita Khrushchev
Clement Attlee
Alexander Dubček
Willy Brandt
David Lange
Achmed Sukarno
Pol Pot

Jan Masaryk
Wladyslaw Gomulka
Marshal Tito
Pierre Trudeau
Lech Walesa
Konrad Adenauer
Leonid Brezhnev
Ho Chi Minh

Match the individual in the list below with the work, movement, or idea with which he is associated by placing the appropriate number in each blank:

1. Claude Lévi-Strauss
2. Andy Warhol
3. Günter Grass
4. Jackson Pollock
5. Ingmar Bergman

_____ postwar human condition portrayed through film

_____ "pop" art

_____ structuralism

_____ *The Tin Drum*

_____ abstract expressionism

STUDY QUESTIONS

1. Why was the Second World War followed so quickly by a "cold war"? Why did the Cold War continue for so long?
2. What factors help account for Stalin's anti-Western policy? What was the basis of his hostility toward and suspicion of the United States?
3. Which of the Eastern European countries achieved the greatest degree of independence from Moscow during the Cold War era?
4. How was rivalry between the superpowers illustrated by, and affected by, the organization of NATO? the division of Germany?
5. What was the nature of the "thaw" under Khrushchev, and what were its limitations?
6. What did the events of 1956 in Poland and Hungary demonstrate about the limits of Soviet tolerance toward satellite states?
7. What reforms became known as the "Prague Spring"?
8. How did relations between the two Germanys change under the administration of the West German chancellor Willy Brandt?
9. What brought on the "Solidarity" movement in Poland in the 1980s?
10. What factors led to the establishment of a military dictatorship in Indonesia?

11. Summarize the stages of U.S. involvement in the Vietnam conflict under Presidents Kennedy, Johnson, and Nixon.

12. Why did the withdrawal of U.S. troops after 1975 not bring peace to Indochina? How did old rivalries resurface? What new rivalries were created?

13. How was superpower rivalry illustrated by the Korean War, the war in Vietnam, and the Soviet invasion of Afghanistan?

14. What accounts for the rapid economic recovery of Western Europe following World War II?

15. Why was economic growth more phenomenal in defeated West Germany than in France or Britain? Why was British growth particularly sluggish?

16. In what ways did economic growth lead to an expansion of social services in Western Europe?

17. Describe the origin and purpose of the European Economic Community. Compare this with efforts at Eastern European economic integration.

18. What changes could be observed in Socialist and other parties of the Left in the postwar period?

19. What policies did Charles de Gaulle pursue as the leader of France? How did his leadership affect France's relations with its neighbors and beyond?

20. How did the Canada Act change Canada's relations with Britain? How did it change Canada's internal administration?

21. Describe ways in which Canada and the United States found their interests increasingly connected in the postwar era.

22. Explain the basis of Québec's claim that it is a "distinct society" within Canada. How have the federal and other provincial governments dealt with Québec's assertion of distinct rights?

23. How and why did Australia's trade and diplomatic relations change after World War II?

24. Outline changes in population in postwar Europe. What were the causes of population shifts? What other changes did population changes produce?

25. What is a "managerial class"? How did this group differ from previous participants in business?

26. How did class consciousness and class relations change following World War II in the advanced economies of the West?

27. Describe some of the ways in which the dilemmas and difficulties of the human condition found voice in postwar American and European literature, film, and other arts.

28. Why did Marxism appeal to a considerable number of European intellectuals?

29. What is meant by "abstract expressionism" in art? What do its practitioners attempt to convey?

PROBLEMS

1. Investigate any of the following:
   a. The theories of Trofim Lysenko
   b. The liberalization movement in Czechoslovakia during the 1960s
   c. The "Solidarity" movement in Poland
   d. The civil war in Cambodia/Kampuchea
   d. The development and operation of the European Economic Community
   e. The de-Stalinization movement and the "thaw" under Khrushchev
   f. The "communications revolution" in the West

2. Read *The Stranger* by Albert Camus, and analyze his view of the dilemma of human existence. Compare his views on the human condition and his approach to political activity with those of Jean-Paul Sartre.

AIDS TO AN UNDERSTANDING OF THE POSTWAR YEARS: RIVALRY AND RECOVERY

Subversion Versus Revolution— A Socialist's View
Isaac Deutscher

But was all the talk about Moscow-inspired subversion so hollow? Behind all that talk there was one real emotion which was and is gripping our ruling classes and our governments to this day: whether subversion threatened or not, our ruling classes were and are really frightened of revolution. They are especially frightened of any revolution behind which there is no Russian and no Chinese hand. The more a revolution is spontaneous, the more a revolution develops by its own momentum, the more are our ruling classes frightened of it. They

have assumed the roles of the gendarmes of counter-revolution, and this is the root of all the trouble. They are the belated twentieth century Metternichs. Metternich sought, after the defeat of Napoleon, to preserve feudalism in Europe and suppressed all revolution, until he was overthrown in 1848. Our present-day Metternichs say, of course, that they are struggling against subversion by offering economic aid to poverty-stricken peoples— they talk of the generosity of Marshall Aid, and so on. We have recently heard how the Vietnamese have been offered economic aid, but if they don't behave well, if they don't respond immediately to our offer, then, of course, the bombing of North Vietnam must be resumed. Either you take my economic aid or I bomb you. This is as in the famous German lines: 'Und willst du nicht mein Bruder sein, da schlag ich dir den Schädel ein.'

Which in a free amateurish English translation means: 'and if you don't want to be my brother and pal, then I am going to smash your wicked skull.'

We have seen how the impotence of the anti-communist containment policy has been revealed again and again. That policy has proved impotent because no weapons, no armed intervention, and no napalm bombing can stop a revolution which develops by its own momentum, a revolution rooted in the faith, the sufferings, and the experience of an entire people or of its working masses. General de Gaulle, who is certainly not the hero of my novel, has learned the lesson in Algeria. He was confronted there with the revolution of a small, primitive, unarmed or badly-armed nation. And half a million (*half a million!*) French soldiers' were fighting against the Algerian insurgents for years; and they had behind them the French section of the Algerian population. Yet they were impotent! Impotent against the revolution of a small and weak nation determined to fight for its existence.

'Ah!' say the defenders of armed intervention, 'But how do you know that such a native revolution is developing in Vietnam by its own force and momentum? Is it not all directed from the North?' There is, I suggest, one infallible test of whether an armed struggle is really the outcome of a genuine, broadly based revolution or not. To get at this test, I suggest that you note the contrast between the wars in Vietnam and Korea. In Southern Korea there was really no genuine revolution when the Northerners invaded it. And so the American troops and the others who participated in the hostilities under the banner of the United Nations had an easy job. They took the whole of Southern Korea in a matter of days almost. Why is it that in Southern Vietnam the troops of intervention are isolated on little bases, surrounded on all sides by the Viet Cong? Those familiar with the characteristics of civil wars in peasant countries know that in such a country no army can hold the ground and win unless it has the support of the peasantry on the spot. Those who are confined to small bases are so confined because the whole surrounding territory is for them 'enemy' territory, because the population of the surrounding areas is against them. Such was the pattern of the Russian civil war and of the Chinese. The Whites, the counter-revolutionary forces, were defeated because every village was for them enemy territory and in every village the ground was burning under their feet. This is what is happening also in South Vietnam, what is happening there to the Americans and the highly unreliable forces of the South Vietnamese government. They are surrounded, hermetically surrounded, by a hostile element; and the hostile element is the peasantry that cooperates with the Viet Cong. Very few newspapers in the west have publicized the fact that the National Liberation Front of South Vietnam has carried out a land reform there and has distributed the estates of the landlords among the peasants. In other words, the peasants have a *vested interest* in the victory of the Viet Cong. They know that if behind American tanks and official South Vietnamese troops the landlords come back, the land will be taken away from the peasants who would also become victims of class revenge.

I still believe that class struggle is the motive force of history, but in this last period, class struggle has all too often sunk into a bloody morass of power politics. On both sides of the great divide, a few ruthless and half-witted oligarchies—capitalist oligarchies here, bureaucratic oligarchies there—hold all the power and make all the decisions, obfuscate the minds and throttle the wills of nations. They even reserve for themselves the roles of our spiritual protagonists and expound for us the great conflicting ideas of our time. The social struggles of our time have degenerated into the unscrupulous contests of the oligarchies. Official Washington speaks for the world's freedom, while official Moscow speaks for the world's socialism. All too long the peoples have failed to contradict these false friends, either of freedom or of socialism. On both sides of the great divide the peoples have been silent too long, and have thus willy-nilly identified themselves with the policies of their governments. The world has thus come very close, dangerously close, to a division between revolutionary and counter-revolutionary nations. This to my mind has been the most alarming result of the cold war. Fortunately, things have begun to change. The Russian people have been shaking off the old conformism and have been regaining a critical attitude towards their rulers. Things are also changing in the United States. They are changing because the world, after all, is something like a system of interconnected vessels where the level of freedom and critical thinking tends to even out. I am sure that without the Russian de-Stalinization there would not have been the amount of freedom and critical thinking that there is in America today. And I am also sure that continued exercise of freedom and continued voicing of criticism and continued critical political action in America will encourage the further progress of freedom in the communist part of the world. Freedom in the Soviet Union was suppressed and stifled mostly during the rise of Nazism. That was the time of the great purges. It was stifled again and trampled over again throughout the cold war or most of the cold war. The more Americans exercise their freedom in opposing their own rulers, the more will the Russians too feel encouraged to speak up critically against the mistakes and blunders of their government.

THE CUBAN MISSILE CRISIS OF 1962
Robert F. Kennedy

On Tuesday morning, October 16, 1962, shortly after 9:00 o'clock, President Kennedy called and asked me to come to the White House. He said only that we were facing great trouble. Shortly afterward, in his office, he told me that a U-2 had just finished a photographic mission and that the Intelligence Community had become convinced that Russia was placing missiles and atomic weapons in Cuba.

That was the beginning of the Cuban missile crisis—a confrontation between the two giant atomic nations, the U.S. and the U.S.S.R., which brought the world to the abyss of nuclear destruction and the end of mankind. From that moment in President Kennedy's office, until Sunday morning, October 28, that was my life—and for Americans and Russians, for the whole world, it was their life as well.

The general feeling in the beginning was that some form of action was required. There were those, although they were a small minority, who felt the missiles did not alter the balance of power and therefore necessitated no action. Most felt, at that stage, that an air strike against the missile sites could be the only course. Listening to the proposals, I passed a note to the President: "I now know how Tojo felt when he was planning Pearl Harbor."

The members of the Joint Chiefs of Staff were unanimous in calling for immediate military action. They forcefully presented their view that the blockade would not be effective. General Curtis LeMay, Air Force Chief of Staff, argued strongly with the President that a military attack was essential. When the President questioned what the response of the Russians might be, General LeMay assured him there would be no reaction. President Kennedy was skeptical. "They, no more than we, can let these things go by without doing something. They can't, after all their statements, permit us to take out their missiles, kill a lot of Russians, and then do nothing. If they don't take action in Cuba, they certainly will in Berlin."

The President went on to say that he recognized the validity of the arguments made by the Joint Chiefs, the danger that more and more missiles would be placed in Cuba, and the likelihood, if we did nothing, that the Russians would move on Berlin and in other areas of the world, feeling the U.S. was completely impotent. Then it would be too late to do anything in Cuba, for by that time all their missiles would be operational.

General David M. Shoup, Commandant of the Marine Corps, summed up everyone's feelings: "You are in a pretty bad fix, Mr. President." The President answered quickly, "You are in it with me." Everyone laughed, and, with no final decision, the meeting adjourned.

Later, Secretary McNamara, although he told the President he disagreed with the Joint Chiefs and favored a blockade rather than an attack, informed him that the necessary planes, men, and ammunition were being deployed and that we could be ready to move with the necessary air bombardments on Tuesday, October 23, if that was to be the decision. The plans called for an initial attack, consisting of five hundred sorties, striking all military targets, including the missile sites, airfields, ports, and gun emplacements.

I supported McNamara's position in favor of a blockade. This was not from a deep conviction that it would be a successful course of action, but a feeling that it had more flexibility and fewer liabilities than a military attack. Most importantly, like others, I could not accept the idea that the United States would rain bombs on Cuba, killing thousands and thousands of civilians in a surprise attack. Maybe the alternatives were not very palatable, but I simply did not see how we could accept that course of action for our country.

With some trepidation, I argued that, whatever validity the military and political arguments were for an attack in preference to a blockade, America's traditions and history would not permit such a course of action. Whatever military reasons he and others could marshal, they were nevertheless, in the last analysis, advocating a surprise attack by a very large nation against a very small one. This, I said, could not be undertaken by the U.S. if we were to maintain our moral position at home and around the globe. Our struggle against Communism throughout the world was far more than physical survival—it had as its essence our heritage and our ideals, and these we must not destroy.

We spent more time on this moral question during the first five days than on any other single matter. At various times, it was proposed that we send a letter to Khrushchev twenty-four hours before the bombardment was to begin, that we send a letter to Castro, that leaflets and pamphlets listing the targets be dropped over Cuba before the attack—all these ideas and more were abandoned for military or other reasons. We struggled and fought with one another and with our consciences, for it was a question that deeply troubled us all.

We met all day Friday [October 19] and Friday night. Then again early Saturday morning we were back at the State Department. I talked to the President several times on Friday. He was hoping to be able to meet with us early enough to decide on a course of action and then broadcast it to the nation Sunday night. Saturday morning at 10:00 o'clock I called the President at the Blackstone Hotel in Chicago and told him we were ready to meet with him. It was now up to one single man. No committee was going to make this decision. He canceled his trip and returned to Washington.

As he was returning to Washington, our armed forces across the world were put on alert. Telephoning from our meeting in the State Department, Secretary McNamara ordered four tactical air squadrons placed at readiness for an air strike, in case the President decided to accept that recommendation.

The President arrived back at the White House at 1:40 P.M. and went for a swim. I sat on the side of the pool, and we talked. At 2:30 we walked up to the Oval Room.

The meeting went on until ten minutes after five. Convened as a formal meeting of the National Security Council, it was a larger group of people who met, some of whom had not participated in the deliberations up to that time. Bob McNamara presented the arguments for the blockade; others presented the arguments for the military attack.

The discussion, for the most part, was able and organized, although, like all meetings of this kind, certain statements were made as accepted truisms, which I, at least, thought were of questionable validity. One member of the Joint Chiefs of Staff, for example, argued that we could use nuclear weapons, on the basis that our adversaries would use theirs against us in an attack. I thought, as I listened, of the many times that I had heard the military take positions which, if wrong, had the advantage that no one would be around at the end to know.

The President made his decision that afternoon in favor of the blockade. There was one final meeting the next morning, with General Walter C. Sweeney, Jr., Commander in Chief of the Tactical Air Command, who told the President that even a major surprise air attack could not be certain of destroying all the missile sites and nuclear weapons in Cuba. That ended the small, lingering doubt that might still have remained in his mind. It had worried him that a blockade would not remove the missiles—now it was clear that an attack could not accomplish that task completely, either.

The strongest argument against the all-out military attack, and one no one could answer to his satisfaction, was that a surprise attack would erode if not destroy the moral position of the United States throughout the world.

The next morning, Wednesday [October 24], the quarantine went into effect, and the reports during the early hours told of the Russian ships coming steadily on toward Cuba. I talked with the President for a few moments before we went in to our regular meeting. He said, "It looks really mean, doesn't it? But then, really there was no other choice. If they get this mean on this one in our part of the world, what will they do on the next?" "I just don't think there was any choice," I said, "and not only that, if you hadn't acted, you would have been impeached." The President thought for a moment and said, "That's what I think—I would have been impeached."

It was now a few minutes after 10:00 o'clock. Secretary McNamara announced that two Russian ships, the *Gagarin* and the *Komiles*, were within a few miles of our quarantine barrier. The interception of both ships would probably be before noon Washington time. Indeed, the expectation was that at least one of the vessels would be stopped and boarded between 10:30 and 11:00 o'clock.

Then came the disturbing Navy report that a Russian submarine had moved into position between the two ships.

It had originally been planned to have a cruiser make the first interception, but, because of the increased danger, it was decided in the past few hours to send in an aircraft carrier supported by helicopters, carrying antisubmarine equipment, hovering overhead. The carrier *Essex* was to signal the submarine by sonar to surface and identify itself. If it refused, said Secretary McNamara, depth charges with a small explosive would be used until the submarine surfaced.

I think these few minutes were the time of gravest concern for the President. Was the world on the brink of a holocaust? Was it our error? A mistake? Was there something further that should have been done? Or not done? His hand went up to his face and covered his mouth. He opened and closed his fist. His face seemed drawn, his eyes pained, almost gray. We stared at each other across the table. For a few fleeting seconds, it was almost as though no one else was there and he was no longer the President.

Then it was 10:25—a messenger brought in a note to John McCone. "Mr. President, we have a preliminary report which seems to indicate that some of the Russian ships have stopped dead in the water."

Stopped dead in the water? Which ships? Are they checking the accuracy of the report? Is it true? I looked at the clock, 10:32. "The report is accurate, Mr. President. Six ships previously on their way to Cuba at the edge of the quarantine line have stopped or have turned back toward the Soviet Union. A representative from the Office of Naval Intelligence is on his way over with the full report." A short time later, the report came that the twenty Russian ships closest to the barrier had stopped and were dead in the water or had turned around.

Friday morning President Kennedy ordered the State Department to proceed with preparations for a crash program on civil government in Cuba to be established after the invasion and occupation of that country. Secretary McNamara reported the

conclusion of the military that we should expect very heavy casualties in an invasion.

The President turned to us all: "We are going to have to face the fact that, if we do invade, by the time we get to these sites, after a very bloody fight, they will be pointed at us. And we must further accept the possibility that when military hostilities first begin, those missiles will be fired."

John McCone said everyone should understand that an invasion was going to be a much more serious undertaking than most people had previously realized. "They have a hell of a lot of equipment," he said. "And it will be damn tough to shoot them out of those hills, as we learned so clearly in Korea."

Despite the heavy pressure on the big decisions, President Kennedy followed every detail. He requested, for instance, the names of all the Cuban doctors in the Miami area, should their services be required in Cuba. Learning that a U.S. military ship with extremely sensitive equipment (similar to the *Liberty*, which was struck by Israel during the Israeli-Arab war) was very close to the coast of Cuba, he ordered it farther out to sea, where it would be less vulnerable to attack. He supervised everything, from the contents of leaflets to be dropped over Cuba to the assembling of ships for the invasion.

In the meantime, we awaited Khrushchev's answer.

At 6:00 o'clock that night the message came.

A great deal has been written about this message, including the allegation that at the time Khrushchev wrote it he must have been so unstable or emotional that he had become incoherent. There was no question that the letter had been written by him personally. It was very long and emotional. But it was not incoherent and the emotion was directed at the death, destruction, and anarchy that nuclear war would bring to his people and all mankind. That, he said again and again and in many different ways, must be avoided.

This is my proposal, he said. No more weapons to Cuba and those within Cuba withdrawn or destroyed, and you reciprocate by withdrawing your blockade and also agree not to invade Cuba. Don't interfere, he said, in a piratical way with Russian ships. "If you have not lost your self-control and sensibly conceive what this might lead to, then, Mr. President, we and you ought not to pull on the ends of the rope in which you have tied the knot of war, because the more the two of us pull, the tighter the knot will be tied. And a moment may come when that knot will be tied so tight that even he who tied it will not have the strength to untie it, and then it will be necessary to cut that knot, and what that would mean is not for me to explain to you, because you yourself understand perfectly of what terrible forces our countries dispose. Consequently, if there is no intention to tighten that knot, and thereby to doom the world to the catastrophe of thermonuclear war, then let us not only relax the forces pulling on the ends of the rope, let us take measures to untie that knot. We are ready for this."

On Saturday morning, October 27, I received a memorandum from J. Edgar Hoover, Director of the Federal Bureau of Investigation, that gave me a feeling of considerable disquiet. He had received information the night before that certain Soviet personnel in New York were apparently preparing to destroy all sensitive documents on the basis that the U.S. would probably be taking military action against Cuba or Soviet ships, and this would mean war. I asked myself as I drove to the White House: If the Soviets were anxious to find an answer to the crisis, why this conduct on the part of Soviet personnel? Did the Khrushchev letter really indicate a solution could be found?

It was therefore with some sense of foreboding that I went to the meeting of our Ex Comm. My concern was justified. A new, this time very formal, letter had arrived from Khrushchev to President Kennedy. It was obviously no longer Mr. Khrushchev personally who was writing, but the Foreign Office of the Kremlin. The letter was quite different from the letter received twelve hours before. "We will remove our missiles from Cuba, you will remove yours from Turkey. . . . The Soviet Union will pledge not to invade or interfere with the internal affairs of Turkey; the U.S. to make the same pledge regarding Cuba."

To add to the feeling of foreboding and gloom, Secretary McNamara reported increasing evidence that the Russians in Cuba were now working day and night, intensifying their efforts on all the missile sites and on the IL-28s. Thus began the most difficult twenty-four hours of the missile crisis.

The change in the language and tenor of the letters from Khrushchev indicated confusion within the Soviet Union; but there was confusion among us as well. At that moment, not knowing exactly what to suggest, some recommended writing to Khrushchev and asking him to clarify his two letters. There was no clear course of action. Yet we realized that, as we sat there, the work was proceeding on the missile sites in Cuba, and we now had the additional consideration that if we destroyed these sites and began an invasion, the door was clearly open for the Soviet Union to take reciprocal action against Turkey.

The NATO countries were supporting our position and recommending that the U.S. be firm; but, President Kennedy said, they did not realize the full implications for them. If we carried out an air strike against Cuba and the Soviet Union answered by attacking Turkey, all NATO was going to be involved. Then, immediately, the President would have to decide whether he would use nuclear weapons against the Soviet Union, and all mankind would be threatened.

The Joint Chiefs of Staff joined the meeting and recommended their solution. It had the attraction of being a very simple next step—an air strike on Monday, followed shortly afterward by an invasion. They pointed out to the President that they had always felt the blockade to be far too weak a course and that military steps were the only ones the Soviet Union would understand. They were not at all surprised that nothing had been achieved by limited force, for this is exactly what they had predicted.

In the midst of these deliberations, another message came, to change the whole course of events and alter history. Major Rudolf Anderson, Jr., from South Carolina, one of the two Air Force pilots who had carried out the original U-2 reconnaissance that uncovered the presence of missiles in Cuba, had since flown several other photo-reconnaissance missions and was flying one that Saturday morning, October 27. Our meeting was interrupted by the report that his plane had been hit by a SAM missile, that it had crashed in Cuba, and that he had been killed.

There was sympathy for Major Anderson and his family. There was the knowledge that we had to take military action to protect our pilots. There was the realization that the Soviet Union and Cuba apparently were preparing to do battle. And there was the feeling that the noose was tightening on all of us, on Americans, on mankind, and that the bridges to escape were crumbling.

The President ordered the Ex Comm to meet again at 9:00 P.M. in the White House. While the letter was being typed and prepared for transmission, he and I sat in his office. He talked about Major Anderson and how it is always the brave and the best who die. The politicians and officials sit home pontificating about great principles and issues, make the decisions, and dine with their wives and families, while the brave and the young die. He talked about the miscalculations that lead to war. War is rarely intentional. The Russians don't wish to fight any more than we do. They do not want to war with us nor we with them. And yet if events continue as they have in the last several days, that struggle—which no one wishes, which will accomplish nothing—will engulf and destroy all mankind.

He wanted to make sure that he had done everything in his power, everything conceivable, to prevent such a catastrophe. Every opportunity was to be given to the Russians to find a peaceful settlement which would not diminish their national security or be a public humiliation. It was not only for Americans that he was concerned, or primarily the older generation of any land. The thought that disturbed him the most, and that made the prospect of war much more fearful than it would otherwise have been, was the specter of the death of the children of this country and all the world—the young people who had no role, who had no say, who knew nothing even of the confrontation, but whose lives would be snuffed out like everyone else's. They would never have a chance to make a decision, to vote in an election, to run for office, to lead a revolution, to determine their own destinies.

Our generation had. But the great tragedy was that, if we erred, we erred not only for ourselves, our futures, our hopes, and our country, but for the lives, futures, hopes, and countries of those who had never been given an opportunity to play a role, to vote aye or nay, to make themselves felt.

I telephoned Ambassador Dobrynin about 7:15 P.M. and asked him to come to the Department of Justice. We met in my office at 7:45. I told him first that we knew that work was continuing on the missile bases in Cuba and that in the last few days it had been expedited. I said that in the last few hours we had learned that our reconnaissance planes flying over Cuba had been fired upon and that one of our U-2s had been shot down and the pilot killed. That for us was a most serious turn of events.

President Kennedy did not want a military conflict. He had done everything possible to avoid a military engagement with Cuba and with the Soviet Union, but now they had forced our hand. Because of the deception of the Soviet Union, our photographic reconnaissance planes would have to continue to fly over Cuba, and if the Cubans or Soviets shot at these planes, then we would have to shoot back. This would inevitably lead to further incidents and to escalation of the conflict, the implications of which were very grave indeed.

I returned to the White House. The President was not optimistic, nor was I. He ordered twenty-four troop-carrier squadrons of the Air Force Reserve to active duty. They would be necessary for an invasion. He had not abandoned hope, but what hope there was now rested with Khrushchev's revising his course within the next few hours. It was a hope, not an expectation. The expectation was a military confrontation by Tuesday and possibly tomorrow. . . .

I had promised my daughters for a long time that I would take them to the Horse Show, and early Sunday morning I went to the Washington Armory to watch the horses jump. In any case, there was nothing I could do but wait. Around 10:00 o'clock, I received a call at the Horse Show. It was Secretary Rusk. He said he had just received word from the Russians that they had agreed to withdraw the missiles from Cuba.

I went immediately to the White House, and there I received a call from Ambassador Dobrynin, saying he would like to visit with me. I met him in my office at 11:00 A.M.

He told me that the message was coming through that Khrushchev had agreed to dismantle and withdraw the missiles under adequate supervision and inspection; that everything was going to work out satisfactorily; and that Mr. Khrushchev wanted to send his best wishes to the President and to me.

It was quite a different meeting from the night before. I went back to the White House and talked to the President for a long time. While I was there, he placed telephone calls to former Presidents Truman and Eisenhower. As I was leaving, he said, making reference to Abraham Lincoln, "This is the night I should go to the theater." I said, "If you go, I want to go with you." As I closed the door, he was seated at the desk writing a letter to Mrs. Anderson. . . .

From Robert F. Kennedy, *Thirteen Days: A Memoir of the Missile Crisis.* Copyright © 1971, 1969 by W. W. Norton & Company, Inc. Copyright © 1968 by The McCall Corporation. Reprinted by permission of W. W. Norton & Company, Inc.

ANALYSIS AND INTERPRETATION OF THE READINGS

1. What does Deutscher mean by saying that the Cold War has led to a "division between revolutionary and counter-revolutionary nations"?

2. At what points during the Cuban missile crisis, as narrated by Robert Kennedy, did events or decisions come closest to precipitating a nuclear war?

CHAPTER 38 | Fragmentation and Change: The End of Postwar Certainties

IDENTIFICATIONS

You should be able to explain the meaning and importance of each of the following terms:

CORE
European Community (EC)
glasnost
perestroika
Civic Forum
Commonwealth of Independent States

Bosnia
"ethnic cleansing"
affirmative action
privatization

You should be able to identify each of the following persons, and explain his or her role in the events and movements discussed in this chapter:

Mikhail Gorbachev
Margaret Thatcher
Malcolm X
Boris Yeltsin

Erich Honecker
François Mitterand
Martin Luther King, Jr.
Václav Havel

Match the individual in the list below with the work, movement, or idea with which he or she is associated by placing the appropriate number in each blank:

1. Boris Pasternak
2. J. R. R. Tolkien
3. Simone de Beauvoir
4. Aleksandr Solzhenitsyn
5. Betty Friedan
6. Herbert Marcuse

_____ *The Second Sex*

_____ *Doctor Zhivago*

_____ women's movement in the United States

_____ *Lord of the Rings*

_____ "one-dimensional" society

_____ *The Gulag Archipelago*

STUDY QUESTIONS

1. Why did both the Soviet Union and the United States become involved in a war in Korea in the early 1950s? What was the outcome of the war?
2. What were the causes behind the protests of young people in France and the United States in the 1960s and 1970s?
3. What were the main issues fueling the women's movement of the postwar years?
4. Summarize the differences between the approaches of Martin Luther King., Jr., and Malcolm X to the problem of black rights.
5. What similarities and what differences do you see between the postwar youth, women's, and black movements?
6. What were the causes of Western economic stagnation in the late 1960s and beyond? How did these causes differ from the causes of economic difficulties in eastern Europe?
7. How did the governments of Margaret Thatcher and François Mitterand differ in their attempts to direct economic recovery in Britain and France, respectively?
8. Why were neither governments of the Right nor those of the Left able to solve economic problems of the postwar era?
9. How do you account for the worldwide spread of terrorism in recent decades? What historical and political factors have helped motivate specific terrorist acts?
10. What was the nature of the reforms that Mikhail Gorbachev sought to promote in the Soviet Union, both in the government and in the Communist party? What were the chief obstacles confronting his reform program?

11. How did *glasnost* affect relations between the Soviet Union and its satellite states?
12. The economy of East Germany was one of the most prosperous in eastern Europe. How, then, do you account for the rapid pace of unification with West Germany in 1989 and 1990?
13. How do you explain the rapid collapse of communist dictatorships in eastern Europe in the late 1980s?
14. What problems were created by the rapid disintegration of the Soviet Union? How did Boris Yeltsin and other leaders attempt to deal with these problems?
15. What have been some of the obstacles to peace and stability in the West following the dramatic changes of the late 1980s and 1990s?
16. How did the conflict in the former Yugoslavia demonstrate the limits of the United Nations' ability to preclude or control conflict?

PROBLEMS

1. Explore the problems of racial integration in Europe, and the prospects for their resolution.
2. Read some of the writings of the Czech playwright-turned-president Václav Havel. What motivated him to accept the presidency of postcommunist Czechoslovakia? How did the experience of living under a communist regime affect his thinking about politics, art, and the relationship between the two?
3. Investigate any of the following:
   a. Mikhail Gorbachev's reform program
   b. Factors prompting the Soviet invasion of Afghanistan and those leading to its end
   c. Ethnic conflicts within the U.S.S.R.
   d. The life and thought of Martin Luther King, Jr.
4. To what extent do the plays of Samuel Beckett or Harold Pinter reflect disillusionment with twentieth-century culture and society? (Study at least one specific example.)

AIDS TO AN UNDERSTANDING OF THE END OF POSTWAR CERTAINTIES

PILGRIMAGE TO NONVIOLENCE
Martin Luther King, Jr.

Often the question has arisen concerning my own intellectual pilgrimage to nonviolence. In order to get at this question it is necessary to go back to my early teens in Atlanta. I had grown up abhorring not only segregation but also the oppressive and barbarous acts that grew out of it. I had passed spots where Negroes had been savagely lynched, and had watched the Ku Klux Klan on its rides at night. I had seen police brutality with my own eyes, and watched Negroes receive the most tragic injustice in the courts. All of these things had done something to my growing personality. I had come perilously close to resenting all white people.

I had also learned that the inseparable twin of racial injustic was economic injustice. Although I came from a home of economic security and relative comfort, I could never get out of my mind the economic insecurity of many of my playmates and the tragic poverty of those living around me. During my late teens I worked two summers, against my father's wishes—he never wanted my brother and me to work around white people because of the oppressive conditions—in a plant that hired both Negroes and whites. Here I saw economic injustice firsthand, and realized that the poor white was exploited just as much as the Negro. Through these early experiences I grew up deeply conscious of the varieties of injustice in our society.

So when I went to Atlanta's Morehouse College as a freshman in 1944 my concern for racial and economic justice was already substantial. During my student days at Morehouse I read Thoreau's *Essay on Civil Disobedience* for the first time. Fascinated by the idea of refusing to cooperate with an evil system, I was so deeply moved that I reread the work several times. This was my first intellectual contact with the theory of nonviolent resistance.

Not until I entered Crozer Theological Seminary in 1948, however, did I begin a serious intellectual quest for a method to eliminate social evil. Although my major interest was in the fields of theology and philosophy, I spent a great deal of time reading the works of the great social philosophers. I came early to Walter Rauschenbusch's *Christianity and the Social Crisis*, which left an indelible imprint on my thinking by giving me a theological basis for the social concern which had already grown up in me as a result of my early experiences. Of course there were points at which I differed with Rauschenbusch. I felt that he had fallen victim to the nineteenth-century "cult of inevitable progress" which led him to a superficial optimism concerning man's nature. Moreover, he came perilously close to identifying the Kingdom of God with a particular social and economic system—a tendency which should never befall the Church. . . .

During the Christmas holidays of 1949, I decided to spend my spare time reading Karl Marx to try to understand the appeal of communism for many people. For the first time I carefully scrutinized *Das Kapital* and *The Communist Manifesto*. I also read some interpretive works on the thinking of Marx and Lenin. In reading such Communist writings I drew certain conclusions that have remained with me as convictions to this day. First, I rejected their materialistic interpretation of history. Communism, avowedly secularistic and materialistic, has no place for God. This I could never accept, for as a Christian I believe that there is a creative personal power in this universe who is the ground and essence of all reality—a power that cannot be explained in materialistic terms. History is ultimately guided by spirit, not matter. Second, I strongly disagreed with communism's ethical relativism. Since for the communist there is no divine government, no absolute moral order, there are no fixed, immutable principles; consequently almost anything—force, violence, murder, lying—is a justifiable means to the "millennial" end. This type of relativism was abhorrent to me. Constructive ends can never give absolute moral justification to destructive means, because in the final analysis the end is pre-existent in the means. Third, I opposed communism's political totalitarianism. In communism the individual ends up in subjection to the state. True, the Marxist would argue that the state is an "interim" reality which is to be eliminated when the classless society emerges; but the state is the end while it lasts, and man only a means to that end. And if any man's so-called rights or liberties stand in the way of that end, they are simply swept aside. His liberties of expression, his freedom to vote, his freedom to listen to what news he likes, or to choose his books are all restricted. Man becomes hardly more, in communism, than a depersonalized cog in the turning wheel of the state.

This deprecation of individual freedom was objectionable to me. I am convinced now, as I was then, that man is an end because he is a child of God. Man is not made for the state; the state is made for man. To deprive man of freedom is to relegate him to the status of a thing, rather than elevate him to the status of a person. Man must never be treated as a means to the end of the state, but always as an end within himself. . . .

During this period I had about despaired of the power of love in solving social problems. Perhaps my faith in love was temporarily shaken by the philosophy of Nietzsche. I had been reading parts of *The Genealogy of Morals* and the whole of *The Will to Power*. Nietzsche's glorification of power—in his theory all life expressed the will to power—was an outgrowth of his contempt for ordinary morals. He attacked the whole of the Hebraic-Christian morality—with its virtues of piety and humility, its other worldliness and its attitude toward suffering—as the glorification of weakness, as making virtues out of necessity and impotence. He looked to the development of a superman who would surpass man as man surpassed the ape.

Then one Sunday afternoon I traveled to Philadelphia to hear a sermon by Dr. Mordecai Johnson, president of Howard University. He was there to preach for the Fellowship House of Philadelphia. Dr. Johnson had just returned from a trip to India, and, to my great interest, he spoke of the life and teachings of Mahatma Gandhi. His message was so profound and electrifying that I left the meeting and bought a half-dozen books on Gandhi's life and works.

Like most people, I had heard of Gandhi, but I had never studied him seriously. As I read I became deeply fascinated by his campaigns of nonviolent resistance. I was particularly moved by the Salt March to the Sea and his numerous fasts. The whole concept of "Satyagraha" (*Satya* is truth which equals love, and *agraha* is force; "Satyagraha," therefore, means truth-force or love-force) was profoundly significant to me. As I delved deeper into the philosophy of Gandhi my skepticism concerning the power of love gradually diminished, and I came to see for the first time its potency in the area of social

reform. Prior to reading Gandhi I had about concluded that the ethics of Jesus were only effective in individual relationship. The "turn the other cheek" philosophy and the "love your enemies" philosophy were only valid, I felt, when individuals were in conflict with other individuals; when racial groups and nations were in conflict a more realistic approach seemed necessary. But after reading Gandhi I saw how utterly mistaken I was.

Gandhi was probably the first person in history to lift the love ethic of Jesus above mere interaction between individuals to a powerful and effective social force on a large scale. Love for Gandhi was a potent instrument for social and collective transformation. It was in this Gandhian emphasis on love and nonviolence that I discovered the method for social reform that I had been seeking for so many months. The intellectual and moral satisfaction that I failed to gain from the utilitarianism of Bentham and Mill, the revolutionary methods of Marx and Lenin, the social-contracts theory of Hobbes, the "back to nature" optimism of Rousseau, and the superman philosophy of Nietzsche, I found in the nonviolent resistance philosophy of Gandhi. I came to feel that this was the only morally and practically sound method open to oppressed people in their struggle for freedom.

THE REVOLUTION AGAINST RACISM
Malcolm X

My thinking had been opened up wide in Mecca. In the long letters I wrote to friends, I tried to convey to them my new insights into the American black man's struggle and his problems, as well as the depths of my search for truth and justice.

"I've had enough of someone else's propaganda," I had written to these friends. "I'm for truth, no matter who tells it. I'm for justice, no matter who it is for or against. I'm a human being first and foremost, and as such I'm for whoever and whatever benefits humanity *as a whole*." . . .

I tried in every speech I made to clarify my new position regarding white people—"I don't speak against the sincere, well-meaning, good white people. I have learned that there are some. I have learned that not all white people are racists. I am speaking against and my fight is against the white *racists*. I firmly believe that Negroes have the right to fight against these racists, by any means that are necessary."

But the white reporters kept wanting me linked with that word "violence." I doubt if I had one interview without having to deal with that accusation.

"I *am* for violence if nonviolence means we continue postponing a solution to the American black man's problem—just to *avoid* violence. I don't go for nonviolence if it also means a delayed solution. To me a delayed solution is a nonsolution. Or I'll say it another way. If it must take violence to get the black man his human rights in this country, I'm *for* violence exactly as you know the Irish, the Poles, or Jews would be if they were flagrantly discriminated against. I am just as they would be in that case, and they would be for violence—no matter what the consequences, no matter who was hurt by the violence."

White society *hates* to hear anybody, especially a black man, talk about the crime the white man has perpetrated on the black man. I have always understood that's why I have been so frequently called "a revolutionist." It sounds as if *I* have done some crime! Well, it may be the American black man does need to become involved in a real revolution. The word for "revolution" in German in *Umwälzung*. What it means is a complete overturn—a complete change. The overthrow of King Farouk in Egypt and the succession of President Nasser is an example of a true revolution. It means the destroying of an old system, and its replacement with a new system. Another example is the Algerian revolution, led by Ben Bella; they threw out the French who had been there over a hundred years. So how does anybody sound talking about the Negro in America waging some "revolution"? Yes, he is condemning a system—but he's not trying to overturn the system, or to destroy it. The Negro's so-called "revolt" is merely an asking to be *accepted* into the existing system! A *true* Negro revolt might entail, for instance, fighting for separate black states within this country—which several groups and individuals have advocated, long before Elijah Muhammad came along. . . .

The only true world solution today is governments guided by true religion—of the spirit. Here in race-torn America, I am convinced that the Islam religion is desperately needed, particularly by the American black man. The black man needs to reflect that he has been America's most fervent Christian—and where has it gotten him? In fact, in the white man's hands, in the white man's interpretation . . . where has Christianity brought this *world*?

It has brought the nonwhite two-thirds of the human population to rebellion. Two-thirds of the human population today is telling the one-third minority white man, "Get out!" And the white man is leaving. And as he leaves, we see the nonwhite peoples returning in a rush to their original religions, which has been labeled "pagan" by the conquering white man. Only one religion—Islam—had the power to stand and fight the white man's Christianity for a *thousand years*! Only Islam could keep white Christianity at bay.

The Africans are returning to Islam and other indigenous religions. The Asians are returning to being Hindus, Buddhists, and Muslims.

As the Christian Crusade once went East, now the Islamic Crusade is going West. With the East—Asia—closed to Christianity, with Africa rapidly being converted to Islam, with Europe rapidly becoming un-Christian, generally today it is accepted that the "Christian" civilization of America—which is propping up the white race around the world—is Christianity's remaining strongest bastion.

Well, if *this* is so—the so-called "Christianity" now being practiced in America displays the best that world Christianity has left to offer—no one in his right mind should need any much greater proof that very close at hand is the *end* of Christianity.

Are you aware that some Protestant theologians, in their writings, are using the phrase "post-Christian era"—and they mean *now*?

And what is the greatest single reason for this Christian church's failure? It is its failure to combat racism. It is the old "You sow, you reap" story. The Christian church sowed racism—blasphemously; now it reaps racism. . . .

"Since I learned the *truth* in Mecca, my dearest friends have come to include *all* kinds—some Christians, Jews, Buddhists, Hindus, agnostics, and even atheists! I have friends who are called capitalists, socialists, and communists! Some of my friends are moderates, conservatives, extremists—some are even Uncle Toms! My friends today are black, brown, red, yellow, and *white*!"

I said to Harlem street audiences that only when mankind would submit to the One God who created all—only then would mankind even approach the "peace" of which so much *talk* could be heard . . . but toward which so little *action* was seen.

I said that on the American racial level we had to approach the black man's struggle against the white man's racism as a human problem, that we had to forget hypocritical politics and propaganda. I said that both races, as human beings, had the obligation, the responsibility, of helping to correct America's human problem. The well-meaning white people, I said, had to combat, actively and directly, the racism in other white people. And the black people had to build within themselves much greater awareness that along with equal rights there had to be the bearing of equal responsibilities. . . .

Sometimes, I have dared to dream to myself that one day, history may even say that my voice—which disturbed the white man's smugness, and his arrogance, and his complacency—that my voice helped to save America from a grave, possibly even a fatal catastrophe.

The goal has always been the same, with the approaches to it as different as mine and Dr. Martin Luther King's nonviolent marching, that dramatizes the brutality and the evil of the white man against defenseless blacks. And in the racial climate of this country today, it is anybody's guess which of the "extremes" in approach to the black man's problems might *personally* meet a fatal catastrophe first—"nonviolent" Dr. King, or so-called "violent" me.

From *The Autobiography of Malcolm X*. Copyright © 1964 by Alex Haley and Malcolm X. Copyright © 1965 by Alex Haley and Betty Shabazz. Reprinted by permission of Grove Press, Inc.

THE ADVENT OF GORBACHEV
Vladimir Pozner

For two decades, up to 1985, thinking people debated whether it was possible for things to change. The writing seemed to be on the wall, Brezhnev and the party apparatus seemed to be entrenched for good in the seat of power, the humanistic ideals of socialism, which had galvanized the nation through periods of terrible hardship, seemed to have degenerated into obscene slogans. There seemed to be no sense in fighting for change, be it within the Party or without, for those who fought were either ignored or punished. The consensus (both in the Soviet Union and abroad) was that fundamental changes were beyond hope. Yet there were those who kept saying that the status quo could not continue, that it was the dark before the dawn.

I was one who held that view, in part because it seemed logical. No society remains static, there must be an up once you have gone down, and, as far as I was concerned, we had hit absolute rock bottom. But more than logic, *I had to believe* change would come. I held on to that faith like a drowning man at sea holds on to a spar. . . .

I remember the sense of excitement created by Gorbachev's election, a feeling in the air, a quickening of the country's pulse. There was absolutely nothing in his official biography that reflected a commitment to radical change, there was no evidence to support the great expectations his election brought to life. But the people knew—as they almost always do. Animals know about the coming hurricane or earthquake, they sense it long before we do. Could it be that we, political animals, have that same sixth sense for approaching social change?

Gorbachev's first speech was different than anything the Soviet people had heard since the time of Lenin. He began by saying what everyone knew, but no official had been willing to admit: the economy was grossly inefficient and in need of fundamental restructuring, labor productivity was extremely low; energy waste was staggering; the production of consumer goods and foodstuffs was well below world standards in both quality and quantity. Radical measures were needed, he said, "to raise the country to a qualitatively new stage of social and economic progress." But Gorbachev went further, tying economic reform to political change: "We have a clear understanding that this task cannot be accomplished without attaining a new level in developing socialist democracy." He added, "Publicity is an inalienable part of socialist democracy and a standard of all public life. Extensive, timely, and frank information is evidence of trust in the people, respect for their intelligence and feelilngs and of their ability to understand events."

To a nation that had lived through decades of strict censorship and information control, that brief sentence, that first call for what would become known throughout the world as glasnost, held the promise of radical transformation. . . .

Many people, myself included, believe capitalism in America was saved by a man of great vision and courage. His name was Franklin Delano Roosevelt. Had it not been for his New Deal, for the laws he pushed through Congress, for such emergency organizations as the National Recovery Administration, for such long-term organizations as the Tennessee Valley Authority, had it not been for his foresight in furnishing Americans with the Social Security Act of 1935, it is quite possible that the American people would have opted for another system. Roosevelt saved capitalism by injecting a healthy dose of socialistic programs to correct the excesses of "free market" capitalism. It was he who propelled the federal government into such things as the regulation of stocks and the banking system. To this day many of America's high and mighty hate Roosevelt because he forced them to share just a little more of the mind-boggling wealth and

put just a little more responsibility for the nation's well-being where it should be—with the federal government.

In a way, Mikhail Gorbachev is our Roosevelt. He is in the process of saving socialism in this country. And he is doing it by injecting some of the things developed in capitalist societies: parliamentary and institutional pluralism, law-based society founded on respect for individual rights, an economic marketplace, a degree of private enterprise and private ownership. And because he is also making sure that the power goes back to where it was always supposed to be, to the people, to the Soviets, there are many who hate him.

It took a war, a tremendous economic shot in the arm, for American capitalism to recover fully. We will have to make our comeback without a war. That's for sure. It will be tough going. But we are on our way. . . .

How exhilarating to see truth break through, to see the tide turn. Yes, there are heavy seas ahead; yes, we still have to sail a long way before we reach our destination. But we are on our way.

And not only the Soviet Union. For nearly half a century, we have all lived in a hostile, bipolar world. In part, that reality was generated by Stalin; in part, by the dictatorial structures and mindset he left behind; in part, by the West stoking those fires. Now, in the Soviet Union, we are building something new, and we are demolishing that legacy in the process. Can the cold war survive without us? I think not.

For all of us, it's a new ball game.

It's breakthrough time.

From Vladimir Pozner. *Parting With Illusions.* Copyright © 1990 by Atlantic Monthly Press. Reprinted by permission of Atlantic Monthly Press.

NEW YEAR'S ADDRESS
Václav Havel

My dear fellow citizens,

For forty years you heard from my predecessors on this day different variations of the same theme: how our country flourished, how many million tons of steel we produced, how happy we all were, how we trusted our government, and what bright perspectives were unfolding in front of us.

I assume you did not propose me for this office so that I, too, would lie to you.

Our country is not flourishing. The enormous creative and spiritual potential of our nations is not being used sensibly. Entire branches of industry are producing goods which are of no interest to anyone, while we are lacking the things we need. A state which calls itself a workers' state humiliates and exploits workers. Our obsolete economy is wasting the little energy we have available. A country that once could be proud of the educational level of its citizens spends so little on education that it ranks today as seventy-second in the world. We have polluted our soil, our rivers and forests, bequeathed to us by our ancestors, and we have today the most contaminated environment in Europe. Adult people in our country die earlier than in most other European countries.

Allow me a little personal observation: when I flew recently to Bratislava, I found time during various discussions to look out of the plane window. I saw the industrial complex of Slovnaft chemical factory and the giant Petržalka housing estate right behind it. The view was enough for me to understand that for decades our statesmen and political leaders did not look or did not want to look out of the windows of their airplanes. No study of statistics available to me would enable me to understand faster and better the situation into which we had gotten ourselves.

But all this is still not the main problem. The worst thing is that we live in a contaminated moral environment. We fell morally ill because we became used to saying something different from what we thought. We learned not to believe in anything, to ignore each other, to care only about ourselves. Concepts such as love, friendship, compassion, humility, or forgiveness lost their depth and dimensions, and for many of us they represented only psychological peculiarities, or they resembled gone-astray greetings from ancient times, a little ridiculous in the era of computers and spaceships. Only a few of us were able to cry out loud that the powers that be should not be all powerful, and that special farms, which produce ecologically pure and top-quality food just for them, should send their produce to schools, children's homes, and hospitals if our agriculture was unable to offer them to all. The previous regime—armed with its arrogant and intolerant ideology—reduced man to a force of production and nature to a tool of production. In this it attacked both their very substance and their mutual relationship. It reduced gifted and autonomous people, skillfully working in their own country, to nuts and bolts of some monstrously huge, noisy, and stinking machine, whose real meaning is not clear to anyone. It cannot do more than slowly but inexorably wear down itself and all its nuts and bolts.

When I talk about contaminated moral atmosphere, I am not talking just about the gentlemen who eat organic vegetables and do not look out of the plane windows. I am talking about all of us. We had all become used to the totalitarian system and accepted it as an unchangeable fact and thus helped to perpetuate it. In other words, we are all—though naturally to differing extents—responsible for the operation of the totalitarian machinery; none of us is just its victim: we are also its co-creators. . . .

In the effort to rectify matters of common concern, we have something to lean on. The recent period—and in particular, the last six weeks of our peaceful revolution—has shown the enormous human, moral, and spiritual potential and civic culture that slumbered in our society under the enforced mask of apathy. Whenever someone categorically claimed that we were this or that, I always objected that society is a very mysterious creature and that it is not wise to trust only the face it presents to you. I am happy that I was not mistaken. Everywhere in the world people wonder where those meek, humiliated, skeptical, and seemingly cynical citizens of Czechoslovakia found the marvelous strength to shake from their shoulders in several weeks and in a decent and peaceful way the totalitarian yoke. And let us ask: from where did the young people who never knew another system take their desire for truth, their love of free thought, their political ideas, their civic courage and civic

prudence? How did it happen that their parents—the very generation that had been considered as lost—joined them? How is it possible that so many people immediately knew what to do and none of them needed any advice or instruction?

I think that there are two main reasons for this hopeful face of our present situation: first of all, people are never just a product of the external world, but are also always able to relate themselves to something superior, however systematically the external world tries to kill that ability in them; second, the humanistic and democratic traditions, about which there had been so much idle talk, did after all slumber in the unconsciousness of our nations and ethnic minorities, and were inconspicuously passed from one generation to another so that each of us could discover them at the right time and transform them into deeds.

We had to pay, however, for our present freedom. Many citizens perished in jails in the fifties, many were executed, thousands of human lives were destroyed, hundreds of thousands of talented people were forced to leave the country. Those who defended the honor of our nations during the Second World War, those who rebelled against totalitarian rule, and those who simply managed to remain themselves and think freely, were all persecuted. We should not forget any of those who paid for our present freedom in one way or another. Independent courts should impartially consider the possible guilt of those who were responsible for the persecutions, so that the truth about our recent past is fully revealed. . . .

Our state should never again be an appendage or a poor relation of anyone else. It is true we must accept and learn many things from others, but we must do this again as their equal partners who also have something to offer. . . .

There are free elections and an election campaign ahead of us. Let us not allow this struggle to dirty the so far clean face of our gentle revolution. Let us not allow the sympathies of the world which we have won so fast to be equally rapidly lost through our becoming entangled in the jungle of skirmishes for power. Let us not allow the desire to serve oneself to bloom once again under the fair mask of the desire to serve the common good. It is not really important now which party, club, or group will prevail in the elections. The important thing is that the winners will be the best of us, in the moral, civic, political, and professional sense, regardless of their political affiliations. The future policies and prestige of our state will depend on the personalities we select and later elect to our representative bodies. . . .

In conclusion, I would like to say that I want to be a president who will speak less and work more. To be a president who will not only look out of the windows of his airplane but who, first and foremost, will always be present among his fellow citizens and listen to them well.

You may ask what kind of a republic I dream of. Let me reply:

I dream of a republic independent, free, and democratic, of a republic economically prosperous and yet socially just, in short, of a humane republic which serves the individual and which therefore holds the hope that the individual will serve it in turn. Of a republic of well-rounded people, because without such it is impossible to solve any of our problems, human, economic, ecological, social, or political.

The most distinguished of my predecessors opened his first speech with a quotation from the great Czech educator Comenius. Allow me to round off my first speech with my own paraphrase of the same statement:

People, your government has returned to you!

————

From Václav Havel, *Open Letters*. Paul Wilson, ed. © 1991 by Alfred A. Knopf, Inc. pp. 390–96.

ANALYSIS AND INTERPRETATION OF THE READINGS

1. To what extent was Martin Luther King, Jr., sympathetic to Marx, and why did he reject Marxism?
2. Contrast the interpretations of Christianity by King and Malcolm X. Was either interpretation acceptable to the majority of white Christians?
3. What parallels does Pozner see between Gorbachev and Franklin Roosevelt?

| # The Middle East and Africa

CHRONOLOGY

Arrange the following items in their proper chronological sequence, supplying the dates of those marked with an asterisk (*):

Formation of Saudi Arabia

Proclamation of first Turkish Republic*

Recognition of independent Algeria*

Proclamation of independent State of Israel*

First Israeli-Arab war*

Beginning of British protectorate in Egypt

U.S. and U.N. intervention in Somalia

Organization of Union of South Africa*

Repeal of last apartheid laws in South Africa*

Agreement between Israel and PLO on autonomous Palestinian regions*

Suez crisis

Military coup in Ghana

Seizure of American hostages in Iran*

IDENTIFICATIONS

You should be able to explain the meaning or importance of each of the following terms:

Kurds	Intifada
the Wafd	mullahs
Aswan High Dam	OPEC
Six-Day War	Arab League
Muslim Brotherhood	Bambata Rebellion
Balfour Declaration (1917)	African National Congress (ANC)
Zionism	"temporary sojourners"
"Eretz Yisrael"	Organization of African Unity
Camp David Accords	Négritude
PLO	

Use the numbers from the following list to indicate, in the blanks below, the name of the person described in each statement:

1. Muhammad Mossadegh
2. Kwame Nkrumah
3. Nelson Mandela
4. Turgut Özal
5. Wole Soyinka
6. Ayatollah Ruholla Khomeini
7. Yitzhak Rabin
8. F. W. de Klerk
9. Steve Biko
10. Saddam Hussein
11. Mustafa Kemal
12. Gamal Abdul Nasser
13. Riza Pahlavi
14. Yasir Arafat
15. Anwar Sadat

_____ As president, dictator, and reformer, he went far toward transforming the western remnant of the discredited Ottoman Empire into a modern state.

_____ This revered leader of the A.N.C.'s struggle against apartheid was released from prison by the South African government in 1990.

_____ This president of the Black People's Convention was killed in jail by police.

_____ This Nigerian playwright and human rights activist won a Nobel Prize.

_____ This military leader, premier, and monarch thwarted British attempts to make his country a protectorate and changed its name to Iran.

_____ This premier was overthrown by a coup when he attempted to nationalize Iran's petroleum industry.

_____ This member of a military junta that overthrew the Egyptian monarchy made a strong bid to become leader of the Arab world.

_____ This conservative Islamic theologian led a revolution that overthrew a Middle Eastern monarchy.

_____ As prime minister of Israel, he forged an agreement with the PLO that allowed for autonomous Palestinian regions in Gaza and the West Bank.

_____ This former World Bank economist led his country through a period that combined industrial growth and political repression.

_____ This Arab leader, with no permanent political base, dedicated his efforts to the cause of the Palestinians.

_____ The son of an illiterate goldsmith in Britain's former Gold Coast colony, he became one of the most prominent leaders of African colonial revolt.

_____ This head of a major Arab country signed a peace treaty with Israel.

_____ The aggressive action of this president of a Middle East state precipitated an international crisis in August 1990.

_____ This South African president first reformed, then repealed, South Africa's apartheid laws.

STUDY QUESTIONS

1. How do you explain Mustafa Kemal's success in effecting a great transformation in Turkey? On what major areas did he focus his reforms?

2. How did the Turkish constitution of 1982 differ from the one that established the Second Turkish Republic in 1961?

3. What are the foundations of democracy in Turkey, and what have been the limitations on its development?

4. How has Turkey's geographic position affected its twentieth-century history?

5. Trace the stages in Britain's involvement in Egypt in the twentieth century. What factors have determined the degree to which Britain has been actively involved in events in Egypt?

6. What were the terms of the Anglo-Egyptian Treaty of Friendship and Alliance (1936)? Why were they never fully realized?

7. What prompted the 1956 Israeli invasion of Egypt? What were the results of the invasion?

8. In what respects were Egyptian presidents Nasser and Sadat successful? Where did they fail?

9. What changes in Egypt's domestic policies were introduced by President Hosni Mubarak?

10. What are the chief economic problems confronting Egypt?

11. What were the causes of the conflict between Arabs and Jews that reached a climax following the Second World War?

12. What prompted Israel's invasion of Lebanon in 1982, and what were the consequences of the invasion?

13. How did the character of the state of Israel change during the first thirty years of its existence?

14. What important steps did Sheik Yamani take to help strengthen the Saudi Arabian state?

15. What were the causes of the Iranian revolution of 1979? What were its unique features?

16. What were some of the key features of the Islamic state in Iran under the Ayatollah Khomeini?

17. What were the causes of the war between Iran and Iraq that began in 1980? What were the results of the war for both sides?

18. What efforts have been made toward pan-Arab unity? Why have they not been more successful?

19. Explain how the discovery of diamonds and gold in South Africa contributed to the coming of the Boer War.

20. Trace the process by which segregationist sentiment became state policy in South Africa.

21. What does *apartheid* mean? What was the basis of apartheid as state policy? Cite some specific programs that resulted from apartheid.

22. How did the 1960 Sharpeville demonstration and its aftermath affect the stance of the ANC? How did it affect the policies of the minority white government of South Africa?

23. Why did the South African constitution of 1984 lead to a new round of violence?

24. Outline the steps in the gradual dismantling of apartheid in South Africa. What factors induced the government to introduce reforms? What groups within South Africa were not satisfied with the way in which apartheid was eliminated as state policy, and why?

25. What was the basis for the economic boom in colonial Africa following World War II? What were some of its results?

26. How do you account for the violence and long duration of the independence struggle in Algeria?

27. What factors have hampered the growth of unity within African states?

28. What have been some of the most serious problems to plague post-independence African states? In what areas have African states made notable progress, and in what areas have they been less successful?

29. What progress toward democratization has been made in Africa? What have been the chief obstacles in the establishment of democratic rule?

30. Describe the role of such international organizations as the World Bank and the International Monetary Fund in the political and economic development of Africa.

31. How do you account for the fact that Africa has continued to be relatively marginalized in international affairs?

32. What factors have limited the sorely needed development of agriculture in Africa? What reasons are there for hope that agricultural prospects may be improving?
33. What have been the causes and consequences of the rapid spread of AIDS in Africa?

PROBLEMS

1. Investigate any of the following topics:
   a. The personality and achievements of Mustafa Kemal (Atatürk)
   b. The history of the Suez Canal
   c. Arab nationalism
   d. The role of oil in the politics of the Middle East
   e. The founding of the state of Israel
   f. The *apartheid* program in South Africa and its effects
   g. The role of the United Nations in the Congo
   h. The career and influence of Jomo Kenyatta
   i. Kurdish minorities in Middle East states

2. After examining the Camp David Accords, the Egyptian-Israeli peace treaty of 1979, and current relations between Israel and the PLO, construct your own formula for achieving peace in the Middle East.
3. "Nationalism proved to be a stronger force than pan-Africanism." Elaborate on this statement. Also, explore the idea of pan-Africanism in both theory and practice, considering both its strengths and its weaknesses.
4. Examine newspaper accounts or other media coverage of current events in the Middle East and Africa. Trace the historical background of the problems presented in news stories.
5. Explore the reasons why so many post-liberation African states at some point in their history were ruled by regimes that were Marxist to a greater or lesser degree.
6. Study the thought of Kwame Nkrumah, J. B. Danquah, Léopold Sédar Senghor, and Julius Nyerere.
7. The Senegalese poet and president Léopold Sédar Senghor once asserted that "*nation* is the first reality of the twentieth century." Discuss this statement with reference to the twentieth-century experience of the Middle East and Africa. Do you agree with Senghor? Explain.

AIDS TO AN UNDERSTANDING OF THE MIDDLE EAST AND AFRICA

TESTIMONY OF REVOLUTIONARIES
Kwame Nkrumah

AUTOBIOGRAPHY

In 1934 when I applied to the Dean for admission to Lincoln University, I quoted from Tennyson's *In Memoriam*:

So many worlds, so much to do,
So little done, such things to be.

This was to me then, as it still is today, an inspiration and a spur. It fired within me a determination to equip myself for the service of my country.

When I wrote that letter, however, I little knew that it would take ten years in America and two-and-a-half years in England, living almost as an exile, to prepare for the struggle that has so far engaged me and which, after nearly eight years, has almost been won.

Those years in America and England were years of sorrow and loneliness, poverty and hard work. But I have never regretted them because the background that they provided has helped me to formulate my philosophy of life and politics. At the end of my student days in America I was offered lectureships in several Negro universities, including Lincoln. This was certainly tempting; it promised an end to my struggle for existence, a pleasurable life without worry in an atmosphere that I had long felt to be a part of me. But I could not dismiss from my mind, in a matter of a few days, the flame of nationalism that had been fanned and kept alight for over ten years.

Independence for the Gold Coast was my aim. It was a colony and I have always regarded colonialism as the policy by which a foreign power binds territories to herself by political ties with the primary object of promoting her own economic advantage. No one need be surprised if this system has led to disturbances and political tension in many territories. There are few people who would not rid themselves of such domination if they could.

At this time I devoted much energy to the study of revolutionaries and their methods. Those who interested me most were Hannibal, Cromwell, Napoleon, Lenin, Mazzini, Gandhi, Mussolini and Hitler. I found much of value to be gleaned and many ideas that were useful to me later in my own campaign against imperialism.

At first I could not understand how Gandhi's philosophy of nonviolence could possibly be effective. It seemed to me to be utterly feeble and without hope of success. The solution of the colonial problem, as I saw it at that time, lay in armed rebellion. How is it possible, I asked myself, for a revolution to succeed without arms and ammunition? After months of studying Gandhi's policy and watching the effect it had, I began to see that, when backed by a strong political organization it could be the solution to the colonial problem. In Jawaharlal Nehru's rise to power I recognized the success of one who, pledged to Socialism, was able to interpret Gandhi's philosophy in practical terms.

The Gold Coast revolt against colonialism is not a new thing. Its roots are deep. There was the Confederation of 1868 when certain chiefs came together to defend themselves not only against their tribal kin the Ashantis, but also against political encroachments from abroad. After the bond of 1844 which gave Britain trading rights the Gold Coast had come increasingly under her control.

The next great move of political cohesion and conscience was the formation of the Aborigines Rights Protection Society by chiefs and literate Africans with the object of defending Gold Coast land. When this collapsed because of an ever-widening rift between the chiefs and the educated people, the latter, binding themselves together and supported by their educated brothers in other West African territories, established the National Congress of British West Africa. This was the first indication of West African nationalism. However, because it lacked the support of the masses, it disintegrated in 1930.

The vacuum that this left in Gold Coast politics was eventually filled by the formation of the United Gold Coast Convention by the merchant and lawyer class of the country. It was when I realized that this movement was doomed to failure because it ignored the interests of the masses, that I broke away in 1949 and formed the Convention People's Party.

I saw that the whole solution to this problem lay in political freedom for our people, for it is only, when a people are politically free that other races can give them the respect that is due to them. It is impossible to talk of equality of races in any other terms. No people without a government of their own can expect to be treated on the same level as peoples of independent sovereign states. It is far better to be free to govern or misgovern yourself than to be governed by anybody else.

From Kwame Nkrumah, *Ghana: The Autobiography of Nkrumah*, Thomas Nelson & Sons, Ltd., 1957. Reprinted by permission of the publisher.

THE RELEVANCE OF WESTERN IDEAS FOR NEW AFRICAN STATES
Thomas L. Hodgkin

If one is concerned with the influence of Western ideas on African societies, one must take into account the Western tradition of social and political thought in its entirety, not simply select some particular aspect of it or theme within it. Marx, Sorel, Pareto belong to this tradition, as much as Locke, Voltaire, or John Stuart Mill. Proletarian democracy is a Western concept as much as parliamentary democracy. Indeed the Marxist branch of this Western tradition is clearly of special significance in a number of modern African states. The antirationalist, elitist, and racist conceptions which became embodied in the ideologies of Fascism and Nazism are also, in another sense, Western ideas, which have had their impact on African societies. Hence

"Western" in its popular, contemporary—and, one hopes, transient—Cold War sense should not be confused with "Western" in the more fundamental sense of the whole body of thinking about the problems of society and political organization which had its origins roughly twenty-four centuries ago in the eastern Mediterranean, and whose influence has during the last two centuries come to be diffused throughout the inhabited world.

This is not simply a matter of language. I am not just saying "Please, in future, for 'Western ideas' substitute 'liberal ideas.'" Indeed, it is, I am sure, the impact of *Western* ideas, in the widest sense of the term, on African societies that we ought to think about, not merely the impact of *liberal* ideas. In the course of their history the peoples of the African continent—particularly, but not exclusively, those social groups which at different times constituted their elites—have been exposed to various aspects of what I have called the Western tradition of political thought. It is worth remembering that, so far as West Africa was concerned, the source from which the Western tradition was first introduced was not our Western Europe, but the Maghrib—the Arab West. By the fourteenth century, I think one could safely say, certain Aristotelian concepts, embedded in Islamic moral, political, and legal theory, had penetrated into the Western and Central Sudan. A tradition of Islamic scholasticism, not totally unlike the tradition of Christian scholasticism in medieval Europe, based on centers of learning such as Timbuktu and Jenne, was well established by the fifteenth and sixteenth centuries. Hence when Commander Clapperton, the first representative from Western Europe to visit the Sokoto Empire, encountered Sultan Muhammad Bello, who had been brought up in this Islamic-scholastic tradition, in 1824, he confessed that he was unable to hold his own with him in theological disputation.

By the end of the fifteenth century those in contact with the earliest Portuguese settlements along the West African coast began to be acquainted with medieval Christian theology, connected by another route with the Platonic-Aristotelian tradition. This particular Western influence was, no doubt, extremely restricted in range—except, perhaps, in the old kingdom of the Congo. But it must be remembered that there are large areas of modern Africa—the former Belgian Congo and the territories under Portuguese rule are obvious examples—where the medieval Christian view of society and social relations, adapted (or distorted) to meet the requirements of the colonial epoch, has been the dominant form in which Western ideas have been officially presented to Africans. The theory that men are "naturally" unequal; that it is "natural"—and therefore right—for society to be hierarchically ordered; that it is right for the irrational many, lacking the capacity for independent moral and political judgment, to submit themselves to the authority of the rational few—this is clearly a theory that is very relevant to the colonial situation and can be used to justify the authoritarian institutions imposed upon an African society by a European administrative, commercial, and ecclesiastical ruling class.

Of course, Africans have been confronted with many versions of the Western authoritarian, elitist theory of the state, of which the modernized medieval-Christian version is only one. In South Africa they have had, and have still, to deal with a peculiarly repulsive racist distortion of Calvinist doctrines.

British empire-builders of the generation of Lugard and Harry Johnston (in his earlier years), more interested as a rule in the practical problems of colonialism than in its presuppositions, tended to combine Tory paternalism, belief in the *Gentleman-Ideal*, with a Social-Darwinist attitude to history. These modes of political thinking, expressed in various patterns of colonial institutions, and in the attitudes of the European ruling classes, were what Western ideas most commonly meant to Africans in *Africa* during the period from the close of the nineteenth century to the end of the Second World War—and, in many African territories, until a much more recent date. These were Western ideas as actually experienced. It was in reaction to ideas of this type, as I shall try to show in more detail later, that the early movements of anticolonial revolt and protest, and at a later stage the nascent national movements, began to construct their own distinctive ideologies—whether revolutionary or reformist, expressed in religious or in secular language. And a literature of protest, expressing these reactions, developed—whose general character can be illustrated by the following short extract from the writings of the late David Diop, a Senegalese poet:

Le Blanc a tué mon père
Mon frère était fort
Le Blanc a violé ma mère
Ma mère était belle
Le Blanc a courbé mon frère sous le soleil des routes
Mon frère était fort
Le Balnc a tourné vers moi
Ses mains rouges de sang
    Noir
Et de sa voix de Maître:
"Hé boy, un berger, une serviette, de l'eau!"

It is, however, also true that, from the end of the eighteenth century, a limited number of Africans, established in Europe or the Americas (for the most part as a consequence of the slave trade), came into contact with this other aspect of Western political thought, "the ideas of European liberalism" (in Harold Laski's sense of the term). But here again it is important to be careful about meanings. The "liberal ideas" in which the intellectuals among the Africans of the Diaspora of the late eighteenth and early nineteenth centuries seem, to judge from their writings, to have been especially interested were, fairly naturally, not the "liberal ideas" that are generally approved in this present age of NATO and the Congress for Cultural Freedom: parliamentary government, two- or multi-party systems, an independent judiciary, a "non-political" civil service, toleration of (non-Communist) minorities, and the like. They were interested in what was doubtless a vaguer—but at the same time a more passionate, more revolutionary—formulation of "liberalism": the idea that "all men are brothers"; that God created men equal, with equal rights to "life, liberty and happiness"; that peoples have an inalienable right to choose their own governors and to "cashier them for misconduct"; that man is "perfectible," and humanity capable of achieving unlimited progress in the arts of living. An interesting outlook (which in these days it is perhaps less confusing to call "revolutionary-democratic" rather than "liberal") and its application by an African to the African situation

occurs in a work by Ottobah Cugoano of Ajumaku (in what is now Ghana), published two years before the French Revolution:

> Those people annually brought away from Guinea are born as free, and are brought up with as great a predilection for their own country, freedom and liberty, as the sons and daughters of fair Britain. Their free subjects are trained up to a kind of military service, not so much by the desire of the chiefs as by their own voluntary inclination. It is looked upon as the greatest respect they can show to their king, to stand up for his and their own defence in time of need. Their different chieftains, which bear a reliance on the great chief, or king, exercise a kind of government something like that feudal institution which prevailed some time in Scotland. In this respect, though the common people are free, they often suffer by the villainy of their different chieftains, and by the wars and feuds which happen among them. . . . Nevertheless their freedom and rights are as dear to them as those privileges are to other people. And it may be said that freedom, and the liberty of enjoying their own privileges, burns with as much zeal and fervour in the breast of an Aethiopian, as in the breast of any inhabitant on the globe.

From *Self-Government in Modernizing Nations*, ed. J. Roland Pennock, Prentice-Hall, Inc., 1964. Reprinted by permission of the publisher.

REBIRTH AND DESTINY OF ISRAEL
David Ben-Gurion

It was destined that the State should rise amid the storms of war, and our liberated people first reveal its fighting quality and military prowess, not its creative and spiritual virtues. In the first months of independence we had to apply all our strength to the main purpose of routing our enemies. In retrospect, that was all to the good. It was well for us, and for history and the world, to know that independence was no gift, that we paid for it the supreme cost of the lives of our dearest sons, and with our own hands set up our State.

We shall have to render up the best of our means and energies for many years to come, to maintain the security of the State. Yet security is only one condition of our existence and independence. Every country must safeguard the peace, prosperity and progress of its inhabitants; Israel is under like obligation, but that is not the main thing. The redemption of the people of Israel comes first.

Even in the hour of crisis, the first months of the State's life, when we were forced to defend ourselves against the armies of six Arab States and, out of Mandatory chaos, establish law and order, services, administration and a Government, even in that tempestuous period the tide of immigration did not ebb, but flooded fuller and higher yet.

When the fighting ended, duty was laid upon us to bring in countless multitudes of our people, to roof them and place them in agriculture, in industry and handicraft; to build new towns and villages to absorb hundreds of thousands, maybe millions. That this might be, we are adjured to carry out a project of colonization far greater than all of the last seventy years. We shall have to devote ourselves on a tremendous scale and at lightning speed to afforesting the hills and flowering the sands. We must install irrigation, improve the soil, and erect farm buildings, dwelling-houses and schools, factories, hospitals and laboratories. We shall have to construct a network of local, national and international communications. We must organize an extensive export and import trade, lay railways and make roads, and much more besides.

But all that is only one side of the coin. We are not just bringing in droves of creatures whom it is enough to employ, feed and house. These are Jewish men and women. This is a people unique, hurled to all the ends of the earth, speaking with many tongues, apprenticed to alien cultures, asunder in different communities and tribes within the House of Israel. We must melt down this fantastically diversified assemblage and cast it afresh in the die of a renewed nationhood. We must break down the barriers of geography and culture, of society and speech, which keep the different sections apart, and endow them with a single language, a single culture, a single citizenship, a single loyalty, with new legislation and new laws. We must give them a new spirit, a culture and literature, science and art. We must draw them into new social and political orbits and attach them to our past and to our vision of sovereignty, in self-government, in liberty, in Jewish unity, in brotherhood, in mutual aid and collective responsibility. And, at the same time, we must take thought for their security, for the security of the State, its freedom and its place among the nations. All this we must do in a tempest-tossed and riven world, when peace hangs by a slender thread and we are encompassed by malevolence and enmity.

How can we get through this immense and difficult task? How lift this heavy load, at once administrative, economic and political, at once cultural and organizational—and we so few? We were hard put to it to garner what little assets we have in the Land; and they are not enough for our multitudinous immigration. We are an oppressed people, the sport of history, we have no material heritage. Yet within a short space of time, with the resources of a little State, there is work to be done which never before we did, which perhaps no other people has ever done. It can only be done by enlisting fully the one superiority we have, our moral and intellectual greatness.

History has robbed us of many things. We did not inherit a spacious land; we were not a numerous people. Political power was not given us. Only now, after seventy years of pioneer striving, have we reached the beginning of independence in a part of our small country. But one thing history granted us from the very start—incomparable moral strength. By this virtue, even in ancient days, we withstood mighty empires which overtopped us not only in numbers and material and military resources, but also, in many respects, in culture. There is no parallel in human memory for a people driven from its native land and dispersed among the nations, yet holding triumphantly to its sworn purpose and independence for thousands of years. Moral strength has made us what we are today. There are nations not inferior in intellectual fibre. There were nations excelling in diverse branches of culture and in the creations of their art and thought. The culture of the Jewish people when it dwelt in its Land was one-sided. In religion, ethics and poetry

we ranked high, but had almost no say in metaphysics, in science, in most of the arts, in architecture and road-making. Perhaps, from that standpoint, the Almighty did right by the people of Israel when he scattered it among the nations. Our life among the peoples of Europe and America enriched us with values we lacked. In our wanderings we imbibed modern culture and took part, too, in its making. Now, in spiritual resource, we are not less than any other nation. The Jewish contribution to the achievements of spirit and science in recent times is as fine as that of the finest nations.

—————

From David Ben-Gurion, *Rebirth and Destiny of Israel*, Philosophical Library, 1954. Reprinted by permission of the publisher.

OPPOSITION TO APARTHEID: Nelson Mandela's Speech at the Rivonia Trial (1964)

I have already mentioned that I was one of the persons who helped to form Umkonto. I, and the others who started the organization, did so for two reasons. Firstly, we believed that as a result of Government policy, violence by the African people had become inevitable, and that unless responsible leadership was given to canalize and control the feelings of our people, there would be outbreaks of terrorism which would produce an intensity of bitterness and hostility between the various races of this country which is not produced even by war. Secondly, we felt that without violence there would be no way open to the African people to succeed in their struggle against the principle of White supremacy. All lawful modes of expressing opposition to this principle had been closed by legislation, and we were placed in a position in which we had either to accept a permanent state of inferiority, or to defy the Government. We chose to defy the law. We first broke the law in a way which avoided any recourse to violence; when this form was legislated against, and then the Government resorted to a show of force to crush opposition to its policies, only then did we decide to answer violence with violence.

But the violence which we chose to adopt was not terrorism. We who formed Umkonto were all members of the African National Congress, and had behind us the ANC tradition of non-violence and negotiation as a means of solving political disputes. We believe that South Africa belonged to all the people who lived in it, and not to one group, be it Black or White. We did not want an interracial war, and tried to avoid it to the last minute. . . .

During the Defiance Campaign, the Public Safety Act and the Criminal Law Amendment Act were passed. These Statutes provided harsher penalties for offences committed by way of protests against laws. Despite this, the protests continued and the ANC adhered to its policy of non-violence. In 1956, 156 leading members of the Congress Alliance, including myself, were arrested on a charge of high treason and charges under the Suppression of Communism Act. The non-violent policy of the ANC was put in issue by the State, but when the Court gave judgement some five years later, it found that the ANC did not have a policy of violence. We were acquitted on all counts, which included a count that the ANC sought to set up a communist state in place of the existing régime. The Government has always sought to label all its opponents as communists. This allegation has been repeated in the present case, but as I will show, the ANC is not, and never has been, a communist organization.

In 1960 there was the shooting at Sharpeville, which resulted in the proclamation of a state of emergency and the declaration of the ANC as an unlawful organization. My colleagues and I, after careful consideration, decided that we would not obey this decree. The African people were not part of the Government and did not make the laws by which they were governed. We believed in the words of the Universal Declaration of Human Rights, that the will of the people shall be the basis of authority of the Government', and for us to accept the banning was equivalent to accepting the silencing of the Africans for all time. The ANC refused to dissolve, but instead went underground. We believed it was our duty to preserve this organization which had been built up with almost fifty years of unremitting toil. I have no doubt that no self-respecting White political organization would disband itself if declared illegal by a government in which it had no say. . . .

I turn now to my own position. I have denied that I am a communist, and I think that in the circumstances I am obliged to state exactly what my political beliefs are.

I have always regarded myself, in the first place, as an African patriot. After all, I was born in Umtata, forty-six years ago. My guardian was my cousin, who was the acting paramount chief of Tembuland, and I am related both to the present paramount chief of Tembuland, Sabata Dalinyebo, and to Kaizer Matanzima, the Chief Minister of the Transkei.

Today I am attracted by the idea of a classless society, an attraction which springs in part from Marxist reading and, in part, from my admiration of the structure and organization of early African societies in this country. The land, then the main means of production, belonged to the tribe. There were no rich or poor and there was no exploitation.

It is true, as I have already stated, that I have been influenced by Marxist thought. But this is also true of many of the leaders of the new independent States. Such widely different persons as Gandhi, Nehru, Nkrumah, and Nasser all acknowledge this fact. We all accept the need for some form of socialism to enable our people to catch up with the advanced countries of this world and to overcome their legacy of extreme poverty. But this does not mean we are Marxists.

Indeed, for my own part, I believe that it is open to debate whether the Communist Party has any specific role to play at this particular stage of our political struggle. The basic task at the present moment is the removal of race discrimination and the attainment of democratic rights on the basis of the Freedom Charter. In so far as that Party furthers this task, I welcome its assistance. I realize that it is one of the means by which people of all races can be drawn into our struggle.

From my reading of Marxist literature and from conversations with Marxists, I have gained the impression that communists regard the parliamentary system of the West as undemocratic and reactionary. But, on the contrary, I am an admirer of such a system. . . .

Africans want to be paid a living wage. Africans want to perform work which they are capable of doing, and not work which the Government declares them to be capable of. Africans want to be allowed to live where they obtain work, and not be endorsed out of an area because they were not born there. Africans want to be allowed to own land in places where they work, and not to be obliged to live in rented houses which they can never call their own. Africans want to be part of the general population, and not confined to living in their own ghettoes. African men want to have their wives and children to live with them where they work, and not be forced into an unnatural existence in men's hostels. African women want to be with their menfolk and not be left permanently widowed in the Reserves. Africans want to be allowed out after eleven o'clock at night and not to be confined to their rooms like little children. Africans want to be allowed to travel in their own country and to seek work where they want to and not where the Labour Bureau tells them to. Africans want a just share in the whole of South Africa; they want security and a stake in society.

Above all, we want equal political rights, because without them our disabilities will be permanent. I know this sounds revolutionary to the Whites in this country, because the majority of voters will be Africans. This makes the White man fear democracy.

But this fear cannot be allowed to stand in the way of the only solution which will guarantee racial harmony and freedom for all. It is not true that the enfranchisement of all will result in racial domination. Political division, based on colour, is entirely artificial and, when it disappears, so will the domination of one colour group by another. The ANC has spent half a century fighting against racialism. When it triumphs it will not change that policy.

This then is what the ANC is fighting. Their struggle is a truly national one. It is a struggle of the African people, inspired by their own suffering and their own experience. It is a struggle for the right to live.

During my lifetime I have dedicated myself to this struggle of the African people. I have fought against White domination, and I have fought against Black domination. I have cherished the ideal of a democratic and free society in which all persons live together in harmony and with equal opportunities. It is an ideal which I hope to live for and to achieve. But if needs be, it is an ideal for which I am prepared to die. . . .

I believe that communists have always played an active role in the fight by colonial countries for their freedom, because the short-term objects of communism would always correspond with the long-term objects of freedom movements. Thus communists have played an important role in the freedom struggles fought in countries such as Malaya, Algeria, and Indonesia, yet none of these States today are communist countries. Similarly in the underground resistance movements which sprung up in Europe during the last World War, communists played an important role. Even General Chiang Kai-Shek, today one of the bitterest enemies of communism, fought together with the communists against the ruling class in the struggle which led to his assumption of power in China in the 1930s.

This pattern of cooperation between communists and non-communists has been repeated in the National Liberation Movement of South Africa. Prior to the banning of the Communist

Party, joint campaigns involving the Communist Party and the Congress movements were accepted practice. African communists could, and did, become members of the ANC, and some served on the National, Provincial, and local committees. . . .

The Government often answers its critics by saying that Africans in South Africa are economically better off than the inhabitants of the other countries in Africa. I do not know whether this statement is true and doubt whether any comparison can be made without having regard to the cost-of-living index in such countries. But even if it is true, as far as the African people are concerned it is irrelevant. Our complaint is not that we are poor by comparison with people in other countries, but that we are poor by comparison with the White people in our own country, and that we are prevented by legislation from altering this imbalance.

The lack of human dignity experienced by Africans is the direct result of the policy of White supremacy. White supremacy implies Black inferiority. Legislation designed to preserve White supremacy entrenches this notion. . . .

From Nelson Mandela, *No Easy Walk to Freedom*. Ruth First, ed. Heineman Publishers, 1965. pp. 166, 180, 182, 187–89.

ANALYSIS AND INTERPRETATION OF THE READINGS

1. What points of agreement and what differences do you find between the viewpoints of Nkrumah and Ben-Gurion?
2. To what extent did Nkrumah modify his philosophy of revolution in response to his experiences?
3. Comment on Nkrumah's assertion that "It is far better to be free to govern or misgovern yourself than to be governed by anybody else."
4. What are the basic differences between "Western Liberalism" and the liberal thinking in new African states?
5. What does Ben-Gurion say are the chief problems confronting the State of Israel and what does he claim to be its greatest asset?
6. What does Nelson Mandela's Rivonia speech reveal about political alignments in South Africa under apartheid? Why does he spend so much time discussing communism? According to Mandela, what were the primary objectives of the opposition movement?

CHAPTER 40 | Independence in South Asia

CHRONOLOGY

Arrange the following events in proper chronological order on the blanks below:

_____ Founding of Indian National Congress
_____ "Noncooperation Movement"
_____ Amritsar Massacre
_____ Indian independence granted
_____ Founding of Muslim League
_____ Storming of Golden Temple
_____ Indira Gandhi becomes prime minister
_____ Secession of East Pakistan
_____ India-China border war
_____ Beginning of Indira Gandhi's "emergency"
_____ Execution of Zulfikar Ali Bhutto

IDENTIFICATIONS

You should be able to identify the following individuals or terms, and explain the historical importance of each:

Allan O. Hume
Lord Curzon
Amritsar Massacre
satyagraha
Lucknow Pact
Government of India Act (1935)
Muslim League
Mohammad Ali Jinnah

"Cripps Offer"
Bangladesh
Rajiv Gandhi
P. D. Narashima Rao
Aung San Suu Kyi
Zulfikar Ali Bhutto
Muhammad Zia ul-Haq

STUDY QUESTIONS

1. "Considering the obstacles in its path, nationalism might never have progressed far had not British rule given it impetus and the framework within which it could develop." Discuss the meaning of this statement and assess its validity. What are the obstacles referred to?

2. From what groups did the Indian National Congress draw its early supporters?

3. In what ways did the Government of India Act of 1919 fall short of expectations?

4. How did the background of Jawaharlal Nehru influence his policies as prime minister of independent India?

5. Trace the changes in the strength and influence of the Congress party, and the reasons for those changes.

6. How did Mohandas K. Gandhi's experience in South Africa affect his thinking and his future course of action?

7. What were the primary principles on which Gandhi based his political activism?

8. Discuss the reasons for the difficulty in forging Hindu-Muslim unity in South Asia.

9. What were the objectives of the "Constructive Program" promoted by Gandhi and others during the 1920s?

10. What was the significance—both symbolic and practical—of the "march to the sea" in 1930?

11. Despite achieving majorities in over half of the British provinces of India in the 1937 election, the Congress party was unable to bring about unity or meaningful reform. Explain the reasons for this.

12. How did the Second World War affect relations between the Congress party and the British government?

13. What factors led to the decision to create two separate states out of British-ruled India? What problems did partition solve? What new problems did it create?

14. What aspects of Gandhi's dream for India were realized? Which were not?

15. Outline the major features of the Indian constitution of 1950.

16. What foundations for substantial economic development can be found in India?

17. Why has the problem of poverty in India proved so difficult to solve?
18. Assess the accomplishments and shortcomings of the rule of Jawaharlal Nehru.
19. Describe the major policies of Indira Gandhi's first term as prime minister. What were the chief excesses of her term in office?
20. How did the events at the Golden Temple in Amritsar in 1984 demonstrate the precarious nature of Indian political and social order?
21. What aspects of Indian industrial and economic development have been relatively successful in the 1980s and 1990s?
22. What are the most visibly persistent social and economic problems in India?
23. Explain the roots of the separation of Bangladesh from Pakistan.
24. What have been the major obstacles to democracy in Pakistan? What has stood in the way of efforts in the past to establish an Islamic republic there?
25. What was unusual about the accession to power of Benazir Bhutto in Pakistan? What initial policies did she pursue, and how did these differ from those of her predecessors?
26. What are the special economic challenges facing Bangladesh?
27. How do you account for the prominent role of women in post-independence politics in South Asia?
28. Briefly describe changes in India's foreign relations, and the reasons for them.

PROBLEMS

1. Compare the ideal society envisioned by Mohandas K. Gandhi with other utopian visions.
2. Compare the personalities and backgrounds of Mohammad Ali Jinnah, Jawaharlal Nehru, and Mohandas K. Gandhi. How were their differences and similarities reflected in their policies and aspirations?
3. Read Gandhi's autobiography and write an essay giving your assessment of his life and ideals.
4. Martin Luther King, Jr., openly acknowledged the influence of Gandhi on his own thinking. Examine the American civil rights leader's writings and actions to see where that influence was most visible.
5. Based on a study of geography, culture, history, and politics, propose a solution to the problem of poverty in South Asia.
6. Study the origin and history of the Sikhs. What has been their role in South Asian history, culture, and politics?
7. Research the question of why Kashmir and Bengal have been the focus of so much controversy and violence.

AIDS TO AN UNDERSTANDING OF INDEPENDENCE IN SOUTH ASIA

INDIAN HOME RULE
Mohandas K. Gandhi

Editorial Note: Gandhi's ideas on various problems in India were presented in the form of a fictive dialogue between a Reader and an Editor. The Editor speaks for Gandhi.

THE HINDUS AND THE MOHAMEDANS

READER: Has the introduction of Mahomedanism not unmade the nation?

EDITOR: India cannot cease to be one nation because people belonging to different religions live in it. The introduction of foreigners does not necessarily destroy the nation; they merge in it. A country is one nation only when such a condition obtains in it. That country must have a faculty for assimilation. India has ever been such a country. In reality, there are as many religions as there are individuals; but those who are conscious of the spirit of nationality do not interfere with one another's religion. If they do, they are not fit to be considered a nation. If the Hindus believe that India should be peopled only by Hindus, they are living in dream-land. The Hindus, the Mahomedans, the Parsis and the Christians who have made India their country are fellow countrymen, and they will have to live in unity, if only for their own interest. In no part of the world are one nationality and one religion synonymous terms; nor has it ever been so in India.

READER: But what about the inborn enmity between Hindus and Mahomedans?

EDITOR: That phrase has been invented by our mutual enemy. When the Hindus and Mahomedans fought against one another, they certainly spoke in that strain. They have long since ceased to fight. How, then, can there be any inborn enmity? Pray remember this too, that we did not cease to fight only after British occupation. The Hindus flourished under Moslem sovereigns and Moslems under the Hindu. Each party recognized that mutual fighting was suicidal, and that neither party would abandon its religion by force of arms. Both parties, therefore, decided to live in peace. With the English advent quarrels recommenced.

The proverbs you have quoted were coined when both were fighting; to quote them now is obviously harmful. Should we not remember that many Hindus and Mahomedans own the same ancestors and the same blood runs through their veins? Do people become enemies because they change their religion? Is the God of the Mahomedan different from the God of the

Hindu? Religions are different roads converging to the same point. What does it matter that we take different roads so long as we reach the same goal? Wherein is the cause for quarrelling? . . .

PASSIVE RESISTANCE

READER: Is there any historical evidence as to the success of what you have called soul-force or truth-force? No instance seems to have happened of any nation having risen through soul-force. I still think that the evil-doers will not cease doing evil without physical punishment.

EDITOR: The poet Tulsidas has said: "Of religion, pity, or love, is the root, as egotism of the body. Therefore, we should not abandon pity so long as we are alive." This appears to me to be a scientific truth. I believe in it as much as I believe in two and two being four. The force of love is the same as the force of the soul or truth. We have evidence of its working at every step. The universe would disappear without the existence of that force. But you ask for historical evidence. It is, therefore, necessary to know what history means. The Gujarati equivalent means: "It so happened." If that is the meaning of history, it is possible to give copious evidence. But, if it means the doings of kings and emperors, there can be no evidence of soul-force or passive resistance in such history. You cannot expect silver ore in a tin mine. History, as we know it, is a record of the wars of the world, and so there is a proverb among Englishmen that a nation which has no history, that is, no wars, is a happy nation. How kings played, how they became enemies of one another, how they murdered one another, is found accurately recorded in history, and if this were all that had happened in the world, it would have been ended long ago. If the story of the universe had commenced with wars, not a man would have been found alive to-day. Those people who have been warred against have disappeared as, for instance, the natives of Australia of whom hardly a man was left alive by the intruders. Mark, please, that these natives did not use soul-force in self-defence, and it does not require much foresight to know that the Australians will share the same fate as their victims. "Those that take the sword shall perish by the sword." With us the proverb is that professional swimmers will find a watery grave.

The fact that there are so many men still alive in the world shows that it is based not on the force of arms but on the force of truth or love. Therefore, the greatest and most unimpeachable evidence of the success of this force is to be found in the fact that, in spite of the wars of the world, it still lives on.

Thousands, indeed tens of thousands, depend for their existence on a very active working of this force. Little quarrels of millions of families in their daily lives disappear before the exercise of this force. Hundreds of nations live in peace. History does not and cannot take note of this fact. History is really a record of every interruption of the even working of the force of love or of the soul. Two brothers quarrel; one of them repents and re-awakens the love that was lying dormant in him; the two again begin to live in peace; nobody takes note of this. But if the two brothers, through the intervention of solicitors or some other reason take up arms or go to law—which is another form of the exhibition of brute force,—their doings would be immediately noticed in the press, they would be the talk of their neighbours and would probably go down to history. And what is true of families and communities is true of nations. There is no reason to believe that there is one law for families and another for nations. History, then, is a record of an interruption of the course of nature. Soul-force, being natural, is not noted in history.

READER: According to what you say, it is plain that instances of this kind of passive resistance are not to be found in history. It is necessary to understand this passive resistance more fully. It will be better, therefore, if you enlarge upon it.

EDITOR: Passive resistance is a method of securing rights by personal suffering; it is the reverse of resistance by arms. When I refuse to do a thing that is repugnant to my conscience, I use soul-force. For instance, the Government of the day has passed a law which is applicable to me. I do not like it. If by using violence I force the Government to repeal the law, I am employing what may be termed body-force. If I do not obey the law and accept the penalty for its breach, I use soul-force. It involves sacrifice of self.

Everybody admits that sacrifice of self is infinitely superior to sacrifice of others. Moreover, if this kind of force is used in a cause that is unjust, only the person using it suffers. He does not make others suffer for his mistakes. Men have before now done many things which were subsequently found to have been wrong. No man can claim that he is absolutely in the right or that a particular thing is wrong because he thinks so, but it is wrong for him so long as that is his deliberate judgment. It is therefore meet that he should not do that which he knows to be wrong, and suffer the consequence whatever it may be. This is the key to the use of soul-force. . . .

READER: From what you say I deduce that passive resistance is a splendid weapon of the weak, but that when they are strong they may take up arms.

EDITOR: This is gross ignorance, Passive resistance, that is, soul-force, is matchless. It is superior to the force of arms. How, then, can it be considered only a weapon of the weak? Physical-force men are strangers to the courage that is requisite in a passive resister. Do you believe that a coward can ever disobey a law that he dislikes? Extremists are considered to be advocates of brute force. Why do they, then, talk about obeying laws? I do not blame them. They can say nothing else. When they succeed in driving out the English and they themselves become governors, they will want you and me to obey their laws. And that is a fitting thing for their constitution. But a passive resister will say he will not obey a law that is against his conscience, even though he may be blown to pieces at the mouth of a cannon.

What do you think? Wherein is courage required—in blowing others to pieces from behind a cannon, or with a smiling face to approach a cannon and be blown to pieces? Who is the true warrior—he who keeps death always as a bosom-friend, or he who controls the death of others? Believe me that a man devoid of courage and manhood can never be a passive resister.

This, however, I will admit: that even a man weak in body is capable of offering this resistance. One man can offer it just as well as millions. Both men and women can indulge in it. It does not require the training of an army; it needs no jiu-jitsu. Control over the mind is alone necessary, and when that is attained, man is free like the king of the forest and his very glance withers the enemy.

Passive resistance is an all-sided sword, it can be used anyhow; it blesses him who uses it and him against whom it is used. Without drawing a drop of blood it produces far-reaching results. It never rusts and cannot be stolen. Competition between passive resisters does not exhaust. The sword of passive resistance does not require a scabbard. It is strange indeed that you should consider such a weapon to be a weapon merely of the weak. . . .

Nature has implanted in the human breast ability to cope with any difficulty or suffering that may come to man unprovoked. These qualities are worth having, even for those who do not wish to serve the country. Let there be no mistake, as those who want to train themselves in the use of arms are also obliged to have these qualities more or less. Everybody does not become a warrior for the wish. A would-be warrior will have to observe chastity and to be satisfied with poverty as his lot. A warrior without fearlessness cannot be conceived of. It may be thought that he would not need to be exactly truthful, but that quality follows real fearlessness. When a man abandons truth, he does so owing to fear in some shape or form. The above four attributes, then, need not frighten anyone. It may be as well here to note that a physical-force man has to have many other useless qualities which a passive resister never needs. And you will find that whatever extra effort a swordsman needs is due to lack of fearlessness. If he is an embodiment of the latter, the sword will drop from his hand that very moment. He does not need its support. One who is free from hatred requires no sword. A man with a stick suddenly came face to face with a lion and instinctively raised his weapon in self-defence. The man saw that he had only prated about fearlessness when there was none in him. That moment he dropped the stick and found himself free from all fear.

From Mohandas K. Gandhi, *Indian Home Rule*. Navajivan, 1939. pp. 23–24, 44–48, 50–51.

INDIA IN THE POSTCOLONIAL WORLD
Jawaharlal Nehru Addresses the United Nations, 1948

You meet here, representatives of all nations of the world, or nearly all. Inevitably, you have behind you and before you the immediate great problems that confront more especially Europe, which has suffered so much.

May I say, as a representative from Asia, that we honour Europe for its culture and for the great advance in human civilization which it represents? May I say that we are equally interested in the solution of European problems, but may I also say that the world is something bigger than Europe, and you will not solve your problems by thinking that the problems of the world are mainly European problems. There are vast tracts of the world which may not in the past, for a few generations, have taken much part in world affairs. But they are awake; their people are moving and they have no intention whatever of being ignored or of being passed by.

It is a simple fact which I think we have to remember, because unless you have the full picture of the world before you, you will not even understand the problem, and if you isolate any single problem in the world from the rest, you do not understand the problem. Today I do venture to submit that Asia counts in world affairs. Tomorrow it will count much more than today. Asia till recently was largely a prey to imperial domination and colonialism; and it is an astonishing thing that any country should still remain unfree; and it is an astonishing thing that any country should still venture to hold and to set forth this doctrine of colonialism, whether it is under direct rule or whether it is indirectly maintained in some form or other. After all that has happened, there is going to be no mere objection to that, but active objection, an active struggle against any and every form of colonialism in any part of the world. That is the first thing to remember.

We in Asia, who have ourselves suffered all these evils of colonialism and of imperial domination, have committed ourselves inevitably to the freedom of every other colonial country. There are neighbouring countries of ours in Asia with whom we are intimately allied. We look to them with sympathy; we look at their struggle with sympathy. Any power, great or small, which in any way prevents the attainment of the freedom of those peoples does an ill turn to world peace.

Great countries like India who have passed out of their colonial stage do not conceive it possible that other countries should remain under the yoke of colonial rule.

We in Asia regard it as a vital problem, because it has been a vital problem for us, and there is a question to which I want to draw attention—that is the question of racial equality, which is something which is laid down in the provisions of the United Nations Charter. It is well to repeat that, because after all this question of racial equality has frequently been spoken about in the Assembly of the United Nations.

I do not think I need dwell on any particular aspect of it, but I would remind this Assembly of the worldwide aspects of this question. Obviously there are large regions of the world which have suffered from this evil of racial inequality. We also feel that there is no part of the world where it can be tolerated in the future, except perhaps because of superior force. It is obviously sowing the seeds of conflict if racial equality is not approved, and a menace to world peace and is in conflict with the principles of the United Nations Charter.

The effects of this inequality in the past have made themselves felt in Asia, Africa and other parts of the world much more than in Europe, leading towards a conflict in the future, and it is a problem which, if it is not properly understood, will not be solved.

It is a strange thing, when the world lacks so many things, food and other necessities in many parts of the world and people are dying from hunger that the attention of this Assembly of Nations is concentrated only on a number of political problems. There are economic problems also. I wonder if it would be possible for this Assembly to take a holiday for a while from some of the acute political problems which face it, and allow men's minds to settle down and look at the vital and urgent economic problems, and look at places in the world where food is lacking.

I feel that today the world is so tied up in fears, apprehensions, some of them justified no doubt, but where a person feels fear, bad consequences and evil consequences follow. Fear is not a good companion. It is surprising to see that this sense of fear is prevailing in great countries—fear, and grave fear of war, and fear of many things. Well, I think that it is admitted, or it will be admitted, that no aggression of any kind can be tolerated, because the very idea of aggression must upset the balance and lead to conflict. Aggression of every type must be resisted.

There are other forms of fear; there is the fear of war. In existing circumstances it is difficult for people to say that they will not defend themselves, because if there is a fear of aggression one has to defend oneself against aggression. We have to defend ourselves, but even in defending ourselves, we must not submit ourselves to this Assembly without clean hands. It is easy to condemn people. Let us not do so, for who are without blame, who cannot themselves be condemned? In a sense, all of us who are gathered here today in this continent of Europe—are there any amongst us who have not been guilty in many ways? We are all guilty men and women. While we are seeking points where error occurs, we should not forget that there is not one of us who is exempt from blame.

If we attend to this problem, and discuss in peace the psychology of fear, if we realize the consequences of what is happening, it is possible that this atmosphere of fear may be dissipated. Why should there be this fear of war? Let us prepare ourselves against any possible aggression, let no one think that any nation, any community can misbehave. The United Nations are here to prevent any fear or hurt, but at the same time let us banish all thought of an aggressive attitude whether by word or deed. However, I feel that few of us can altogether avoid this attitude, whether it is in the course of discussions before this Assembly or elsewhere. One tries to make one's points in the course of discussion, but there always rests a bitterness which complicates the problem still further. As I have already said, I ask this Assembly to remember that such great problems cannot be solved if our eyes are bloodshot and our minds are obscured by passion.

I have no doubt that this Assembly is going to solve our problems. I am not afraid of the future. I have no fear in my mind, and I have no fear, even though India, from a military point of view, is of no great consequence. I am not afraid of the bigness of great powers, and their armies, their fleets and their atom bombs. That is the lesson which my Master taught me. We stood as an unarmed people against a great country and a powerful empire. We were supported and strengthened, because throughout all this period we decided not to submit to evil, and I think that is the lesson which I have before me and which is before us today. I do not know if it is possible to apply this to the problems which face the world today. It is a terrible problem, but I think if we banish this fear, if we have confidence, even though we may take risks of trust rather than risk violent language, violent actions and in the end war, I think those risks are worth taking.

In any event, there are risks—and great risks. If it is a question of taking risks, why take risks which inevitably lead to greater conflict? Take the other risks, while always preparing yourself to meet any possible contingency that may arise.

We do not think that the problems of the world or of India can be solved by thinking in terms of aggression or war or vio-

lence. We are frail mortals, and we cannot always live up to the teaching of the great man who led our nation to freedom. But that lesson has sunk deep into our souls and, so long as we remember it, I am sure we shall be on the right path. And, if I may venture to suggest this to the General Assembly, I think that if the essentials of that lesson are kept in mind, perhaps our approach to the problems of today will be different; perhaps the conflicts that always hang over us will appear a little less deep than they are and actually will gradually fade away.

UN speech by Nehru, 1948, from *Jawaharal Nehru*. Publications Division of the Ministry of Information and Broadcasting, Govt. of India. pp. 57–59.

COLONIAL RULE AND THE INTELLECTUAL:
The View from Burma
Aung San Suu Kyi

A comparison of the intellectual life of Burma and India under colonialism shows two very different societies facing the onslaught of alien forces in their own different ways. In India there was an initial enthusiasm for western ideas and institutions among its leadership. This early admiration was a major factor in the birth of the Indian Renaissance which was to influence intellectual development and political thought in the country right up to the time of independence. The language of the rulers not only helped to spread western ideas but also acted as a unifying factor in the multilingual subcontinent. English became so much a part of Indian intellectual life that Indo-Anglian works acquired their own place in the literature of the nation after independence. Even when Indian attitudes towards the British had changed to resentment and hostility, the intellectual impulse that sought a harmonious fusion of the east and west did not die out completely. And English continued to be accepted as the political language of the nation.

Leftist thought was not without its fascination for the intellectuals of India, where social conditions were such as to make the promises of a communist society seem most attractive. But the majority of the nationalist leaders, who still ascribed to the Renaissance view that social, religious and political factors were but different facets of the indivisible life of civilized man, preferred to select critically from the wide range of socialist ideas (in particular those with an economic bearing) rather than to accept whole ideologies in their entirety.

Looking from the Indian situation to that of Burma, there is the almost surreal impression of a time warp. Colonized at a much later date and for a much shorter period, the Burmese experience of British rule is in some ways a concertinaed version of developments in India. But there were also developments which took their own individual course, explainable not so much by the colonial experience common to many Asian and African countries of that era as by the distinct cultural and historical background of Burma.

The Burmese people lacked a leadership which could have helped them to face the challenges posed by their confrontation with alien values. They learnt to adjust to new conditions slowly, almost imperceptibility. Towards the end of British rule some leaders arose who saw the need to adopt a broad assimilative approach and to develop a philosophy which could cope with modern developments. But on the whole, such changes as came about in the traditional values of the Burmese took place because the people themselves willed it and not because they were carried along by the force of dynamic leaders. The leaders that they did follow willingly were those who could communicate with them in their own language. As the founder of the Dohbama Asiayone had realized, language, together with race and religion, were the mainsprings of the Burmese sense of their unique identity. Even when the revolutionary young politicians dropped the notions of race and religion from their concept of modern nationhood, the validity of the Burmese language as a unifying factor was tacitly retained.

The aspects of intellectual life on which this study has focused reveals a strong link between nationalism and intellectual developments in Burma and India under colonialism. Indian society accustomed to the tradition of privileged castes, readily accepted the intellectual elite born of the Indian Renaissance which provided many of its national leaders. This elite led the movement which sought a harmonious union between western thought and Hindu philosophy in the search for nationalist ideals. In Burma, however, traditional attitudes shaped by an essentially egalitarian society militated against the acceptance of an elite. Moreover, the early generation of Burmese who acquired their education under the colonial system were largely ignorant of the classical learning of their own country. As a result they found themselves distanced from the traditional scholars as well as from the people in general. Western education and traditional learning began to merge only in the 1930s when the study of Burmese language and literature became an integral part of the education system. The younger leaders who were the products of this system strived to give to nationalist aspirations an ideological framework which would be acceptable not only to the Burmese but to all the peoples of Burma. There always

remained an intellectual, one might almost say a cultural, gap between the old leadership and the young politicians who were to carry on the independence movement after the war.

The situation in neither country could be said to have been wholly satisfactory. In India the elite demonstrated that Indians could reach the topmost ranks of intellectual excellence which combined the best in their own traditions with those of the best that the west had to offer. But the gap between the elite and the common people was so large that the momentum of the Renaissance could not be sustained. The forces which had provided the nationalist movement with ideas and ideals had already begun to dissipate before India became independent.

In Burma, the lack of an elite meant that there was little to guide and spur on the people to reach out for greater achievements. The younger generation of leaders appeared too late to bring about effective changes before the outbreak of the Second World War. Developments in Burma after 1940 took many abrupt twists and turns, and to this day, it still remains a society waiting for its true potential to be realized.

From Aung San Suu Kyi, *Burma and India: Some Aspects of Intellectual Life under Colonialism*. Indian Institute of Advanced Study, 1990. pp. 73–75.

ANALYSIS AND INTERPRETATION OF THE READINGS

1. Why was Gandhi so careful to point out that passive resistance was not "only a weapon of the weak"?
2. On the basis of your reading of Gandhi, explain the differences between passive resistance as a strategy and passive resistance as a moral principle.
3. According to Nehru, what fundamental issues confronted the world in 1948? What did he feel the experience of India could contribute to solving world problems?

CHAPTER 41 | Eruption in East Asia

CHRONOLOGY

In the blanks below, provide the correct date (year or specific date, as appropriate) for each of the following events.

_____ Qing dynasty overthrown

_____ Beginning of "May Fourth Movement"

_____ Paris Peace Conference

_____ Japanese army attacks Chinese positions in Manchuria

_____ U.S. passes Oriental Exclusion law

_____ Beginning of Chinese civil war

_____ Year agreed to in treaty for return of Hong Kong to China

_____ "Northern Expedition"

_____ U.S.–Japan Security Treaty

_____ Japan withdraws from the League of Nations

_____ China detonates its first atomic bomb

_____ Huge famine in China

_____ LDP loses parliamentary majority in Japan

_____ Tiananmen Square demonstrations

_____ Formation of Chinese Communist Party

_____ Full diplomatic relations between Japan and China

_____ New Japanese constitution promulgated

_____ Beginning of Second World War in Asia

_____ Great Leap Forward

_____ Chinese "Cultural Revolution"

_____ People's Republic of China established

_____ China and the U.S. establish formal diplomatic relations

_____ First Five Year Plan in China

IDENTIFICATIONS

You should understand the role of the following individuals in twentieth-century East Asia:

Yuan Shikai

Chiang Kai-shek

Zhou Enlai

Liu Shaoqi

Ding Ling

Douglas MacArthur

Zhang Xueliang

Jiang Qing

Sun Yat-sen

Michael Borodin

Mao Zedong

Lin Biao

Fang Lizhi

Deng Xiaoping

Nakasone Yasuhiro

Lu Xun

Chiang Ching-kuo

You should also know the importance of the following:

May Fourth Movement

Tiananmen Square

Guomindang

Three Principles of the People

Long March

communes (China)

Great Leap Forward

"Cultural Revolution" (China)

Red Guards

Gang of Four

"four modernizations"

Oriental Exclusion Law

zaibatsu

Manchukuo

"Greater East Asia Co-Prosperity Sphere"

SCAP

Security Treaty of 1951

Liberal Democratic Party (LDP)

burakumin

"Nixon shock"

STUDY QUESTIONS

1. What were the causes of the decline of central authority in China in the nineteenth and early twentieth centuries?
2. What was the spark for the "May Fourth Movement"? Into what areas did its momentum carry it beyond its original cause? What effects did the movement have on China in later decades?
3. Explain the reasons why the Soviet Union assisted the Guomindang. What was the primary Soviet interest in China? Why was the Western-leaning, noncommunist Sun Yat-sen receptive to Soviet offers of assistance?
4. What were Sun Yat-sen's *Three Principles of the People*? What was the actual content of each of the principles?
5. Why did cooperation between the Guomindang and the Communists end so abruptly in 1927?
6. What were the successes of the Guomindang as the government of China? What were the major obstacles Chiang Kai-shek and his party had to overcome? What were the chief weaknesses in the regime and its program?
7. What were the reasons for Japan's attack on the Chinese in Manchuria in 1931? What were the results of this incident?
8. How did the Second World War in Asia contribute to the ultimate victory of the Communist party in China?
9. How did Mao Zedong's conception of the role of peasants in revolution differ from that of Lenin and other earlier revolutionaries?
10. What did Mao mean by calling the Long March of 1934–1935 a "seeding machine"?
11. How did the Chinese Communists win over the peasants of China? How did they differ from the Guomindang in their policies in rural China?
12. How do you account for the triumph of the Communists in China's civil war despite the initial advantages enjoyed by the Nationalists?
13. What was the significance (both short-term and long-term) of the Chinese Communist Party's purge of the rural, landholding elite?
14. What problems did the new People's Republic of China solve in the short term?
15. Describe the purposes behind the "Great Leap Forward," and explain why it failed to achieve those purposes. What were the actual results of this campaign?
16. What were the reasons for, and the effects of, China's "Cultural Revolution" of 1966–1976?
17. How can Mao's changing relationship with Lin Biao be seen as reflecting changes in Mao's approach to the continuing revolution in China?
18. Explain the reasons for the deterioration of relations between China and the Soviet Union in the late 1950s.
19. What changes in economic policy were introduced by Deng Xiaoping? How successful were they?
20. What brought about the massive demonstrations in Tiananmen Square in the spring and summer of 1989?

What were the concerns of the demonstrators? How did the 1989 demonstrations differ from other demonstrations in China's history? What resulted from the demonstrations?

21. Why did China embark on its disastrous attack on Vietnam in 1979?
22. Why has Taiwan been a source of international tension, and why does it continue to be?
23. What was the cause of the hyperinflation that plagued China in the 1940s? How did the government of the new People's Republic deal with this problem?
24. What changes were instituted with the first Five-Year Plan in China? How successful was the plan? What economic policies resulted in stagnation by the 1970s?
25. Despite their ideological differences, why have economic ties increased between Taiwan and the People's Republic of China?
26. What do the authors of the text mean in referring to post-1949 social changes in China as "one of the most profound transformations in its entire history"?
27. Trace the gains and setbacks for women in China since 1949, and the reasons for them.
28. What real and potential environmental problems does China face in the late 20th century?
29. What was the contribution of Lu Xun to China's cultural development?
30. How and why did art and literature in China change after 1949?
31. What new problems did China face as it reemerged in world affairs in the late twentieth century?
32. Why did the representatives at the Paris Peace Conference and the League of Nations allow Japan to retain former German holdings it seized in the First World War?
33. What factors or circumstances encouraged liberal tendencies in Japan following the First World War?
34. What were the obstacles, external and internal, to the establishment of a genuinely democratic regime in Japan between the two World Wars?
35. Explain the origins of the idea of a "Greater East Asian Co-Prosperity Sphere."
36. What are the remarkable features of the Japanese Constitution of 1946? How was the position of the emperor redefined by this Constitution?
37. Of the various reforms inaugurated in postwar Japan, which seem to be most successful and which least successful?
38. What are the distinctive features of the Japanese political system? In what respects is it democratic?
39. Explain how the LDP was able to stay in power for so long.
40. How do you account for Japan's phenomenal economic recovery and expansion since 1945? In which fields has Japan achieved greatest success? What outstanding economic problems remain?

41. "Japan has only one-twentieth as many lawyers per capita as the United States." Why?
42. What problems—economic, social, or environmental—have accompanied Japan's industrial expansion?
43. Outline the ways in which Japan's relations with its former enemies and colonies have changed since the end of the Second World War.
44. What are the bases of the repeated trade disputes between the U.S. and Japan?
45. Why were the Japanese elections of July 1993 so momentous?

PROBLEMS

1. "For the last two hundred years of the modern world, nationalism has been the angel of unity and the devil of despair." Examine how this statement applies to East Asia.
2. Study Sun Yat-sen's *Three Principles of the People* in detail, noting possible influences on Sun's thinking.
3. Numerous first-person accounts have been produced in English of life in Mao's China (particularly during the Cultural Revolution). Read and compare two or more of these accounts, and analyze the differences in background, outlook, and experience of the authors. What circumstances influenced the way in which the events of the Cultural Revolution affected the different authors?
4. It has been suggested that Mao was "a good leader who lived too long." What might be meant by such a statement? Do you agree or disagree?
5. Assess the ongoing efforts in the People's Republic of China to come to terms with the legacy of Mao Zedong. How have changing conditions since Mao's death led to the need for the ruling party to reinterpret his contribution? What aspects of his legacy seem more open to revision than others, and why?
6. Compare the May Fourth Movement of 1919 with the Tiananmen Square demonstrations of 1989, noting both similarities and differences.
7. Read, in English translation, Lu Xun's "The True Story of Ah Q," and analyze it as a work condemning problems in the China of Lu Xun's time. What is the focus of the author's critique?
8. Examine the policies and dynamics of the American occupation in Japan. In particular, analyze ways in which American forces worked with Japanese individuals and institutions.
9. Study the role of the Japanese emperor in the war, surrender, occupation, and beyond.
10. Investigate any of the following:
    a. The life and work of Sun Yat-sen
    b. The career of Chiang Kai-shek
    c. Mao Zedong's philosophy of revolution
    d. Sino-Soviet relations, 1923 to the present
    e. Industrial development in the PRC
    f. Educational changes in China
    g. The "Cultural Revolution" in China
    h. The changing role of women in Japan
    i. Changing U.S.-Chinese relations since 1949
    j. The rise of militant nationalism in Japan
    k. Liberal and antiwar sentiment in Japan during the period 1919–1941
    l. Industrial and technological developments in postwar Japan
    m. The character and role of political parties in Japan
    n. Japanese-American relations since the Occupation
    o. Taiwan under Chinese Nationalist rule

AIDS TO AN UNDERSTANDING OF ERUPTION IN EAST ASIA

MAO ZEDONG ON THE DICTATORSHIP OF THE PEOPLE'S DEMOCRACY (1949)

"**Y**ou are dictatorial." Dear sirs, you are right; that is exactly what we are. The experience of several decades, amassed by the Chinese people, tells us to carry out the people's democratic dictatorship. That is, the right of reactionaries to voice their opinions must be abolished and only the people are allowed to have the right of voicing their opinions.

Who are the "people"? At the present stage in China, they are the working class, the peasant class, the petty bourgeoisie, and national bourgeoisie. Under the leadership of the working class and the Communist Party, these classes unite together to form their own state and elect their own government (so as to) carry out a dictatorship over the lackeys of imperialism—the land-lord class, the bureaucratic capitalist class, and the Kuomintang reactionaries and their henchmen representing these classes—to suppress them, allowing them only to behave properly and not to talk and act wildly. If they talk and act wildly their [action] will be prohibited and punished immediately. The democratic system is to be carried out within the ranks of the people, giving them freedom of speech, assembly, and association. The right to vote is given only to the people and not to the reactionaries. These two aspects, namely, democracy among the people and dictatorship over the reactionaries, combine to form the people's democratic dictatorship. . . .

The [function of the] people's state is to protect the people. Only when there is the people's state, is it possible for the people to use democratic methods on a nationwide and all-round scale to educate and reform themselves, to free themselves from the influence of reactionaries at home and abroad (this influence is at present still very great and will exist for a long time and cannot be eliminated quickly), to unlearn the bad habits and ideas acquired from the old society and not to let themselves travel on the erroneous path pointed out by the reactionaries, but to continue to advance and develop towards a socialist and communist society accomplishing the historic mission of completely eliminating classes and advancing towards a universal fraternity.

The methods we use in this field are democratic; that is, methods of persuasion and not coercion. When people break the law they will be punished, imprisoned, or even sentenced to death. But these are individual cases and are different in principle from the dictatorship over the reactionary class as a class.

From C. Brandt, B. Schwartz, and J. K. Fairbank, *A Documentary History of Chinese Communism*, Harvard University Press, 1952. Reprinted by permission of the publisher.

The Cultural Revolution: A Chinese Newspaper Reports on the Red Guards in Action

According to a *Kwangsi Daily* report, on August 23, Red Guards and revolutionary teachers and students in the city of Nan-ning, inspired by the revolutionary spirit of revolt shown by the Red Guards in the capital, and filled with great revolutionary pride, took to the streets to post revolutionary leaflets and big-character posters and carry out oral propaganda. Using the thought of Mao Tse-tung as a weapon, they violently attacked all old ideas, old culture, old customs and old habits. They demanded that Nan-ning be built into a great school of Mao Tse-tung's thought.

A group of Red Guards in the Second Middle School in Nanning climbed up to a traffic policeman's stand and, through the medium of loudspeakers, read aloud to the people their Manifesto of Revolt: "Today, the clarion call for the Great Proletarian Cultural Revolution has been sounded, and the battle between the proletariat and the bourgeoisie has begun. We must promote the fearless spirit of the proletariat—the spirit of staining our bayonets with blood—and the revolt against feudalism, capitalism, and all demons and monsters. Backed by Chairman Mao and the Party Central Committee, this revolt is sure to succeed. Let the thought of Mao Tse-tung shine upon every corner. . . ."

Revolutionary "young generals" of the Kwangsi College of Arts formed four propaganda teams for the purpose of replacing bourgeois ideology with proletarian ideology and getting rid of the old to make way for the new. In no time they composed a revolutionary song entitled "Raise the Iron Broom of the Revolution," and sang it in the streets and shops. With revolutionary pride, they sang: "Sweep and break. Raise the iron broom of the revolution to sweep away the vestiges of feudalism, uproot the bourgeois ideology, hold aloft the red banner of the thought of Mao Tse-tung, establish proletarian and destroy bourgeois ideology, destroy a lot and build a lot, and construct a new socialist country." The masses around them sang with them.

Red Guards of the Kwangsi Nationality College in a remote suburban area arrived in the morning at the Station for the Re-

ception of the Masses operated according to the revolutionary rules. These Red Guards proposed to change the names of streets, places, and stores—such as People's Livelihood Road, People's Rights Road, Emperor Ridge, and White Dragon Bridge—into new names with revolutionary content. They proposed getting rid of all poisonous things in barber shops, tailor shops, and book-lending shops immediately. In shops that the Red Guards of the Nan-ning Ninth Middle School and revolutionary teachers and students visited, they were received warmly by the workers and employees, who were determined to respond to their revolutionary proposals.

The workers of the Handicraft Product Center of Nan-ning said, "We have long wanted to discard artistic products decorated with emperors, kings, generals, prime ministers, scholars, and beauties. Now that you have come to support us, we'll take immediate action." They immediately tucked away the carved standing screens and hanging screens and hung more portraits of Chairman Mao in the shop.

The workers of the New South Barber Shop at the suggestion of the Red Guards took down the pictures showing decadent bourgeois hair styles such as the "wave-type" and "big western style" and indicated that they would in future refuse to do such bizarre hair styles for their clients.

Fourteen Chinese and Western medicine shops under the Medical Company of Nan-ning held workers' forums one after the other and, after discussion, that same night adopted new signboards expressing revolutionary ideas.

The revolutionary masses of the city's cultural palace and museum listened to the broadcasts at eight o'clock in the morning and by nine had posted a big-character poster at Prince Liu Park. They thought that the term "Prince Liu" reflected feudal bureaucratic ideas and was incompatible with the spirit of the times. They thought the name should be changed into "People's Park," so immediately wrote "People's" on a piece of paper and pasted it on top. This suggestion was warmly supported by the revolutionary masses passing by.

From *Chinese Civilization and Society*, Patricia Buckley Ebrey, ed. pp. 393–94. The Free Press, 1981.

A Japanese View of the American Occupation and Its Effects
Kawai Kazuo

The thoroughness of their defeat was one important factor in the receptivity of the Japanese to the Occupation. Their world, as they had known it, had collapsed. Not only were their cities in ruins, their economy shattered, and their manpower mangled and strewn over nearly half the globe, but the dreams of national greatness which had sustained their spirits had evaporated. They were disillusioned, demoralized, and paralyzed. Although traditional controls largely stifled overt expressions of defeatism, the horrors of the last few months of the war had reduced many of the Japanese to an inner state bordering on panic. The surrender came to them as a heaven-sent relief; the Occupation became a welcome symbol of deliverance from annihilation.

Their unpreparedness for defeat was another important factor in the reaction of the Japanese. Never having been successfully invaded in all their long history, they had never even imagined the possibility of an enemy occupation. When suddenly confronted with a situation for which their social conditioning had provided no preparation, they found themselves utterly bewildered. While they were thus off balance, they were easily susceptible to any new influence that might be directed upon them. . . .

While their ancient history still inevitably exerts a strong conservative drag on their lives, more important is the fact that the bewilderingly rapid changes of the past hundred years have left the Japanese people with no deeply rooted convictions of their own. Cast adrift from their traditional moorings, some individuals struggle stubbornly to retrieve the past, while others cling hopefully to some new faith which they have found. But the vast majority, drifting aimlessly while troubled with feelings of instability and insecurity, clutch constantly at anything new that comes along in the hope that it can give them anchorage. In a sense, as the entire past century has been for them an unexpected situation to which their traditional book of rules could not apply, so the entire past century has been a hectic search by trial and error for new sets of rules. The Occupation represented only an intensified phase of this historic process rather than a wholly extraneous experience. As militarism was earlier, so was the Occupation in its turn eagerly welcomed by the Japanese as still another experiment that might yield them the truth which would rescue them from their uneasy flux. It was not simple fickleness or hypocrisy; it was the perennial quest of the modern Japanese for salvation. While this restless search might augur ill for the permanence of Japanese attraction to the Occupation program, at least it served to facilitate their initial acceptance of the Occupation. . . .

Japanese readiness to accept the Occupation was also aided by the fact that from the time of Commodore Perry to the outbreak of the war the United States had influenced Japan more profoundly than any other foreign country. Japanese intellectuals might admire Europe more; political difficulties with the United States and nationalist reaction in Japan might at times and in some fields substantially curb American influence. But in general America, popularly idealized as the model of progress and enlightenment, had continuously exercised the preeminent influence in the making of modern Japan. Feelings of inferiority and envy were not lacking; sometimes they erupted into anti-Americanism in some sections of the Japanese public. But the predominant attitude of the Japanese toward America for nearly a century had been that of an eager pupil toward a benevolent teacher. With the new demonstration of American superiority which the war had given, it was easy for the Japanese to fall back into the familiar pattern of tutelage to America. . . .

Many Japanese were also attracted to the Occupation program because a considerable portion of it represented the fulfillment of their own long-felt desires. Undistinguished as democratic development had been in prewar Japan, there had

been in the past some spontaneous indigenous democratic trends. These had reached fairly substantial proportions in the comparatively liberal decade of the 1920's before interruption by the rise of the militarists in the 1930's. When it was seen that the Occupation program sought to restore and extend the trends which had existed in the 1920's, it naturally appealed to the Japanese elements which had supported them then. While some of the Occupation measures represented a forcible imposition of alien ideas which the Japanese did not welcome, enough of the Occupation's program coincided with desirable indigenous historic trends to enable the Occupation to ride on the wave of a substantial popular native support.

The Occupation program, moreover, created in Japanese society new vested interests which came to have a vital stake in supporting and perpetuating the new regime. While the former ruling classes naturally did not welcome the Occupation, the segments of Japanese society which felt themselves liberated and endowed with new power by the Occupation quickly came to constitute a pillar of support for the Occupation. Even when some of these new vested interests—like organized labor—clashed with specific Occupation policies and eventually turned against the Occupation, they comprised new countervailing forces in Japanese society which weakened the "Old Guard" and indirectly helped to advance the long-range democratic objectives of the Occupation. . . .

Finally, in addition to all the theoretical explanations of Japanese conduct was the simple fact that the Japanese were realistic enough to see that co-operation with the Occupation was the only practicable course open to them. While they might have had the power to sabotage the Occupation, they realized that no advantage could come to them through such action. Hence, turning necessity into a virtue, they made the best of the situation that confronted them. . . .

Social change in Japan has not been seriously hampered by loyalty to old standards, nor has it been particularly inspired by new Western models. The generally non-doctrinaire, pragmatic inclination of most Japanese has resulted in neither a status quo nor a sweeping revolution but in a succession of gradual changes in response to specific situations, producing over the years a significant transformation in the nature of Japanese society. The postwar period has added nothing essentially different to this historic pattern of change, although the Occupation vastly speeded up the tempo of change for a short while. Such a pattern of social change would seem to indicate that the Japanese response to the stimulus of the Occupation is having gradual but profound long-range consequences. There was no immediate wholesale adoption of the American example; attempts to foist such an example bodily on the Japanese were quietly resisted or circumvented. But neither was there a blind and stubborn clinging to the past. The changes stimulated by the Occupation will undoubtedly be all the more permanently assimilated into Japanese life insofar as they were accepted by the Japanese of their own volition as suitable to their situation.

From Kawai Kazuo, *Japan's American Interlude,* University of Chicago Press, 1960. Reprinted by permission of the publisher.

ANALYSIS AND INTERPRETATION
OF THE READINGS

1. How does Mao Zedong explain the combination of "dictatorship" and "democracy" in his regime? How does he define "the people"?

2. In what ways does the newspaper report on Red Guard activities reflect Mao's 1949 description of "the people"? In what ways does it reflect changes in China's social and political situation from the 1940s to the 1960s?

3. Explain Kawai's statement that to many Japanese the Occupation "represented the fulfillment of their own long-felt desires."

CHAPTER 42 | Progress, Poverty, and Revolution in Latin America

IDENTIFICATIONS

You should be able to explain the meaning and importance of each of the following terms:

ejido
Institutional Revolutionary Party (PRI)
Mercosur
descamisados
peronistas
Falkland Islands (Malvinas)
"Shining Path"
Andean Group
Bay of Pigs
"liberation theology"
Sandinistas
contras
Alliance for Progress
Panama Canal treaties of 1977
Summit of the Americas

You should also be able to explain the role of each of the following in Latin America's history:

Getúlio Vargas	General Andrés Rodríguez
Alfredo Stroessner	José Batlle y Ordóñez
Patricio Aylwin	Anastasio Somoza
Fernando Collor de Mello	José Napoleon Duarte
Oscar Arias Sanchez	Isabel Perón
Fulgencio Batista	Violetta Barrios de Chamorro
Jean-Bertrand Aristide	General Manuel Noriega

In the blanks provided, write the letter corresponding to the most accurate completion of each of the following statements:

_____ 1. The great Mexican Revolution began in: (a) 1810; (b) 1868; (c) 1910–1911; (d) 1930.

_____ 2. The popular Mexican president Lázaro Cárdenas: (a) attempted to set aside the Constitution of 1917; (b) was overthrown by the military; (c) severed relations with the United States; (d) nationalized the oil industry.

_____ 3. President João Goulart of Brazil: (a) abolished slavery; (b) built the new capital of Brasília; (c) suppressed labor unions; (d) was overthrown by a *coup d'état* that inaugurated over two decades of military rule.

_____ 4. The "dirty war" of the late 1970s was carried on by a military junta governing: (a) Brazil; (b) Mexico; (c) Argentina; (d) Paraguay.

_____ 5. Latin America's leading oil exporters are: (a) Venezuela and Ecuador; (b) Venezuela and Mexico; (c) Mexico and Brazil; (d) Colombia and Chile.

_____ 6. The poorest Latin American state is: (a) Cuba; (b) Paraguay; (c) Panama; (d) Haiti.

_____ 7. President Raúl Alfonsín of Argentina: (a) greatly reduced the national debt; (b) recovered the Falkland Islands; (c) brought high-ranking military officers to trial; (d) brought inflation under control.

_____ 8. The victor in Peru's presidential election of June 1990 was: (a) a popular novelist; (b) a general; (c) Alán García Pérez; (d) the son of Japanese immigrants.

STUDY QUESTIONS

1. From what groups did Pancho Villa and Emiliano Zapata draw their primary support? Why were these groups dissatisfied with the established regime?

2. Several of the larger Latin American states have experienced upheavals that have brought a change in government. What is the justification for saying that only Mexico had a genuine revolution?

3. What were the objectives of the Mexican Constitution of 1917? In what ways were attempts made to realize those objectives? To what extent were those attempts successful?

4. Describe the reform program of President Lázaro Cárdenas.

5. What problems accompanied the industrial expansion beginning in the 1940s in Mexico?

6. Describe the consequences of the Mexican government's miscalculations following the discovery of oil and gas in 1976.

7. Identify the root causes of social and political unrest in Mexico.

8. What were the major achievements of Carlos Salinas as president of Mexico?

9. To what extent are Brazil's problems typical of industrializing societies? To what extent are they typical of many Latin American societies?

10. What were the major features of Brazil's economic boom beginning in the 1960s? What were the frailties of this period of growth?

11. What led to Brazil's hyperinflation of the 1980s? What were its political consequences?

12. What natural advantages does Argentina possess?

13. What factors have led to instability, inequality, and conflict in Argentina in the twentieth century?

14. What were the bases of Juan Perón's political support? What was the character of his rule, and what were its consequences?

15. What circumstances brought about the fall in 1983 of the military junta that had ruled Argentina for seven years?

16. How do you explain Argentina's decline from prosperity to near bankruptcy within the span of a century?

17. What measures did President Carlos Saúl Menem take to bring Argentina's inflation under control and improve Argentina's economy? How successful were his policies?

18. What were the major changes pursued by Salvador Allende as president of Chile?

19. How do you account for the violent overthrow of Chile's democratically elected president in September 1973?

20. Why, in your judgment, was General Pinochet able to retain power longer than several other contemporary dictators?

21. How do you explain the trend toward military dictatorships in much of Latin America after the Second World War?

22. In what respects was Peru's military dictatorship of the 1970s different from other military regimes?

23. What factors have promoted the expansion of coca cultivation in northeastern Peru? What hazards (both domestic and international) does it pose?

24. What did Alberto Fujimori do to try to turn the Peruvian economy around? What signs of success can you point to?

25. How do you explain Uruguay's turn from a relatively high level of democracy to dictatorship and repression by the 1970s?

26. "Bolivia could be viewed as a working model of the problems and frustrations confronting Latin American nations." Explain this statement.

27. What are some of the general weaknesses common to many Latin American economies?

28. What were the objectives of the "Twenty-sixth of July Movement" in Cuba?

29. Despite successes in some areas, what have been the roadblocks to the achievement of all of Fidel Castro's dream for Cuba?

30. What circumstances delayed the coming of revolution in Central America?

31. In 1979 dictators were expelled both from Nicaragua and El Salvador. How has the subsequent regime in El Salvador differed from Nicaragua's?

32. Compare or contrast the objectives of the Sandinistas with those of (a) the Mexican revolution; (b) the Cuban revolution.

33. Explain why the United States' position with regard to Panama changed from cooperation with the government of General Omar Torrijos to conflict with the government of General Manuel Noriega.

34. What are some of the indicators that could give hope for greater stability and prosperity in Latin America in the future?

PROBLEMS

1. Investigate any of the following:
   a. Argentina during the Perón decade
   b. Economic and educational progress in Mexico
   c. Relations between the United States and Latin America in recent decades
   d. The role of foreign investments in the economies of Latin America
   e. Conflicting interpretations of the Cuban revolution
   f. The 1965 crisis in the Dominican Republic
   g. Latin American contributions to literature, art, or music
   h. The career of Salvador Allende
   i. The Organization of American States
   j. The Falkland Islands war
   k. The controversy over negotiation of the Panama Canal treaties of 1977
   l. The application or nonapplication of the Monroe Doctrine since its formulation in 1823
   m. Reasons for, and outcomes of, U.S. intervention in Latin America in the twentieth century

2. Explore the competing interests in Latin America's rain forest. On the basis of your reading and your personal priorities, propose a solution to the problem.

AIDS TO AN UNDERSTANDING OF PROGRESS, POVERTY, AND REVOLUTION IN LATIN AMERICA

A VICTIM OF ARGENTINA'S "DIRTY WAR"
Jacobo Timerman

The peephole of my cell opens and the face of the corporal on guard appears. He smiles, and tosses something into the cell. "Congratulations, Jacobo."

This is the first time anyone has spoken to me. Until now, the discipline in this place to which I was brought a few days ago has been extremely severe. With each change of guard, the light is turned on from outside and they shout out: "Name?" This means that the peephole gets opened four times a day, every six hours. I'm cursorily addressed at other times, when the three dishes of hot liquid that constitute breakfast, lunch, and dinner are delivered. The peephole is opened, and I'm asked: "Are you going to eat?"

So the guard's present remark is startling. My initial reaction, whenever a new event occurs, is always: What will happen to me now? True, I'm in a legal prison at central headquarters of the Federal Police in Buenos Aires. The cell measures nearly two meters in width and three in length. Furthermore, it has a privy in it so that I needn't ask permission to go to the toilet, and it has a tap with drinking water. I can also wash up, but have no soap or towel. There's a cement bed without mattress, though I was promised one. I have a blanket, but gusts of cold air penetrate from the space above the wall, and I must walk for hours in an attempt to keep warm. If I calculate carefully the longest diagonal extending from the hole in the ground to the other end of the cell, I'm able to take seven steps. I've already covered a thousand laps.

It's better, much better, than in a clandestine prison. But no one talks to me. I don't know what's going to happen; the peephole is always shut. Everything is utterly still, except for the sounds and voices that penetrate from outside. Before dawn, while it's still dark, I can hear the bugle, commanding orders, and the sound of a formation under my window. Then the sounds of courtyards being washed; also tin pots. This takes place alongside what might be called the window—a mere hole in a wide wall, with a double row of iron bars. I climb on the bed to look outside, but am unable to see anything because the wall is so thick. From the corridor on the other side of the peephole, I can also hear shouts—not commands but insults. Prisoners, no doubt, washing the passageway and being yelled at and struck by the corporal. Often I hear prisoners weeping. One of the punishments meted out to those who don't do a good scrubbing job is to force them to undress, lean over with their index finger on the ground, and have them rotate round and round, dragging their finger on the ground without lifting it. This is called "looking for oil." You feel as if your kidneys are bursting. But it's even more entertaining to place a prisoner near the wall and have five hefty policemen form a little train by lining up in single file and holding onto the hips of the person in front. They come down the passage making the sound of a locomotive and, picking up speed, hurl themselves like a dead weight on the prisoner, plastering him against the wall. This is called the "choo-choo shock." When they're busy, though, they simply order the prisoner to run naked along the passageway, which is fifty meters from one end to the other, reciting aloud sayings dictated to him. He has to repeat these without stopping until they invent others. *My mother's a whore. . . . The whore who gave birth to me. . . . I masturbate. . . . I must respect the corporal on guard. . . . The police love me. . . .*

The prisoner who is incommunicado is envious of all this. He longs to see a face. His need engenders a series of skills. From his isolation, he begins to comprehend the architecture of the outside world, a faceless architecture that he pieces together like a puzzle. Although he is a blind man, a dextrous blind man who comes to the end of his task without a happy conclusion providing him any relief, he remains, in the end, blind, never able to see the vital part. There are long silences that must be linked with whispers. (A soft voice asks, "Who's there?" and, softly, I reply, "Timerman," and the voice lets out a burst of laughter. Then another voice slowly asks, "Who's there?" and this time I don't answer: but another time I say, "Timerman," and he murmurs, "Be strong.") Then, too, one must find a place in the puzzle for the shouts, insults, and hard beatings meted out to prisoners, the jokes toward homosexuals; all must be incorporated in order to have an idea of what's going on. The police need to shout—shouting helps them. They have orders from their superiors to shout all the time in order to intimidate and confuse prisoners. Therefore, whenever they talk, they shout, which adds to the puzzle, to the effort of constructing the outside world, the only world apart from the cell.

And then there are other pieces: The policeman who negotiates with a homosexual to rent a cell in the isolation ward so that the latter can receive alternating prisoners from another ward, the one for petty criminals and thieves who are in for sixty or ninety days, entitled to use their money for food, and glad to pay for this hour of male prostitution inside a cell located in the heart of Buenos Aires, a hallucinatory brothel administered by the Federal Police, which Juan Domingo Perón pronounced the best police force in the world.

Adding further to the puzzle are the big cleaning days when a commissioner will be coming for inspection and the cells are disinfected. But since those who are held incommunicado cannot be let out, a man in white opens the door and fumigates the cell with puffs of white powder. The chemical smell engulfs me for days, though I no longer fear choking, like the first time. Then there are the typical Sunday sounds, when the names of prisoners with visiting rights are called out, and you hear radio broadcasts of soccer matches and smell the odor of different foods, that of the guards no doubt; there are days, too, when you hear the droning sound of a religious service.

And that is why I am startled now. The sound that just dropped into my cell has destroyed the puzzle and doesn't fit into the despair of the cell, nor into my effort to compensate for that despair by my slow, laborious, ardent reconstruction of the exterior architecture, the blind man's stubborn obsession with his puzzle.

I pick up a letter and two candies. The letter, a few brief lines, is from my wife. Dated May 20, 1977. We've been married today for twenty-seven years. I leave everything on the bed and go back to my task as blind architect: She's undoubtedly contacted one of our army friends, one of those who came to our house so often, or one of the retired officers who worked on my newspaper, perhaps someone who spent vacations at our beach house. . . . And yet, this doesn't fit into the heightened sensibility of a blind man whose sightless eyes are gazing at an unknown world. No military man nowadays would dare to speak to my wife. More likely one of the policemen, a ward guard, went to visit her and offered, for a sum of money, to bring something to me. At this point the blind architect starts reconstructing the scene. My house, the entrance, the doorbell, my wife's face. . . . But no, the image of my wife's face is unbearable in this place.

How I cursed my wife that day! How many times I told myself I wouldn't read her letter, I wouldn't eat the candies. After so many efforts to forget, to refrain from loving and desiring, to refrain from thinking, the entire painstaking edifice constructed by the blind architect collapses over his head. Already I'd begun to belong to the world around me, the one I actually belonged to, the imprisoned world where my heart and blood were installed: this world I've already accepted and that is real, that corresponds to the inscriptions on the wall, the odor of the latrine matching that emitted by my skin and clothes, and those drab colors, the sounds of metal and violence, the harsh, shrill, hysterical voices. And now this world, so heavily armored, so solid and irreplaceable, without cracks, has been penetrated by a letter and two candies. Risha, why have you done this to me?

She tells me that if she could she'd give me heaven with all its stars and clouds, all the air in the world, all her love, all her tenderness. She says that she'd kiss me a thousand times if she could. But that is what she fails to understand: she cannot. In a rage, I throw the letter into the latrine, and with equal rage stick the two candies into my mouth. But already I'm lost, for the flavor is overpowering, as is my wife's face, her scent almost; and my realization that I've been married today for twenty-seven years and have been sequestered for forty days.

How can a blind architect fit into his unknown edifice—that structure he can neither see nor touch—the face of his wife, the taste of two candies, his wedding anniversary? Anywhere I place them, the structure collapses. Then, once again, I sit down on the stone bed, and when the guard opens the peephole to ask me my name, once again I arouse myself from the submerging debris, grasping for a life jacket to reconstruct my reality. I don't reply, and the guard kicks the steel door with his heavy boots. "Name, son of a whore!"

The blind architect goes to work trying to fit the meaning of this insult into his world. He no longer needs to remember. At this juncture I feel as if I've passed the first serious test, worse than torture, and that I'll survive. For it is here that you must survive, not in the outside world. And the chief enemy is not the electric shocks, but penetration from the outside world, with all its memories.

ASPHYXIATION BY PROGRESS
Carlos Fuentes

The dripping sky is one of the constants in Mexico City; it rains incessantly, a black, oily, carboniferous rain that darkens the grandest neon signs, the sensation of a veiled, dark sky in whose fogs fade the skeletons of the buildings, many of them unfinished, many just rusted steel beams, truncated towers, the temples of underdevelopment, skyscrapirontemples, others mere canvas, others just cubes of cardboard dripping acid rain, but very few real, inhabited structures: the city lives by moving, permanence has become secret, only movement is visible, the stands along the old Paseo de la Reforma, fried foods, fruit stands, wilted flowers, black candy, sweetmeats, burro heads, pigsfeet, muguey worms (perpetual humidity of the city, immense breeding ground for mildew, moss, rot), and the files of figures bent over devouring the tacos sold along Reforma in front of the tents illuminated by naked bulbs and burning mosquito repellant. But these details can only be seen with a microscope because from above the city is an immense, ulcerated crater, a cavity in the universe, uban gangrene, the chancre of the Americas, the hemorrhoid of the Tropic of Cancer.

Since the earthquake of '85, tens of thousands of the homeless have taken over the traffic circle islands and medians along Reforma and other main, divided arteries: shacks and puptents, little shops and stalls: With each passing day the capital of Mexico looks more and more like a hick town in the provinces.

The slow collapse of all hydraulic systems—Lerma, Mexcala, Usumacinta—have been compensated for by the constant acid misting caused by the industrialization of this high, burning, and enclosed valley.

"The problem is water," said don Fernando Benítez to Minister Robles Chacón. "You make people think it's the air just to distract their attention from the real problem, then you make up this Disneyland story about the Dome that's going to protect us from pollution and give a fair share of pure air to every inhabitant of the city. You miserable rats lie and lie and lie! The problem is the water, because every single drop of water that reaches this city costs millions of pesos."

"Don't you worry about it, don Fernando," answered the minister in a calm, friendly voice. "We know how to distribute our reserves and how to ration out that precious liquid. How are your water tubs doing, tell me. Have you had any problems? Haven't we taken care of you just as you deserve?"

"Like everyone else, I'm saving as much water in them as I can, so my tubs are just fine," said Benítez despondently. Then he quickly recovered his fighting spirit: "And how's your mom?"

"Blind and buried," said Robles Chacón unflinchingly.

"Well, let's hope you have enough water to keep the flowers on her grave alive," said Benítez before leaving.

The minister looked incredulously at his feet and called his aide-de-camp, the statistician he kept hidden in the armoire:

"Let's see now," Minister Robles Chacón snapped his fingers explosively, "get out here and catch me that rat, and make it snappy! A rat in the office of the Secretary of Patrimony and Vehicles . . . But get a move on, you jerk, what's your problem?" shouted the minister to the little man who'd emerged from the closet at the sound of that betitled and superior snap, and who then skulked his way through the furniture bought in Roche-Bobois, hunting for the rat and explaining that Mexico City has thirty million human inhabitants, but it has one hundred and twenty eight million rats. He fell on his knees and stretched his hand under a table made of aluminum and transparent glass, a model people in the luxury market called the New York Table—they inhabit sewers, Mr. Secretary, drains, and mountains of garbage, every year they contaminate more than ten million people with parasitosis and other intestinal ailments.

"And they consume thirty tons of corn and other cereals every two weeks. These rats are murderers, sir, but they themselves die mysteriously when they eat certain grains."

"Mounds of dead rodents have been found, dead from eating imported corn. And the cats, coyotes, and other animals that eat those dead rats also suffer serious sicknesses."

"Then aren't those grain importers taking part in the deratification campaign?" inquired Robles Chacón.

The diminutive statistician dressed in his tuxedo cleaned his breath and drool off the bottom of the glass table in the French furnished office of the minister:

"No, sir, because rats breed every twenty-one days."

He got to his feet with difficulty, adding, as he smoothed his hair into place, "Perhaps the importers simply contribute to the . . ."

"Statistics, no moral judgments," said the minister to the statistician.

IMPRESSIONS OF THE SANDINISTA REVOLUTION
Julio Cortázar

RECONSTRUCTION

The liberation of the Nicaraguan people on July 19, 1979, was immediately manifest in a will to *reconstruct* which went far beyond the material sense of that word. When the national leadership calls itself a government of reconstruction, it uses that term knowing it is fully understood by those who have experienced the bitter costs of ignorance in their own flesh and blood. It's no surprise that accomplished poets and intellectuals such as Ernesto Cardenal, Sergio Ramírez and Tomás Borge are members of this government. For them, reconstruction means not simply raising the country out of smoking ruins but raising all the children and all the adults to a level of full participation—conscious, critical participation—in the work ahead. Speak with any of these leaders and you'll see how their sense of reconstruction begins with the idea of the Nicaraguan citizen as an active worker in this process, fully capable of understanding the job to be done, why it is necessary, and how it ought to be carried out. The devastating notion of a passive people, brutally enforced by Somoza, has shifted to a nationwide dynamic of participation and consultation, a process unimaginable without a minimum of intellectual preparation.

This preparation involves the reassessment of atavistic and traditional beliefs, making use of them when they seem positive, or leaving them definitively behind when they contribute to regression and stagnation.

All this should make it easy to understand the intense energy now pouring into the literacy campaign in Nicaragua. Since even the most elementary tools were lacking, from pencils to textbooks, it was obvious to the entire population that the campaign could not advance without the aid which would have to come from friendly nations. In this connection, I should point out that UNESCO's call for funds was a wholehearted response to Nicaragua's decision, in the race of which indifference or hesitation are impossible. However, in the 1960s in Cuba it was another story entirely. At that time UNESCO sat back, awaiting the outcome of the campaign, stepping in only to verify the results and announce them with enthusiastic praise. Now UNESCO is no longer hesitating but calling out for worldwide assistance, thus demonstrating its full confidence that one more Latin American country will have the strength to emerge from underdevelopment.

A YOUNG REVOLUTIONARY

Two nights ago I was in one of the women's wards of the Dávila Bolaños Hospital in Managua, visiting a fifteen-year-old girl, a high school sophomore. I recognized her immediately, though the room was crowded with women patients, because her picture has been in the papers here every day, and hers is not a face to be forgotten or confused with anybody else's.

Everybody's talking about her smile, the same generous smile which was on her lips as I approached her bed. People speak of Brenda Rocha with a mixture of love and admiration, but you can also sense their horror and, above all, their outrage at the reason why this child is in a hospital bed. Only a few days ago Brenda lost her right arm. It was amputated five inches from the shoulder.

In one of the most inaccessible regions of the country, near the mineral deposits of Siuna. La Rosita and Bonanza, there's a little town called Salto Grande. Like all the isolated communities of the interior, it is frequently threatened by bands of Somoza's ex-Guard. Armed with weapons from abroad, these roving bands have been murdering campesinos, robbing and destroying their villages and attacking the Sandinista militia which defend their towns. Brenda Rocha and a small group of *compañeros* from Bonanza were the militia responsible for the defense of Salto Grande. At age fifteen she had already taken part in the literacy campaign and joined the Sandinista Youth. She then became a member of the militia. As she herself says, with great naturalness, her task was to be ready for anything. On July 24 she was standing guard with her *compañeros* when a Somocista squad, superior in numbers and weaponry, stormed out of the hills and opened fire on the town.

In the ensuing battle, seven militia fighters died: six men and one woman. Bullets ripped through Brenda's right arm, but she went right on firing with her left. Finally, weak from loss of blood, she had to stop. By then the Somocistas were inside the town.

Lying face down on the ground, she pretended to be dead, and the attackers, fearing the arrival of Sandinista reinforcements, withdrew without touching her. Immediately the townspeople rushed to her aid, taking care of her until she could be moved to Managua, where it was necessary to amputate her arm. By the end of the month, the doctors say, she'll be able to go to the Soviet Union, where, by means of the most advanced surgical techniques, she'll be fitted with a prosthesis. For Brenda this means only one thing: being able to come home to her work, to carry on with her duties as a militiawoman.

ANALYSIS AND INTERPRETATION OF THE READINGS

1. Why does the imprisoned Timerman call himself a blind architect?
2. Where does Fuentes seem to be placing the blame for urban pollution?
3. What do you suppose Julio Cortázar intended to show with the story of Brenda Rocha?

CHAPTER 43 | Epilogue: Problems of World Civilization

STUDY QUESTIONS

1. How are the problems of the less-developed world affected by the demographic revolution?
2. Cite examples of ecological problems resulting from advanced technology and industrialization.
3. What technological projects involve an impairment of the land as a natural resource?
4. What are the causes of the "greenhouse effect"? What are its possible consequences?
5. What is the "demographic revolution"? Explain its causes.
6. In what regions of the world has population growth been the highest in recent decades? What problems has this raised?
7. Why has the progress of science brought new problems while solving some old ones? Cite specific examples.
8. What have been the chief accomplishments in preventive medicine since the Second World War?
9. What successes have there been in efforts to reduce stockpiles of nuclear weapons throughout the world? Why have these efforts not been more successful?
10. Explain how automation differs from mechanization. What are the advantages of automation? Is it accompanied by any disadvantages?
11. How did the views on technology of Jean Baudrillard and Jean-François Lyotard differ? Which view is closer to your own?

PROBLEMS

1. Investigate any of the following:
   a. The discovery of the structure of DNA by Crick and Watson
   b. The effects of automation in eliminating and in creating jobs
   c. Proposals for meeting the crisis of ecology
   d. Birth control programs in India and China
2. Develop arguments to affirm or deny the proposition that science and technology created, but can also solve, many of the problems that threaten our civilization.
3. Write an essay in which you discuss ways in which the advent of the personal computer has affected your life.
4. On what basis can the claim be made that for an understanding of the workings of human nature, "there is no better source than history"? How can history instruct us regarding human nature? How can the study of the past assist us as we try to find solutions to the problems of the present?

AIDS TO AN UNDERSTANDING OF PROBLEMS OF WORLD CIVILIZATION

THE UNITED NATIONS UNIVERSAL DECLARATION OF HUMAN RIGHTS (1948)

PREAMBLE

*W*hereas recognition of the inherent dignity and of the equal and inalienable rights of all members of the human family is the foundation of freedom, justice and peace in the world,

Whereas disregard and contempt for human rights have resulted in barbarous acts which have outraged the conscience of mankind, and the advent of a world in which human beings shall enjoy freedom of speech and belief and freedom from fear and want has been proclaimed as the highest aspiration of the common people,

Whereas it is essential, if man is not to be compelled to have recourse, as a last resort, to rebellion against tyranny and oppression, that human rights should be protected by the rule of law,

Whereas it is essential to promote the development of friendly relations between nations,

Whereas the peoples of the United Nations have in the Charter reaffirmed their faith in fundamental human rights, in the dignity and worth of the human person and in the equal rights of men and women and have determined to promote social progress and better standards of life in larger freedom,

Whereas Member States have pledged themselves to achieve, in cooperation with the United Nations, the promotion of universal respect for and observance of human rights and fundamental freedoms,

Whereas a common understanding of these rights and freedoms is of the greatest importance for the full realization of this pledge,

Now, therefore,

The General Assembly

Proclaims this Universal Declaration of Human Rights as a common standard of achievement for all peoples and all nations, to the end that every individual and every organ of society, keeping this Declaration constantly in mind, shall strive by teaching and education to promote respect for these rights and freedoms and by progressive measures, national and international, to secure their universal and effective recognition and observance, both among the peoples of Member States themselves and among the peoples of territories under their jurisdiction.

ARTICLE 1

All human beings are born free and equal in dignity and rights. They are endowed with reason and conscience and should act towards one another in a spirit of brotherhood.

ARTICLE 2

Everyone is entitled to all the rights and freedoms set forth in this Declaration, without distinction of any kind, such as race, colour, sex, language, religion, political or other opinion, national or social origin, property, birth or other status.

Furthermore, no distinction shall be made on the basis of the political, jurisdictional or international status of the country or territory to which a person belongs, whether it be independent, trust, non-self-governing or under any other limitation of sovereignty.

ARTICLE 3

Everyone has the right to life, liberty and the security of person.

ARTICLE 4

No one shall be held in slavery or servitude; slavery and the slave trade shall be prohibited in all their forms.

ARTICLE 5

No one shall be subjected to torture or to cruel, inhuman or degrading treatment or punishment.

ARTICLE 6

Everyone has the right to recognition everywhere as a person before the law.

ARTICLE 7

All are equal before the law and are entitled without any discrimination to equal protection of the law. All are entitled to equal protection against any discrimination in violation of this Declaration and against any incitement to such discrimination.

ARTICLE 8

Everyone has the right to an effective remedy by the competent national tribunals for acts violating the fundamental rights granted him by the constitution or by law.

ARTICLE 9

No one shall be subjected to arbitrary arrest, detention or exile.

ARTICLE 10

Everyone is entitled in full equality to a fair, and public hearing by an independent and impartial tribunal, in the determination of his rights and obligations and of any criminal charge against him.

ARTICLE 11

1. Everyone charged with a penal offence has the right to be presumed innocent until proved guilty according to law in a public trial at which he has had all the guarantees necessary for his defence.
2. No one shall be held guilty of any penal offence on account of any act or omission which did not constitute a penal offence, under national or international law, at the time when it was committed. Nor shall a heavier penalty be imposed than the one that was applicable at the time the penal offence was committed.

ARTICLE 12

No one shall be subjected to arbitrary interference with his privacy, family, home or correspondence, nor to attacks upon his honour and reputation. Everyone has the right to the protection of the law against such interference or attacks.

ARTICLE 13

1. Everyone has the right to freedom of movement and residence within the borders of each State.
2. Everyone has the right to leave any country, including his own, and to return to his country.

ARTICLE 14

1. Everyone has the right to seek and to enjoy in other countries asylum from persecution.

2. This right may not be invoked in the case of prosecutions genuinely arising from non-political crimes or from acts contrary to the purposes and principles of the United Nations.

ARTICLE 15

1. Everyone has the right to a nationality.
2. No one shall be arbitrarily deprived of his nationality nor denied the right to change his nationality.

ARTICLE 16

1. Men and women of full age, without any limitation due to race, nationality or religion, have the right to marry and to found a family. They are entitled to equal rights as to marriage, during marriage and at its dissolution.
2. Marriage shall be entered into only with the free and full consent of the intending spouses.
3. The family is the natural and fundamental group unit of society and is entitled to protection by society and the State.

ARTICLE 17

1. Everyone has the right to own property alone as well as in association with others.
2. No one shall be arbitrarily deprived of his property.

ARTICLE 18

Everyone has the right to freedom of thought, conscience and religion; this right includes freedom to change his religion or belief, and freedom, either alone or in community with others and in public or private, to manifest his religion or belief in teaching, practice, worship and observance.

ARTICLE 19

Everyone has the right to freedom of opinion and expression; this right includes freedom to hold opinions without interference and to seek, receive and impart information and ideas through any media and regardless of frontiers.

ARTICLE 20

1. Everyone has the right to freedom of peaceful assembly and association.
2. No one may be compelled to belong to an association.

ARTICLE 21

1. Everyone has the right to take part in the government of his country, directly or through freely chosen representatives.
2. Everyone has the right of equal access to public service in his country.
3. The will of the people shall be the basis of the authority of government; this will shall be expressed in periodic and genuine elections which shall be by universal and equal suffrage and shall be held by secret vote or by equivalent free voting procedures.

ARTICLE 22

Everyone, as a member of society, has the right to social security and is entitled to realization, through national effort and international co-operation and in accordance with the organization and resources of each State, of the economic, social and cultural rights indispensable for his dignity and the free development of his personality.

ARTICLE 23

1. Everyone has the right to work, to free choice of employment, to just and favourable conditions of work and to protection against unemployment.
2. Everyone, without any discrimination, has the right to equal pay for equal work.
3. Everyone who works has the right to just and favourable remuneration ensuring for himself and his family an existence worthy of human dignity, and supplemented, if necessary, by other means of social protection.
4. Everyone has the right to form and to join trade unions for the protection of his interests.

ARTICLE 24

Everyone has the right to rest and leisure, including reasonable limitation of working hours and periodic holidays with pay.

ARTICLE 25

1. Everyone has the right to a standard of living adequate for the health and well-being of himself and of his family, including food, clothing, housing and medical care and necessary social services, and the right to security in the event of unemployment, sickness, disability, widowhood, old age or other lack of livelihood in circumstances beyond his control.
2. Motherhood and childhood are entitled to special care and assistance. All children, whether born in or out of wedlock, shall enjoy the same social protection.

ARTICLE 26

1. Everyone has the right to education. Education shall be free, at least in the elementary and fundamental stages. Elementary education shall be compulsory. Technical and professional education shall be made generally available and higher education shall be equally accessible to all on the basis of merit.
2. Education shall be directed to the full development of the human personality and to the strengthening of respect for human rights and fundamental freedoms. It shall promote understanding, tolerance and friendship among all nations, racial or religious groups, and shall further the activities of the United Nations for the maintenance of peace.
3. Parents have a prior right to choose the kind of education that shall be given to their children.

ARTICLE 27

1. Everyone has the right freely to participate in the cultural life of the community, to enjoy the arts and to share in scientific advancement and its benefits.

2. Everyone has the right to the protection of the moral and material interests resulting from any scientific, literary or artistic production of which he is the author.

ARTICLE 28

Everyone is entitled to a social and international order in which the rights and freedoms set forth in this Declaration can be fully realized.

ARTICLE 29

1. Everyone has duties to the community in which alone the free and full development of his personality is possible.
2. In the exercise of his rights and freedoms, everyone shall be subject only to such limitations as are determined by law solely for the purpose of securing due recognition and respect for the rights and freedoms of others and of meeting the just requirements of morality, public order and the general welfare in a democratic society.
3. These rights and freedoms may in no case be exercised contrary to the purposes and principles of the United Nations.

ARTICLE 30

Nothing in this Declaration may be interpreted as implying for any State, group or person any right to engage in any activity or to perform any act aimed at the destruction of any of the rights and freedoms set forth herein.

From *Sources of World Civilization.* vol. 2. Oliver A. Johnson, ed. Prentice-Hall, 1994. pp. 424–28.

THE RETURN OF HISTORY
Freimut Duve

The striking image of the Berlin Wall's destruction lends great emotional power to the idyllic view of a New Europe that is reconciled, de-ideologized and peaceful. Yet, there is no utopian mirage as dangerous as this one.

To confuse the end of the Cold War with the end of war, or the end of History with the end of the ideological wrestle between capitalism and socialism, would be the worst possible manner for us to approach the difficult times ahead. I'm sure that the future that awaits us will be quite discordant with this harmonious lullaby.

All of these learned pronouncements of the End—delivered in such fashionably apocalyptic tones, heralding in the West the end of politics, of ideology, of art, of the novel, of History, of the Subject—share the same basic flaw of perceiving the new dawn as a dying twilight.

Clearly, the modern era is setting. But what if another day is dawning? What if history cannot be diagrammed simply by one, and only one, path of Salvation—from Original Sin to the Last Judgement? What if history is not linear, but characterized by a spiral of avatars and analogues, with curves connecting identical points of waves of varying heights and lengths, with destinies not entirely the same, but not entirely different?

Rather than setting once and for all on history's horizon, maybe Hegel's "world spirit," which was to find its final embodiment in the liberal institutions of the West, is reemerging in the East. After all, the great wave of hi-tech prosperity did not stop in California. The yen is pressing the dollar for supremacy and Japan is moving rapidly to surpass an America wounded by declining industries, flagging technological progress and deteriorating trade balances. The North Pacific is displacing the Atlantic as the core of the world economy; China has merely slowed this momentum by an irrational, and quite temporary, retreat.

In what our unerring experts persist in calling the "Eastern Bloc," a new day has finally dawned, but in the East, not the West. The democratizing light emanates from Moscow toward Berlin, not from Prague toward Moscow.

Further, what our philosophers have called "the end of ideology" has for a long while obscured the resurgence of religions—the primary and fundamental forms of ideology. This new religious upsurge has also spread from East to West, from Shi'ite to Sunni Islam, coursing through Judaism and onward to Roman Catholicism. In Hegelian terms, religion over the centuries became secularized ideology in passing from heave to earth, and from East to West. At the end of the 20th century, the materialized "world spirit" has risen back to the heavens to reappear in the East as religion.

We can see today a similar inversion with respect to ideological and strategic rivalries. The end of East-West rivalry will not lead to a glorious Pentecost of "one world democracy under God" where the primary issue will be the equitable distribution of VCRs among households. Rather, it will lead to a return to the world of empires and nations just as we had left them in Central Europe before Yalta, and in the Soviet Union before 1917.

Those tired terms "totalitarianism" and "liberalism," as clumsy as false teeth, were never the true historical categories that ideologues on both sides of the divide had us believe. The true historical subjects, as a handful of die-hard Gaullists have always insisted, are peoples and their cultures in their unending, prosaic, and stubborn diversity.

As long as the Cold War remained, the superpowers could mutually agree that stifling regional conflicts would accommodate their own interests. But, without the cold breath of ideological hostility between the blocs, the era of nations, religions and cultures is again beginning to smolder.

As we welcome the rebirth of a diverse Europe, let us not forget that this rebirth brings with it the pangs of our old nationalisms. In short, the 19th century awaits us at the dawning of the 21st. Contemporary Europe has abandoned its imposture and is once again revealing its true character: Austria-Hungary, the German Federation, Holy Russia, the Baltic nations, Christian Armenia, Muslim Turkestan, Catholic Poland. Once again, we are faced with the matrix of the great European conflicts that the strategic renewal of conventional forces and the proliferation of nuclear arms have rendered all the more tempting.

From Freimut Duve, "The 21st Century Will Resemble the 19th," *New Perspectives Quarterly.* Vol. 7, no. 1 (1990). Reprinted by permission of *New Perspectives Quarterly.*

BLOOD AND BELONGING
Michael Ignatieff

CIVIC AND ETHNIC NATIONALISM

As a political doctrine, nationalism is the belief that the world's people are divided into nations, and that each of these nations has the right of self-determination, either as self-governing units within existing nation-states or as nation-states of their own.

As a cultural ideal, nationalism is the claim that while men and women have many identities, it is the nation that provides them with their primary form of belonging.

As a moral ideal, nationalism is an ethic of heroic sacrifice, justifying the use of violence in the defense of one's nation against enemies, internal or external.

These claims—political, moral, and cultural—underwrite each other. The moral claim that nations are entitled to be defended by force or violence depends on the cultural claim that the needs they satisfy for security and belonging are uniquely important. The political idea that all peoples should struggle for nationhood depends on the cultural claim that only nations can satisfy these needs. The cultural idea in turn underwrites the political claim that these needs cannot be satisfied without self-determination.

Each one of these claims is contestable and none is intuitively obvious. Many of the world's tribal peoples and ethnic minorities do not think of themselves as nations; many do not seek or require a state of their own. It is not obvious, furthermore, why national identity should be a more important element of personal identity than any other; nor is it obvious why defense of the nation justifies the use of violence.

But for the moment, what matters is that nationalism is centrally concerned to define the conditions under which force or violence is justified in a people's defense, when their right of self-determination is threatened or denied. Self-determination here may mean either democratic self-rule or the exercise of cultural autonomy, depending on whether the national group in question believes it can achieve its goals within the framework of an existing state or seeks a state of its own.

All forms of nationalism vest political sovereignty in "the people"—indeed, the word "nation" is often a synonym for "the people"—but not all nationalist movements create democratic regimes, because not all nationalisms include all of the people in their definition of who constitutes the nation.

One type, civic nationalism, maintains that the nation should be composed of all those—regardless of race, color, creed, gender, language, or ethnicity—who subscribe to the nation's political creed. This nationalism is called civic because it envisages the nation as a community of equal, rights-bearing citizens, united in patriotic attachment to a shared set of political practices and values. This nationalism is necessarily democratic, since it vests sovereignty in all of the people. Some elements of this ideal were first achieved in Great Britain. By the mid-eighteenth century, Britain was already a nation-state composed of four nations—the Irish, the Scots, the Welsh, and the English—united by a civic rather than an ethnic definition of belonging, i.e., by shared attachment to certain institutions: the Crown, Parliament, and the rule of law. But it was not until the French and American revolutions, and the creation of the French and American republics, that civic nationalism set out to conquer the world. . . .

Of these two types of nationalism, the civic has a greater claim to sociological realism. Most societies are not mono-ethnic; and even when they are, common ethnicity does not of itself obliterate division, because ethnicity is only one of the many claims on an individual's loyalty. According to the civic nationalistic creed, what holds a society together is not common roots but law. By subscribing to a set of democratic procedures and values, individuals can reconcile their right to shape their own lives with their need to belong to a community. This in turn assumes that national belonging can be a form of rational attachment.

Ethnic nationalism claims, by contrast, that an individual's deepest attachments are inherited, not chosen. It is the national community that defines the individual, not the individuals who define the national community. This psychology of belonging may have greater depth than civic nationalism's, but the sociology that accompanies it is a good deal less realistic. The fact, for example, that two Serbs share Serbian ethnic identity may unite them against Croats, but it will do nothing to stop them fighting each other over jobs, spouses, scarce resources, and so on. Common ethnicity, by itself, does not create social cohesion or community, and when it fails to do so, as it must, nationalistic regimes are necessarily impelled toward maintaining unity by force rather than be consent. This is one reason why ethnic nationalist regimes are more authoritarian than democratic. . . .

There is also a host of examples—Northern Ireland, India, and Canada, to name three—where ethnic nationalism flourishes within states formally committed to civic democracy. In Northern Ireland, between 1920 and 1972, the Loyalist Protestant majority used the British parliamentary system to maintain a comprehensive form of majoritarian tyranny against the Catholic minority. Being steeped in the British democratic and legal tradition did nothing to stop Loyalists from bending democracy to nationalist ends. In India, forty-five years of civic democracy have barely contained the ethnic and religious nationalisms that are currently tearing the country's federal system apart. In Canada, the picture is more optimistic, but the analytical point is the same. Full inclusion within a federal democratic system has not abated the force of Quebecois nationalism.

In all these places, the fundamental appeal of ethnic nationalism is as a rationale for ethnic majority rule, for keeping one's enemies in their place or for overturning some legacy of cultural subordination. In the nations of Eastern Europe, ethnic nationalism offers something more. For when the Soviet empire and its satellite regimes collapsed, the nation-state structures of the region also collapsed, leaving hundreds of ethnic groups at the mercy of each other. Since none of these groups had the slightest experience of conciliating their disagreements by democratic discussion, violence or force became their arbiter. Nationalist rhetoric swept through these regions like wildfire because it provided warlords and gunmen with a vocabulary of opportunistic self-justification. In the fear and panic which swept the ruins of the Communist states, people began to ask: So who will protect me now? Faced with a situation of political and economic chaos, people wanted to know whom to trust, and whom to call their own. Ethnic nationalism provided an answer that was intuitively obvious: Only trust those of your own blood.

From Michael Ignatieff, *Blood and Belonging*. New York: Farrar, Straus & Giroux. 1993. pp. 5–9.

THE FATE OF THE EARTH
Jonathan Schell

In recent years, scientists in many fields have accumulated enough knowledge to begin to look on the earth as a single, concrete mechanism, and to at least begin to ask how it works. One of their discoveries has been that life and life's inanimate terrestrial surroundings have a strong reciprocal influence on each other. For life, the land, oceans, and air have been the environment, but, equally, for the land, oceans, and air life has been the environment—the conditioning force. The injection of oxygen into the atmosphere by living things, which led to the formation of an ozone layer, which, in turn, shut out lethal ultraviolet rays from the sun and permitted the rise of multicellular organisms, was only one of life's large-scale interventions. The more closely scientists look at life and its evolution, the less they find it possible to draw a sharp distinction between "life," on the one hand, and an inanimate "environment" in which it exists, on the other hand. Rather, "the environment" of the present day appears to be a house of unimaginable intricacy which life has to a very great extent built and furnished for its own use. It seems that life even regulates and maintains the chemical environment of the earth in a way that turns out to suit its own needs. In a far-reaching speculative article entitled "Chemical Processes in the Solar System: A Kinetic Perspective," Dr. McElroy has described the terrestrial cycles by which the most important elements of the atmosphere—oxygen, carbon, and nitrogen—are kept in proportions that are favorable to life. He finds that in each case life itself—its birth, metabolism, and decay—is chiefly responsible for maintaining the balance. For example, he calculates that if for some reason respiration and decay were suddenly cut off, photosynthesis would devour all the inorganic carbon on the surface of the ocean and in the atmosphere within forty years. Thereafter, carbon welling up form the deep ocean would fuel photosynthesis in the oceans for another thousand years, but then "life as we know it would terminate." Dr. McElroy also observes that the amount of ozone in the stratosphere is influenced by the amount of organic decay, and thus by the amount of life, on earth. Nitrous oxide is a product of organic decay, and because it produces nitric oxide—one of the compounds responsible for ozone depletion—it plays the role of regulator. In the absence of human intervention, living things are largely responsible for introducing nitrous oxide into the atmosphere. When life is exceptionally abundant, it releases more nitrous oxide into the atmosphere, and may thus act to cut back on the ozone, and that cutback lets in more ultraviolet rays. On the other hand, when life is sparse and depleted, nitrous-oxide production is reduced, the ozone layer builds up, and ultraviolet rays are cut back. These speculative glimpses of what might be called the metabolism of the earth give substance to the growing conviction among scientists that the earth, like a single cell or a single organism, is a systemic whole, and in a general way they tend to confirm the fear that ny large man-made perturbation of terrestrial nature could lead to a catastrophic systemic breakdown. Nuclear explosions are far from being the only perturbations in question; a heating of the global atmosphere through an increased greenhouse effect, which could be caused by the injection of vast amounts of carbon dioxide into the air (for instance, from the increased burning of coal), is another notable peril of this kind. But a nuclear holocaust would be unique in its suddenness, which would permit no observation of slowly building environmental damage before the full—and, for man, perhaps the final—catastrophe occurred. The geological record does not sustain the fear that sudden perturbations can extinguish all life on earth (if it did, we would not be here to reflect on the subject), but it does suggest that sudden, drastic ecological collapse is possible. It suggests that life as a whole, if it is given hundreds of millions of years in which to recuperate and send out new evolutionary lines, has an astounding resilience, and an ability to bring forth new and ever more impressive life forms, but it also suggests that abrupt interventions can radically disrupt any particular evolutionary configuration and dispatch hundreds of thousand of species into extinction.

The view of the earth as a single system, or organism, has only recently proceeded from poetic metaphor to actual scientific investigation, and on the whole Dr. Thomas's observation that "we do not really understand nature, at all" still holds. It is as much on the basis of this ignorance, whose scope we are only now in a position to grasp, as on the basis of the particular items of knowledge in our possession that I believe that the following judgment can be made: Bearing in mind that the possible consequences of the detonations of thousand s of megatons of nuclear explosives include the blinding of insects, birds, and beasts all over the world; the extinction of many ocean species, among them some at the base of the food chain; the temporary or permanent alteration of the climate of the globe, with the outside chance of "dramatic" and "major" alterations in the structure of the atmosphere; the pollution of the whole ecosphere with oxides of nitrogen; the incapacitation in ten minutes of unprotected people who go out into the sunlight; the blinding of people who go out into the sunlight; a significant decrease in photosynthesis in plants around the world; the scalding and killing of many crops; the increase in rates of cancer and mutation around the world, but especially in the targeted zones, and the attendant risk of global epidemics; the possible poisoning of all vertebrates by sharply increased levels of Vitamin D in their skin as a result of increased ultraviolet light; and the outright slaughter on all targeted continents of most human beings and other living things by the initial nuclear radiation, the fireballs, the thermal pulses, the blast waves, the mass fires, and the fallout from the explosions; and, considering that these consequences with all interact with one another in unguessable ways and, furthermore, are in all likelihood and incomplete list, which will be added to as our knowledge of the earth increases, one must conclude that a full-scale nuclear holocaust could lead to the extinction of mankind.

ANALYSIS AND INTERPRETATION
OF THE READINGS

1. What problems continue to stand in the way of the realization of the ideals contained in the "Universal Declaration of Human Rights"?

2. What historic forces does Freimut Duve foresee as returning with the end of the Cold War?

3. Of the two types of nationalism that Michael Ignatieff describes, which do you see as playing a larger role in world affairs today?

4. According to Jonathan Schell, what is the relationship between life and the environment? What are some of the threats to that relationship?

The Middle East Today

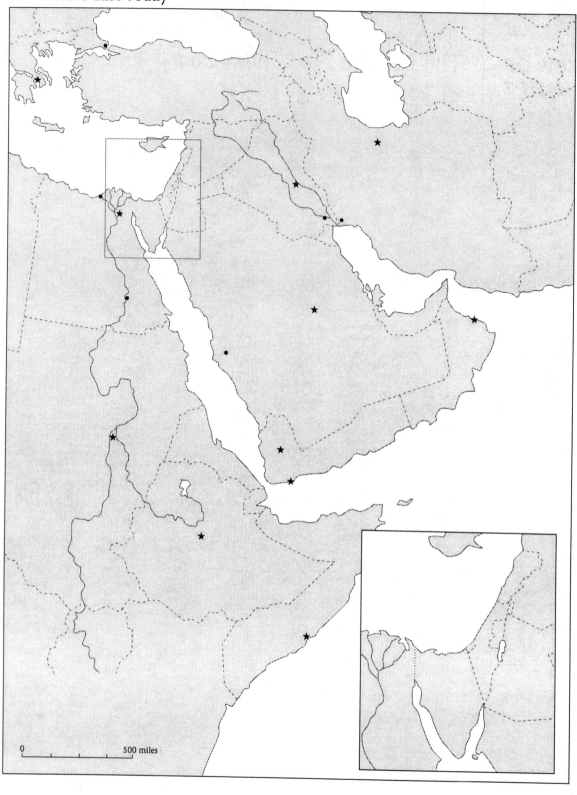

0   500 miles

REVIEW OF PART 7

The Middle East Today and The New Africa, 1990

THE MIDDLE EAST TODAY

1. On the "Middle East Today" map (see page 154 opposite), identify the following countries:

Jordan	Lebanon
Israel	Syria
Turkey	United Arab Emirates
Saudi Arabia	Iran
Iraq	Kuwait
Egypt	Oman

2. Mark the following cities:

Jerusalem	Beirut
Damascus	Cairo
Riyadh	Baghdad
Tehran	

3. Label the following:

Aswan High Dam	Nile River
Suez Canal	Persian Gulf
Red Sea	Gaza Strip

THE NEW AFRICA, 1990

1. On the "New Africa" map (see page 156), label the following:

Kenya	South Africa
Chad	Libya
Liberia	Rwanda
Zaire	Sudan
Zimbabwe	Ethiopia
Somalia	Algeria
Ghana	Nigeria
Uganda	Mozambique

2. Circle the states from the list above that were independent prior to 1945.

The New Africa, 1990

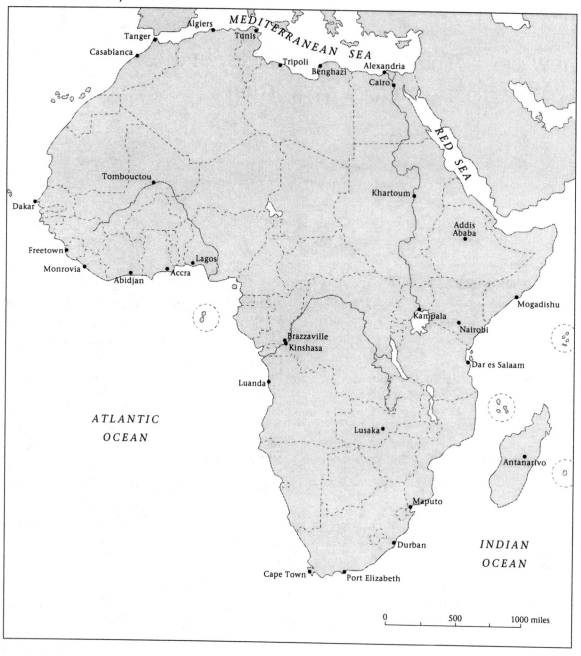

MEDITERRANEAN SEA

Algiers
Tanger
Casablanca
Tunis
Tripoli
Benghazi
Alexandria
Cairo

RED SEA

Tombouctou
Khartoum

Dakar
Addis
Ababa

Freetown
Lagos
Monrovia
Accra
Abidjan

Mogadishu

Brazzaville
Kinshasa
Kampala
Nairobi

Dar es Salaam

Luanda

ATLANTIC
OCEAN

Lusaka

Antanarivo

Maputo

Durban

INDIAN
OCEAN

Cape Town
Port Elizabeth

0   500   1000 miles

NOTES

NOTES

NOTES

NOTES

NOTES

NOTES

NOTES

NOTES

NOTES

NOTES

NOTES

NOTES

Study Guide
to accompany

WORLD CIVILIZATIONS
NINTH EDITION • VOLUME 2

Philip Lee Ralph
Robert E. Lerner
Northwestern University

Standish Meacham
University of Texas at Austin
Alan T. Wood
University of Washington, Bothell Campus

Richard W. Hull
New York University
Edward McNall Burns

by J. Michael Allen

The primary purpose of this **Study Guide** is to assist students in mastering the material in the Ninth Edition of **World Civilizations** and to provide them with a means whereby they can test their mastery. It also affords a convenient guide for review as well as a basis for classroom discussion and tests.

The same general pattern is followed in each chapter, but the nature of the exercise material varies somewhat from chapter to chapter in accordance with the character and content of the corresponding chapter in the text. Each chapter usually begins with a **review of chronology** that aims to give the same emphasis to dates that the pertinent textual discussion does. This section is followed by identifications that include **completion questions, matching questions,** and **multiple-choice questions**. These elements, including **map exercises,** are reinforced in reviews that appear at the end of each of the seven major parts of the text.

The objective questions in each chapter are complemented by **study questions** calling for short essays based on discussions in the text. More elaborate **problems** offer controversial or speculative questions and suggest topics of inquiry that often extend beyond the discussions in the text. Finally, every chapter contains a selection of brief **readings** drawn from original and secondary sources. Since the readings have been chosen with the organization and emphasis of the text constantly in mind, they will help students visualize and better understand the material they are studying. To this end, questions to assist in analyzing the readings are provided.

To ensure that the **Study Guide** accompanying the Ninth Edition of **World Civilizations** can be used with equal facility in a range of courses, chapter 21 appears in both volumes.

Cover art: Ando Hiroshige, *Fireworks Over Ryoguku Bridge*, from the series *One Hundred Famous Views of Edo*, ca. 1857. Oban woodblock print (detail). Credit: Honolulu Academy of Arts; the James A. Michener Collection (HAA 22, 792).

Cover design: Bernadette Evangelist © 1997 Robert Anthony, Inc.

W·W·NORTON

NEW YORK · LONDON

ISBN 0-393-96883-9

90000

9 780393 968835

TangleEasy
Vintage Ico

BEN KWOK

Design templates for Zentangle® coloring, and more

DO#1157   DO#1158   DO#1159   DO#1160

DO#1161   DO#1162   DO#1163   DO#1164

DO#1165   DO#1166   DO#1167   DO#1168

DO#1169   DO#1170   DO#1171   DO#1172

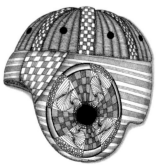

TangleEasy
Vintage Icons

Design templates for Zentangle® coloring, and more

By Darla Tjelmeland (DO#1165)

BEN KWOK

DESIGN ORIGINALS
an Imprint of Fox Chapel Publishing
www.d-originals.com

By Elaine Sampson (DO#1181)

About the Templates

Welcome to *TangleEasy Vintage Icons*, a book filled with templates that you can use to create stunning colored and patterned art. Each template has been numbered (DO#1181, for example) for ease of reference. My name is Ben Kwok, and I'm so excited to share these designs with you.

Art has always been a big part of my life. I've been drawing since I was four years old, keeping myself busy for endless hours when I was young by drawing on scrap pieces of paper. I am a very visual person, and while I was not good at some things, I always excelled at art. It seems to be an ingrained part of my personality. You could say I was born to be an artist, so art has always made sense to me, even at a young age.

I received a Bachelor of Fine Arts in Illustration from California State University, Long Beach and have worked as a graphic artist in the apparel industry for more than ten years. I've had the opportunity to work with several major brands, including Disney, Converse, and Lucky Brand. I find I most enjoy art that takes a very high skill level to accomplish. Some people like art to tell a story, but I personally like perfectly executed work. A good example is work by David A. Smith and Aaron Horkey. To me, these artists are the best in the world, and I am constantly inspired by them. I always strive for the same level of quality and perfection. I also like Art Nouveau, Biomechanics, Tattoo Flash, and Gig Posters.

In addition to my passion for art, I have a great love for animals and animal conservation. I regularly donate to the World Wildlife Fund and the Wildlife Conservation Network. Recently I've focused on the Save the Elephants project through WCN, an incredibly important effort in elephant conservation.

I started creating templates like the ones included in this book when I encountered Zentangle art. I noticed the Zentangle community was growing rapidly and producing lots of amazing work. While a lot of Zentangle art is abstract, there are also many who like to make Zentangle art in the shape of a particular object or animal. Many times these tanglers like to have an outline or other starting point to work from so they can focus on adding their intricate designs and not worry about having to sketch a realistic fish or other shape. I saw this missing piece in the puzzle, so I decided to start creating templates for Zentangle enthusiasts and doodlers alike to create intricately patterned artwork that had a distinct shape when they were finished. It seemed like a perfect fit.

ISBN 978-1-4972-0040-1

© 2016 by Ben Kwok and New Design Originals Corporation, *www.d-originals.com*, an imprint of Fox Chapel Publishing, 800-457-9112, 1970 Broad Street, East Petersburg, PA 17520.

Cover and back cover art: Christine Bates (guitar), Angela Cater (crown), Annie Jump (cassette), Linda McMillen (roses), Elaine Sampson (ice cream cone), Darla Tjelmeland (jukebox, tea set, VW bus)

Printed in the United States of America
First printing

When I started creating these templates, I had hopes of building a community centered on them, but the feedback and love I received was completely unexpected. I had no idea the templates would be so popular, or that they would have such a positive impact on the lives of others. I've received so many stories about the way working, drawing, and creating with the templates has helped people through difficult times. People like the templates because they allow them to create amazing, beautiful art, even if they're just beginners or can't draw like a professional. One of the reasons I offer the templates is because I see the motivation in these aspiring artists, and I wanted to give them an easier way to create art they could be proud of. I also love creating these templates because I want to give back to the art community and help out my fellow artists. The road to a successful art career can be very tough. Whether you are a professional or an amateur doesn't matter to me. I feel like it's my duty to give back.

There are so many wonderful things that have come out of the creation of these templates, but my favorite by far is the feedback I receive from those who use them. To me, being appreciated for my efforts is priceless. I feel like I'm making a difference in people's lives, and that's a great feeling.

If you've picked up this book, you have the itch to create something amazing, and this is a great place to start. Some advice I always try to offer is to treat the template guidelines as just that: guides. Fight the temptation to follow the lines exactly. Although you can, you certainly don't have to. I think many people, especially if they are new to patterning, follow along the lines because they are afraid of what might happen if they deviate from the template. Don't be afraid to break away and explore what you can do beyond the lines. I think that's where the true magic and creativity happens. Use your imagination and see where you can go.

Through these templates, I want to continue nurturing the artist spirit that we all share. There are lots of hopes that I have for the future—in the spirit of continuing to give back, I'm considering ways to use the templates to support animal conservation. This seems like a fitting role for these designs. And of course, I'm

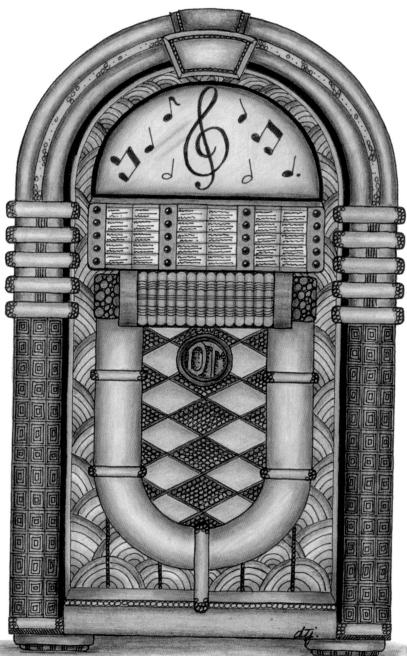

By Darla Tjelmeland (DO#1179)

very excited about what you'll do with the templates in this book.

Please visit *www.TangleEasy.com*, where you can see my latest work, access free template downloads, and explore a gallery of finished art created using my designs. For a glimpse at my own work as an artist, visit *www.BIOWORKZ.com*.

Go create!
—Ben

Adding Color

There are so many ways you can color the templates in this book. Use your favorite medium—colored pencils, markers, pens, gel pens, watercolors—or combine different mediums to create unique effects. Remember, there is no right or wrong way to add color. If you're feeling a little unsure, take a look at the color wheel. Some very light research into color theory can give you loads of ideas for creating color palettes. Also, be sure to check out the color examples on the pages that follow for inspiration.

When purchasing coloring supplies, try to get the highest quality you can afford. You'll be much happier with the results. Test your purchases in a scrapbook to see how you like the color and quality. Make notes so you know what you liked and what you didn't for your next shopping trip. Have fun experimenting!

Color Theory

Color gives sensational beauty to the world around you. Color allows you to tell the difference between various objects and landscapes. There are even scientific studies that show how different colors can affect your mood. Color is everything! Let's explore the ins and outs of color itself and how to use it to make your artwork the best that it can be. From the primary colors we all grew up with to color schemes you may not be so familiar with, these pages will show you how to take your coloring to the next level.

Here you see the age-old color wheel. Thanks to art classes from elementary school, it is easy to point out each of the familiar, essential colors of the wheel like red, yellow, green, blue, and purple. However, to best understand the color wheel in full, you should learn the various categories of color that it illustrates.

Categories of Color

Primary Colors: red, yellow, and blue. Primary colors are the three widely recognized colors on the wheel that cannot be created by mixing other colors together.

Secondary Colors: purple, orange, and green. Secondary colors are the colors you can create from mixing two primary hues together. Mixing the primary colors red and blue creates purple; mixing red and yellow creates orange; mixing blue and yellow creates green.

Tertiary Colors. Tertiary colors are the colors made by combining a primary (p) with a secondary (s) color. Mixing red (p) and purple (s) creates the tertiary color red-violet/magenta; mixing blue (p) and green (s) creates blue-green/teal; mixing yellow (p) and green (s) creates yellow-green/chartreuse, etc.

Color Schemes

It's time to delve even deeper into the universe of coloring to explore the different color schemes you can make from primary, secondary, and tertiary colors. Here are a few combinations to try:

Analogous: An analogous color scheme uses colors that are right next to each other on the wheel to create a completely harmonious range of color. Analogous color schemes commonly include a primary color paired with two of its tertiary neighbors. An example of an analogous color scheme is blue-green, green, and yellow-green.

Monochromatic: A monochromatic color scheme revolves around different shades and tints of one single color. Try using light, medium, and dark greens to create an earthy color scheme or all different yellows and golds to create a picture full of sunshine.

Complementary: Complementary colors are two hues that are directly across from one another on the color wheel; when placed together, these colors create a striking contrast that will make any project pop. Examples of complementary color schemes are red and green, yellow and purple, and blue and orange.

With this guide to the basics of color theory, your art projects will become masterpieces in no time! Don't forget to come back to these pages often to look at your color wheel while you're coloring. Consider printing one out to have on hand at all times! Explore different color schemes—if you like it, try it.

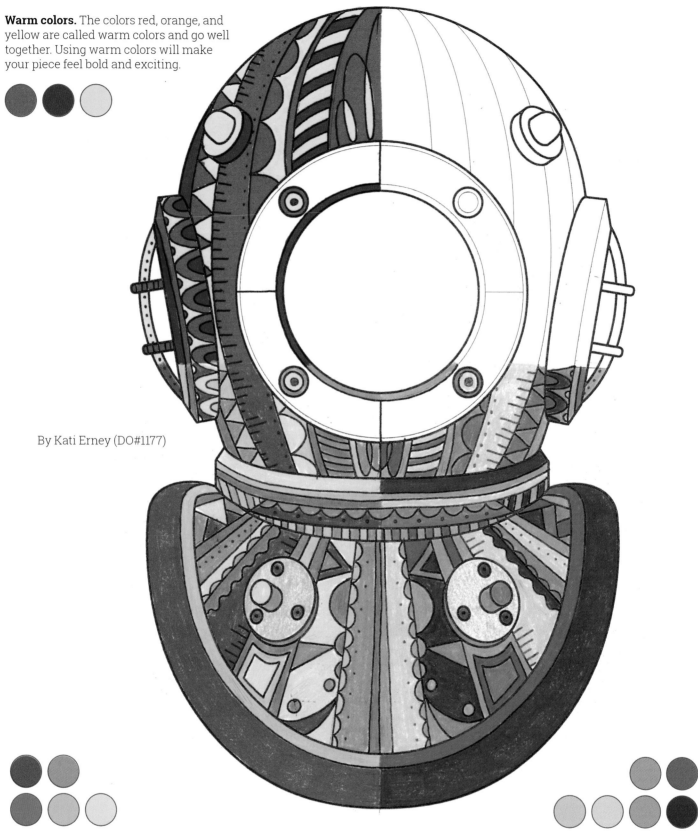

Warm colors. The colors red, orange, and yellow are called warm colors and go well together. Using warm colors will make your piece feel bold and exciting.

By Kati Erney (DO#1177)

Complementary colors. Colors opposite one another on the color wheel are complementary, meaning they pair well together. A color will also stand out more against its complement than against any other color. Note that complementary pairs always contain a warm color and a cool color. Complementary pairings include red/green, orange/blue, and yellow/purple.

Cool colors. The colors purple, blue, and green are called cool colors and go well together. Using cool colors will make your piece feel calm and soft.

Markers. Markers are a great way to cover lots of ground and fill in large areas. Dual-tip markers come with a large brush end for big spaces and a felt-tip end for small areas. Some markers can be layered for unique blending and shading effects. Experiment with water-based and alcohol-based options and a variety of brands to see which suits you best!

By Kati Erney (DO#1177)

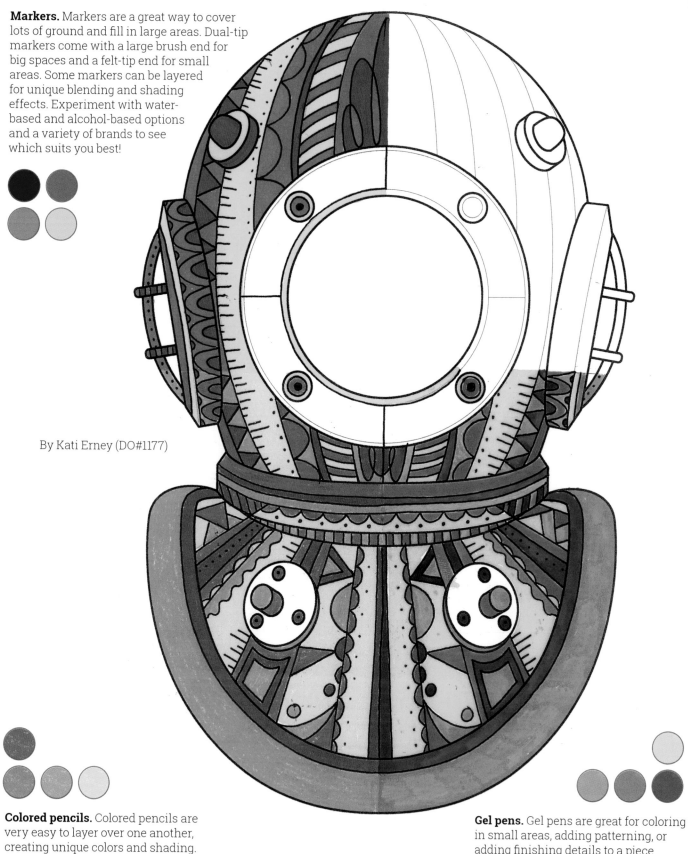

Colored pencils. Colored pencils are very easy to layer over one another, creating unique colors and shading. They can be used to fill in large areas or sharpened to a fine point for detail work. Experiment with watercolor pencils to give your piece a painted effect.

Gel pens. Gel pens are great for coloring in small areas, adding patterning, or adding finishing details to a piece already colored with a different medium. There are lots of varieties available, including neon, metallic, sparkle, and pastel.

Adding Patterns

These templates were made to be embellished with patterning, and there are so many different ways to do it. The Zentangle method offers wonderful step-by-step designs, called tangles, to make patterning accessible for anyone. Try using some of the tangles on the following pages to fill a template. If you'd like to learn more about the Zentangle method, check out *Zentangle Basics, Expanded Workbook Edition*, or *Joy of Zentangle* to get started.

Simple patterning. You don't have to add a different pattern to every section in a template to create a beautiful finished piece. All of the sections in this lighthouse were filled with a triangle pattern. The artist varied the size of the patterning depending on the space available and also left some open spaces between the areas of patterning. Try picking just one pattern that you like and add it to all of the sections of a template.

By Kati Erney (DO#1186)

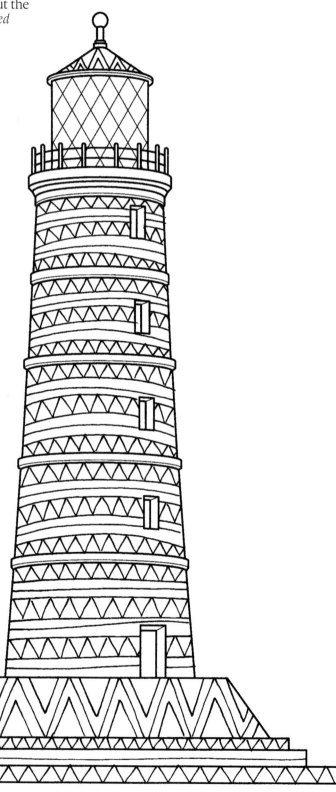

Shading with color. Another simple way to create stunning art is to enhance your patterning with color shading. As with the lighthouse on the previous page, this guitar is embellished with very simple patterning. Then, shading was added using yellow and orange colored pencil. More pressure and the addition of orange was used to create dark areas, and light pressure was used to create light areas. The simple patterning and shading create a beautifully realistic piece.

By Kati Erney (DO#1163)

Multiple patterns. As you become more comfortable with patterning, try adding a different pattern to each section of a template. This gramophone is filled with tangles.

Pigma Micron 01 black pens are the preferred drawing medium for tanglers. For any coloring or patterning, purchase the highest-quality supplies you can. You'll be much happier with the results.

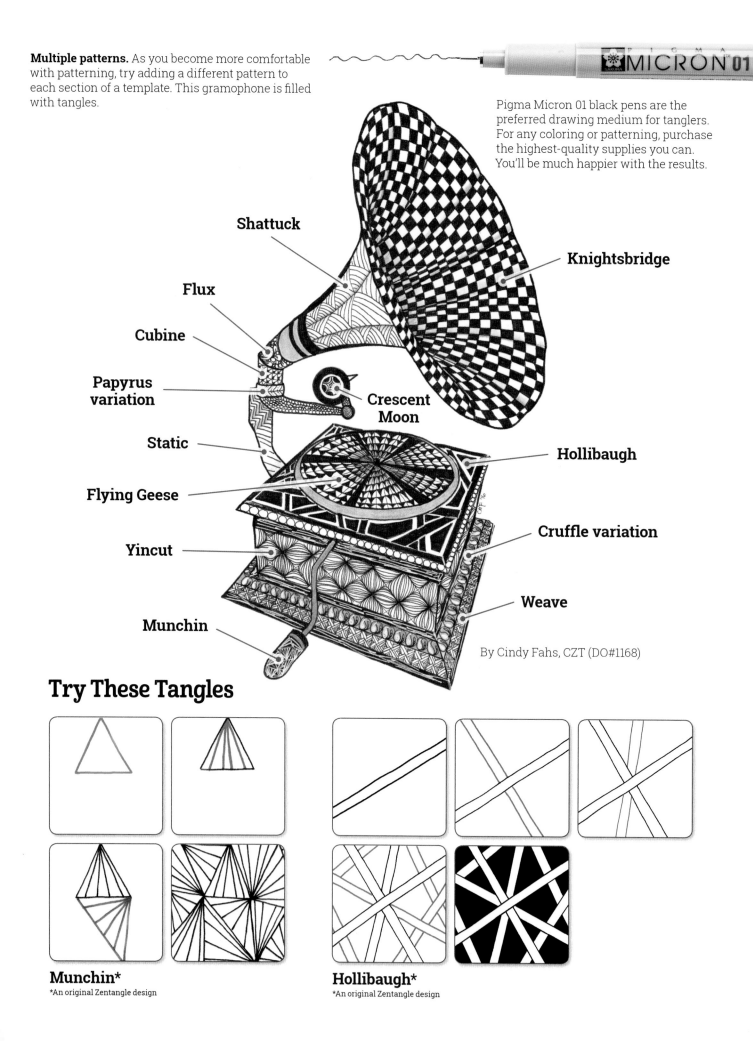

Shattuck

Flux

Cubine

Papyrus variation

Static

Flying Geese

Yincut

Munchin

Crescent Moon

Knightsbridge

Hollibaugh

Cruffle variation

Weave

By Cindy Fahs, CZT (DO#1168)

Try These Tangles

Munchin*
*An original Zentangle design

Hollibaugh*
*An original Zentangle design

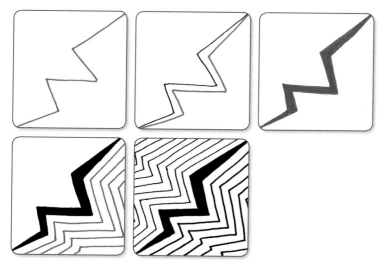

Static*
*An original Zentangle design

Crescent Moon*
*An original Zentangle design

Yincut*
*An original Zentangle design

Knightsbridge*
*An original Zentangle design

Weave
Tangle by Sandy Steen Bartholomew, CZT

Flying Geese
Tangle by Suzanne McNeill, CZT

Design Your Own Patterns

You can also add patterning by creating your own designs using simple shapes and lines. Checkerboards, polka dots, and stripes are all patterns that anyone can draw. Check out some of the freehand patterns below to get some ideas.

Stripes. Draw parallel lines to create stripes. You can use even spacing between the lines, or vary the spacing. Lines drawn close together will create dark areas, while lines drawn further apart will create light areas.

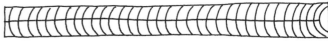

Varied stripes. You can make stripes curved or wavy for added interest. Add extra dots or lines for complexity.

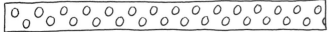

Circles. Fill a template section with circles. You can draw them in orderly rows as shown, or add them in a completely random pattern. Vary the size of the circles or keep them uniform; fill them in or leave them open; allow them to overlap or keep them separated.

Checkerboard. Draw a grid and fill in alternating boxes for a checkerboard pattern. Use square or rectangular boxes. Or, draw a grid with curved lines for added interest.

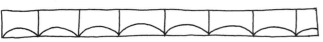

Crescents. Crescent shapes are easy to repeat along a line. Build on your design by adding more rows of crescents, or draw dots or lines between each crescent as shown.

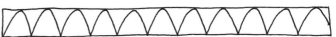

Extended crescents. These tall crescents make a great border around the edges of a section in a template.

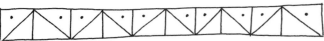

Triangles. Draw a series of triangles next to each other. Divide the triangles in half as shown, or add more lines to divide the triangles into thirds or fourths. You can also add dots and circles.

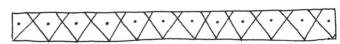

Overlapping triangles. Draw a series of triangles so that they overlap. Add extra lines and dots for complexity.

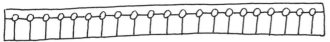

Circles and lines. Draw a series of circles. Then connect each one with a line. You can add more lines coming out from the circles. The lines can be straight and parallel, or go in any direction and crisscross.

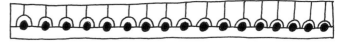

Varied circles and lines. Add more complexity to the circles and lines design by filling in the circles and adding semi-circle outlines.

Inspirational Gallery

We asked people to share the amazing art they've been creating using the templates found in this book. We've featured their beautiful work here to spark your creativity and get ready to create some art of your own. Notice how the same template can look completely different depending on the way each artist used the guidelines and the patterns or colors added. Remember to put your individual touch and style on every piece you create. Have fun!

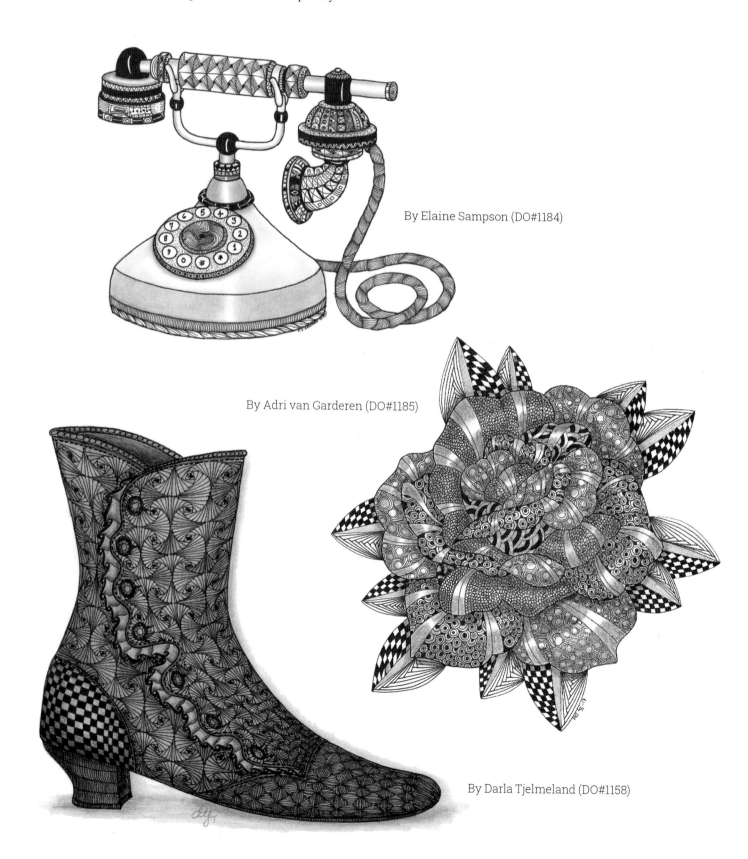

By Elaine Sampson (DO#1184)

By Adri van Garderen (DO#1185)

By Darla Tjelmeland (DO#1158)

By Annie Jump (DO#1182)

By Annie Jump (DO#1167)

By Angela Cater (DO#1174)

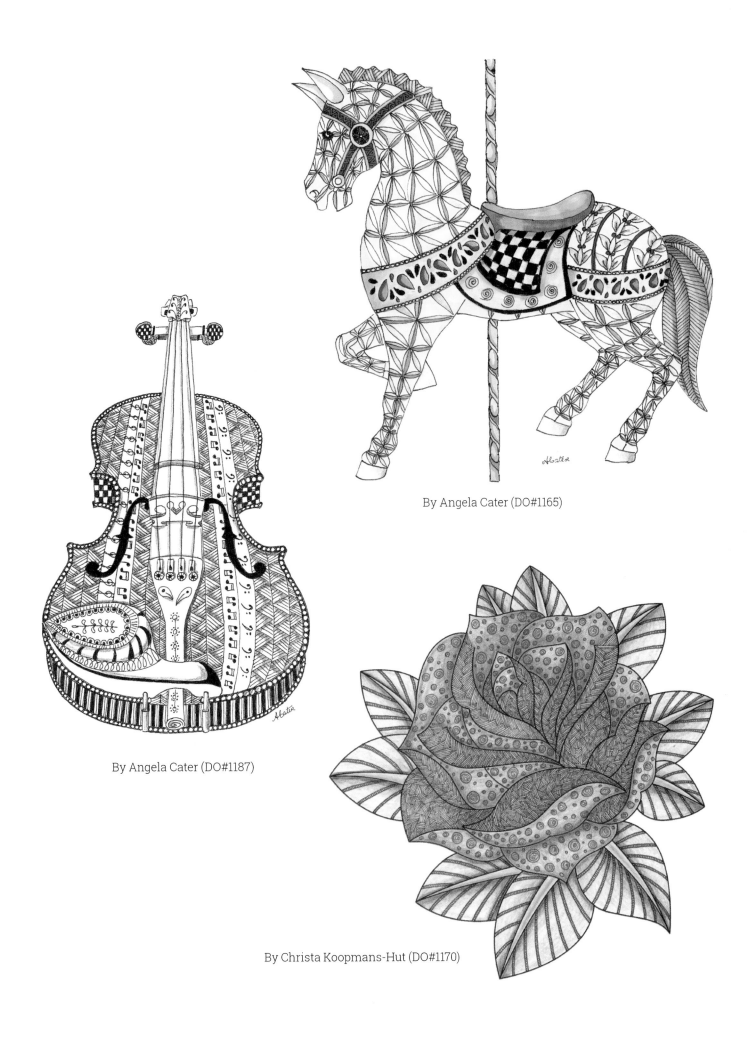

By Angela Cater (DO#1165)

By Angela Cater (DO#1187)

By Christa Koopmans-Hut (DO#1170)

By Christa Koopmans-Hut (DO#1178)

By Christa Koopmans-Hut (DO#1168)

By Christa Koopmans-Hut (DO#1160)

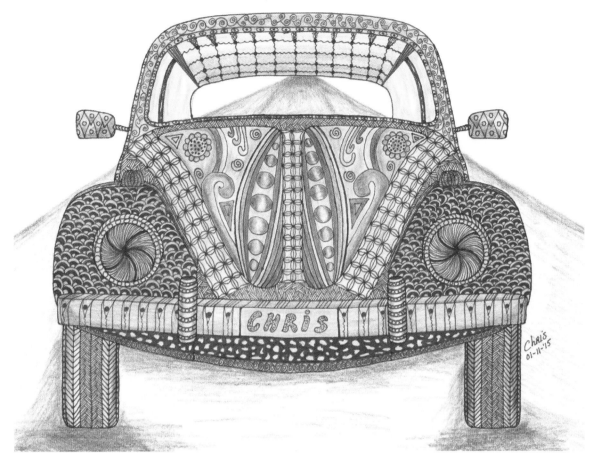

By Christa Koopmans-Hut (DO#1188)

By Elaine Sampson (DO#1159)

By Christine Bates (DO#1163)

By Darla Tjelmeland (DO#1160)

By Darla Tjelmeland (DO#1172)

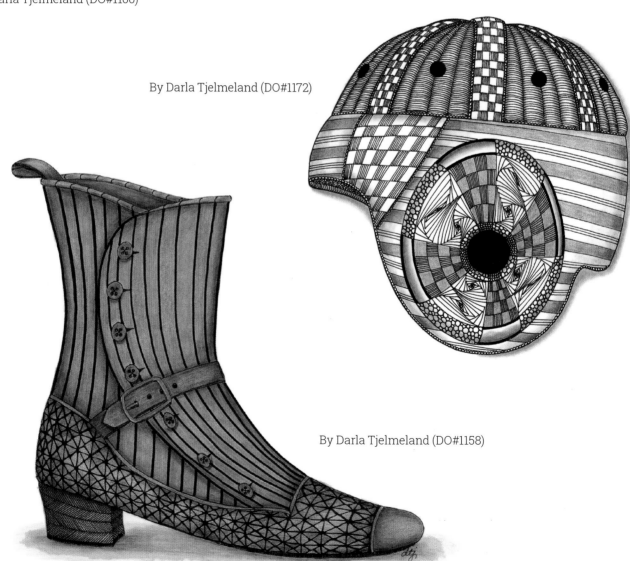

By Darla Tjelmeland (DO#1158)

By Darla Tjelmeland (DO#1165)

By Diane Jennings (DO#1180)

By Darla Tjelmeland (DO#1176)

By Diane Jennings (DO#1180)

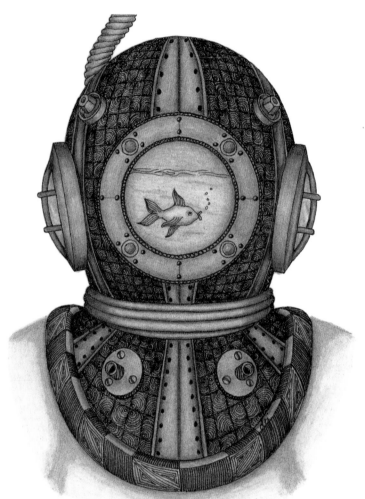

By Darla Tjelmeland (DO#1177)

By Christine Hood (DO#1171)

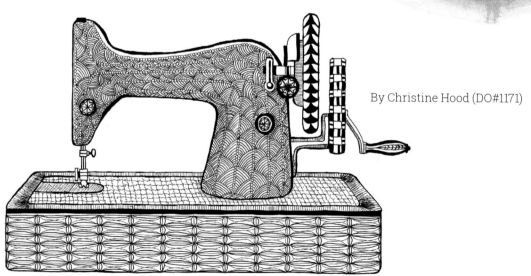

By Angela Cater (DO#1178)

By Angela Cater (DO#1164)

By Darla Tjelmeland (DO#1179)

By Darla Tjelmeland (DO#1159)

By Darla Tjelmeland (DO#1173)

By Darla Tjelmeland (DO#1186)

By LeeAnn Denzer (DO#1165)

By Karen Grayczk (DO#1184)

By Jessica Madore (DO#1180)

By Diane Jennings (DO#1180)

By Elaine Sampson (DO#1175)

By Darla Tjelmeland (DO#1157)

By Dusty Darrah (DO#1188)

By Elaine Sampson (DO#1162)

By Elaine Sampson (DO#1163)

By LeeAnn Denzer (DO#1169)

By Karen Aicken (DO#1165)

By Linda McMillen (DO#1162)

By Kelly Kidd (DO#1186)

By Dusty Darrah (DO#1160)

By Ninna Hellman (DO#1169)

By Ninna Hellman (DO#1163)

By Darla Tjelmeland (DO#1171)

By Lorraine O'Hare (DO#1181)

By Darla Tjelmeland (DO#1187)

By Ninna Hellman (DO#1173)

By Ninna Hellman (DO#1161)

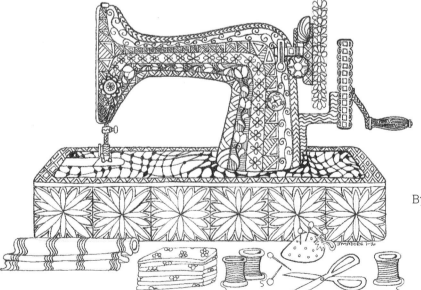

By Jessica Madore (DO#1171)

By Christa Koopmans-Hut (DO#1183)

By Elaine Sampson (DO#1181)

By Elaine Sampson (DO#1166)

By Ninna Hellman (DO#1157)

In a gentle way, you can shake the world.

—Mahatma Gandhi

DO#1157, Volkswagen Bus:
This vehicle first appeared in the 1950s
and is an iconic symbol of the 1960s and 1970s era.

It is better to fail in originality
than to succeed in imitation.

—Herman Melville

DO#1158, Boot:

At one time, only women wore shoes; men wore boots.

Together is a wonderful place to be.

—Unknown

DO#1159, Tea Set:
Tea party etiquette dictates that each guest should receive a spoon
for stirring sugar into his or her tea, but that the sugar bowl
should have its own spoon for adding sugar.

Hope anchors the soul.

—Unknown

DO#1160, Anchor:
Before the advent of the modern-day anchor,
stones, sandbags, or logs were used.

The best things in life are sweet.

—Unknown

DO#1161, Cupcake:

Depending on your location in the world, you might hear cupcakes referred to as fairy cakes, butterfly cakes, or patty cakes.

Deep in their roots all flowers keep the light.

—Theodore Roethke

DO#1162, Rose:

There are more than 100 species of roses.

Music can change the world because it can change people.

—Bono

DO#1163, Electric Guitar:

While the electric guitar is commonly associated with rock and roll,
jazz, blues, and country artists first championed the instrument.

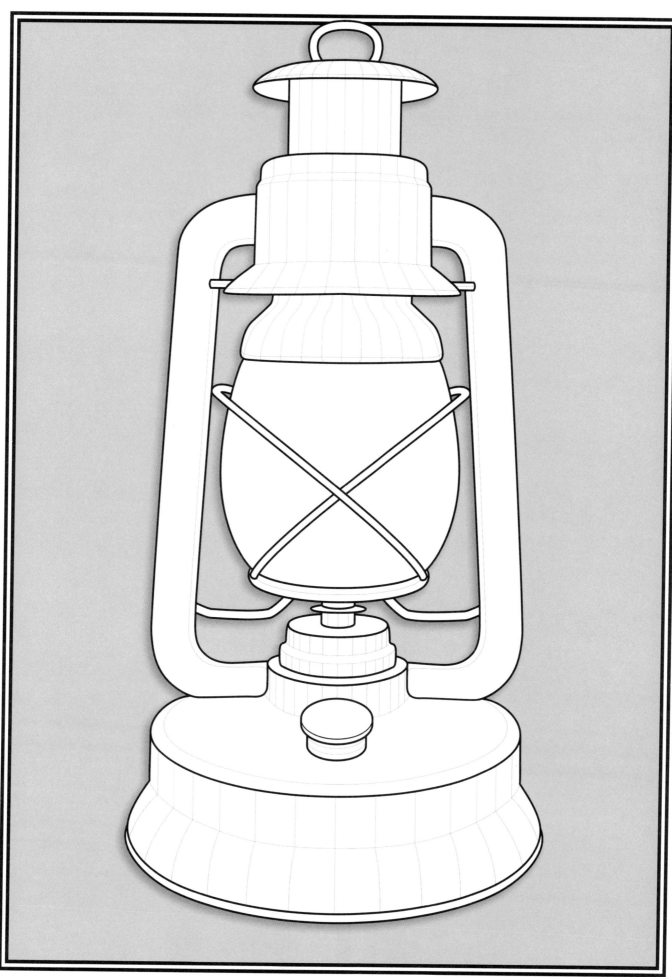

© Ben Kwok, From *TangleEasy Vintage Icons* © Design Originals, www.D-Originals.com

Nothing can dim the light that shines from within.

—Maya Angelou

DO#1164, Lantern:

Before the advent of batteries or electricity,
candle or fuel lanterns were the essential devices for illumination.

We didn't realize we were making memories,
we just knew we were having fun.

—Unknown

The history of the carousel's brass ring dates all the way back to
a ring-spearing competition popular among Arabian and Turkish horsemen.

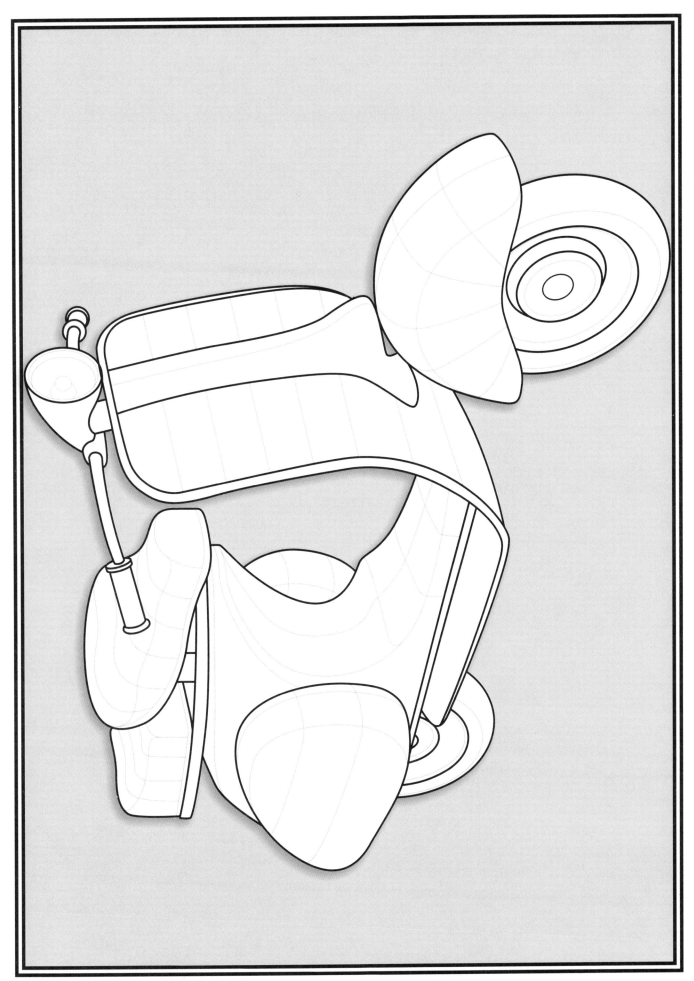

There was nowhere to go but everywhere,
so just keep on rolling under the stars.

—Jack Kerouac, *On the Road: The Original Scroll*

DO#1166, Scooter:

One tank of gas will take you more than 200 miles on a Vespa.

Blessed are the gypsies, the makers of music,
the artists, writers, dreamers of dreams, wanderers,
and vagabonds, children and misfits, for they teach us
to see the world through beautiful eyes.

—Unknown

DO#1167, Cassette Tape:
The cassette tape was originally intended to be
a recording device for dictation, not music.

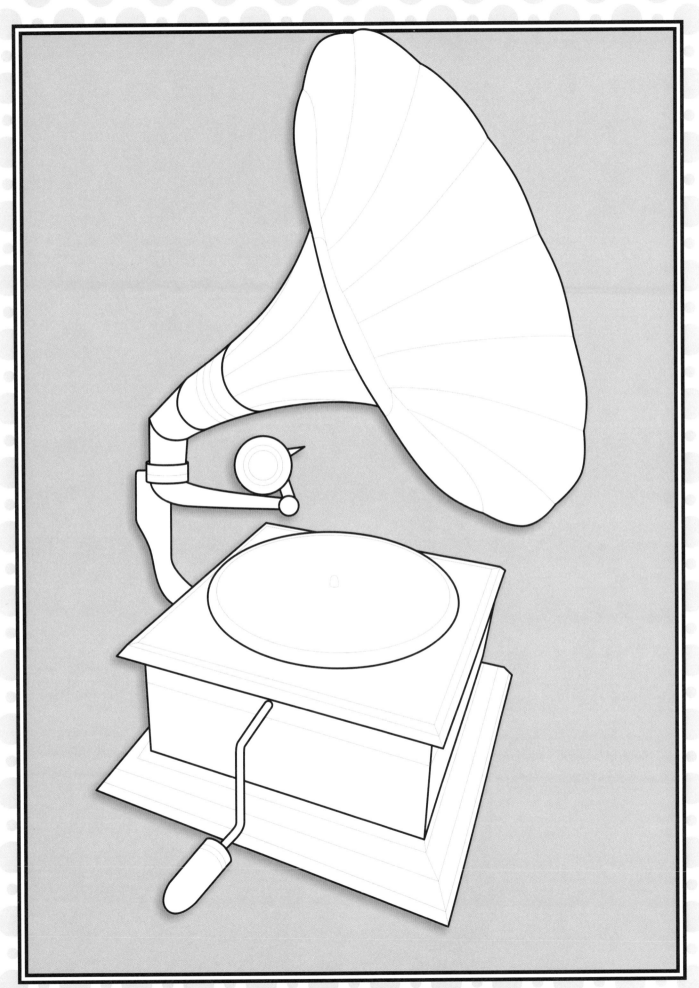

Where words fail, music speaks.

—Hans Christian Andersen

DO#1168, Gramophone:
Predecessors of the gramophone recorded sound on cylinders.
The gramophone was the first device to use flat discs.

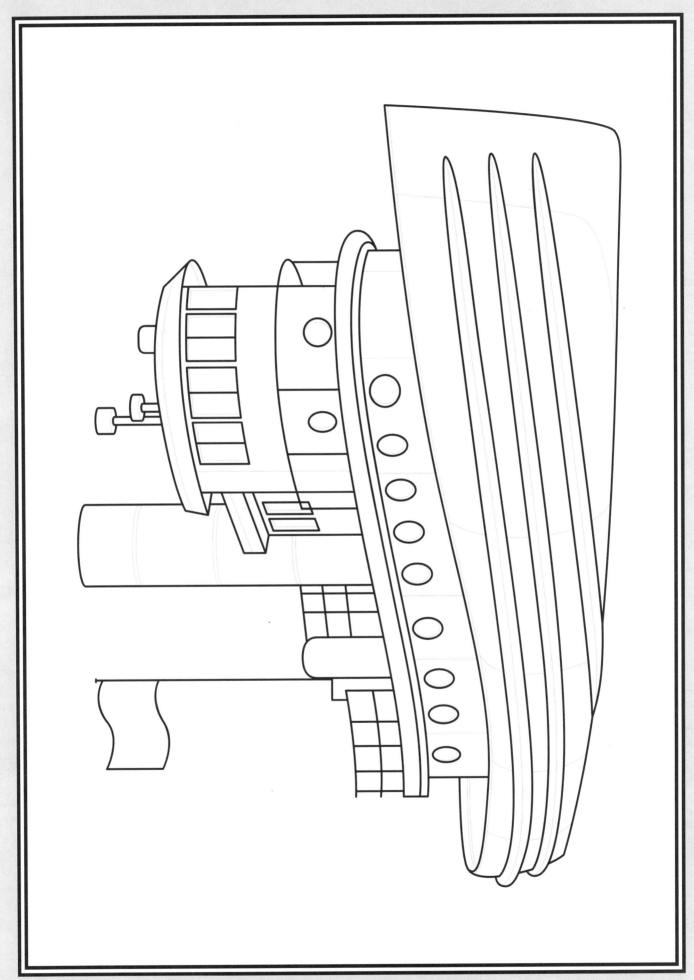

A smooth sea never made a skilled sailor.

—Unknown

DO#1169, Tugboat:
Although usually small, tugboats are exceptionally powerful,
built to tow or guide much larger vessels.

If you look the right way, you can see that the whole world is a garden.

—Frances Hodgson Burnett, *The Secret Garden*

DO#1170, Rose:

A rose's fruit is called a rose hip.

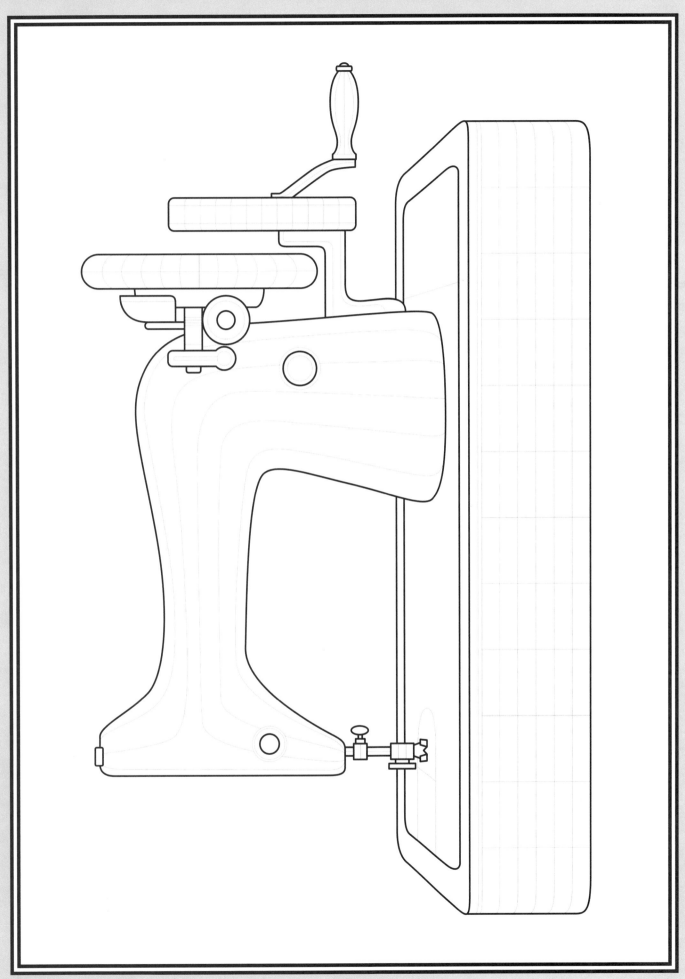

There is nothing like a dream to create the future.

—Victor Hugo, *Les Misérables*

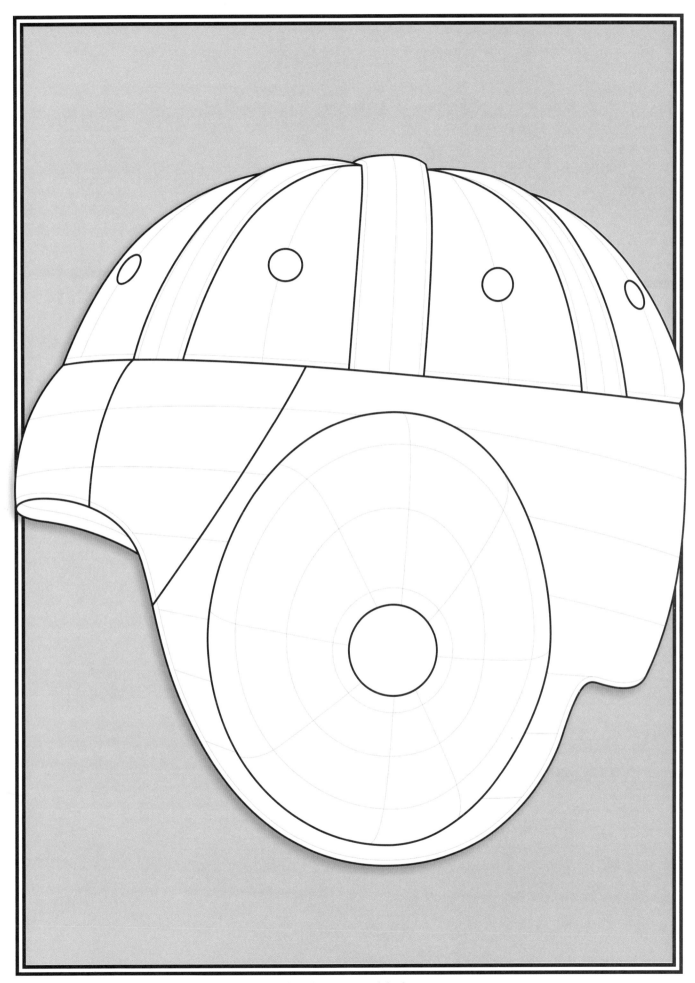

May you always be courageous. Stand upright and be strong.
May you stay forever young.

—Bob Dylan, *Forever Young*

DO#1172, Football Helmet:
The first football helmets were made of soft leather
and provided almost no protection compared to today's polycarbonate gear.

Faith is the bird that feels the light
and sings when the dawn is still dark.

—Rabindranath Tagore

DO#1173, Lamp:

Thomas Edison developed the first long-lasting

incandescent bulb in the late 1800s.

© Ben Kwok, From *TangleEasy Vintage Icons* © Design Originals, www.D-Originals.com

Sometimes the smallest things
take up the most room in your heart.

—Winnie-the-Pooh

DO#1174, Baby Carriage:
Revolutionary changes to the baby carriage/stroller in the late 1800s
included the development of independently moving wheels,
and a seat that could be turned to face backwards or forwards.

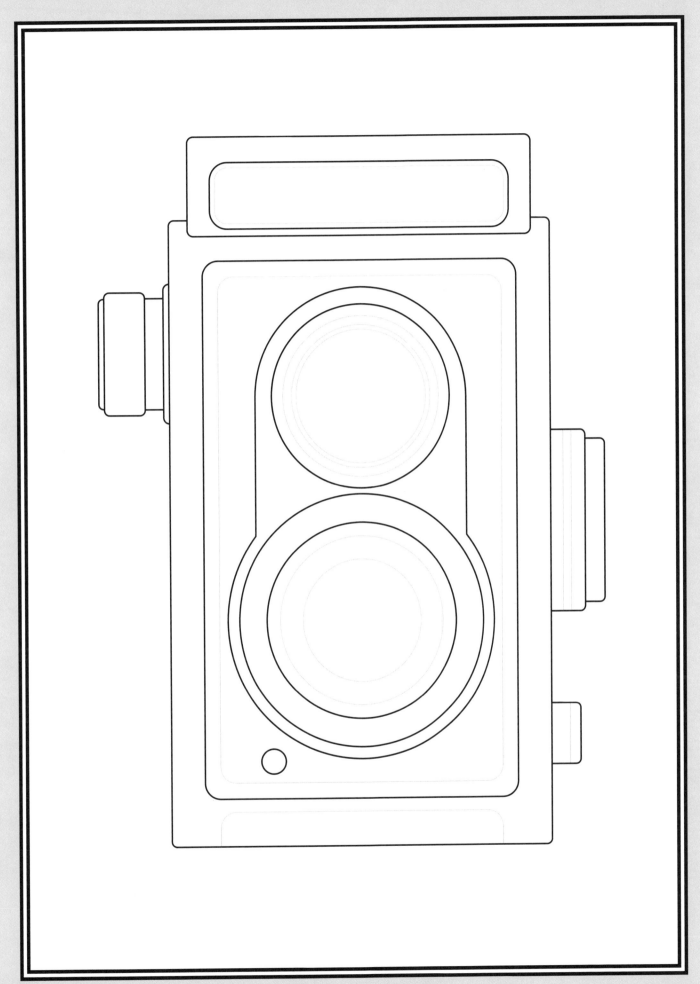

Life is like a camera. Just focus on what's important, capture the good times, develop from the negatives, and if things don't turn out—take another shot.

—Unknown

DO#1175, Camera:

George Eastman founded the Eastman Kodak Company in 1888.

We are all visitors to this time, this place.
We are just passing through. Our purpose here is to observe,
to learn, to grow, to love... and then we return home.

—Australian aboriginal proverb

DO#1176, Grandfather Clock:
"Grandfather clock" is the common term for the long-case clock,
which uses a pendulum as the driving device.

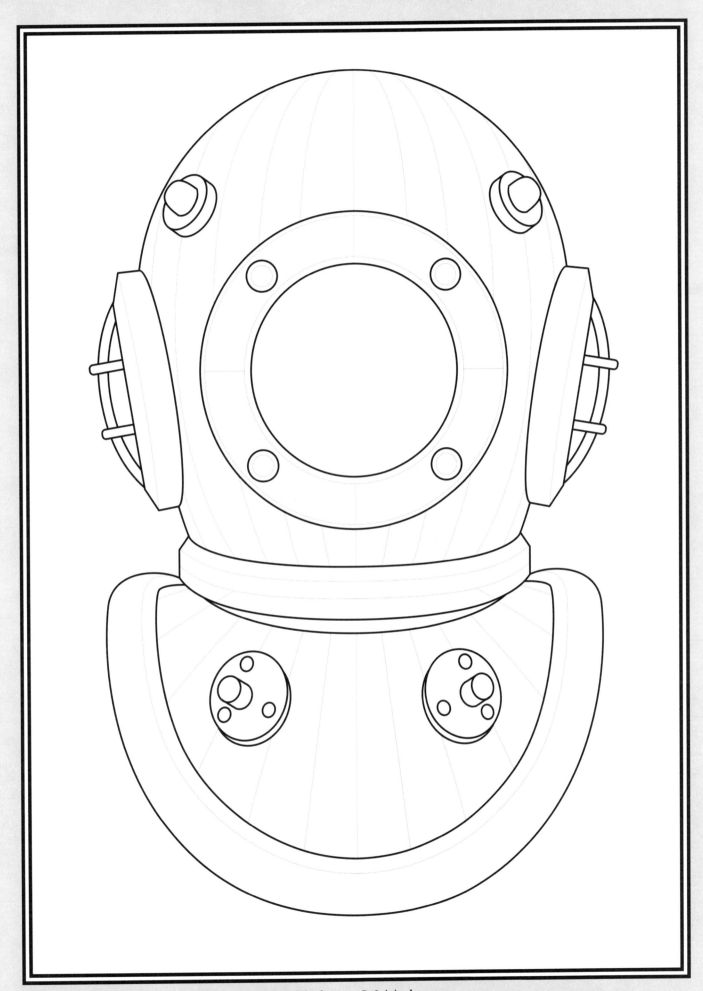

Every time I slip into the ocean, it's like going home.

—Sylvia Earle

DO#1177, Diving Helmet:

Before the invention of scuba gear,
divers had to rely on air pumped down to them from the surface.

Whatever you do, be different.

—Unknown

DO#1178, Crown:

Crowns are commonly associated with monarchs, but historically, decorative headgear might also represent triumph, honor, and glory, as well as power and authority.

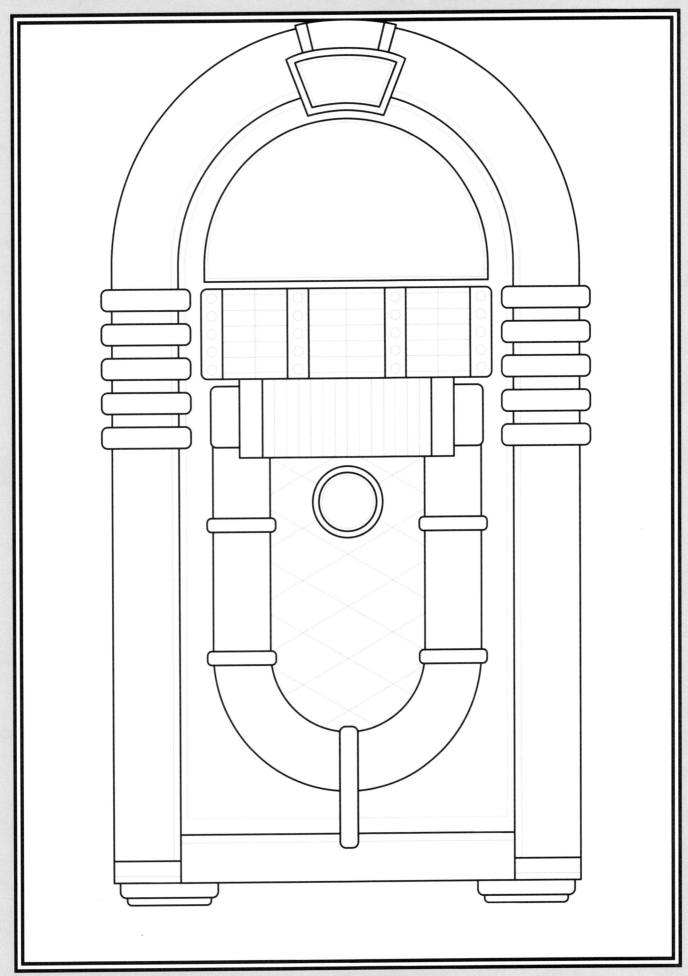

Do it with passion or not at all.

—Unknown

DO#1179, Jukebox:

Early jukeboxes were fitted with "listening tubes,"
much like those on stethoscopes.

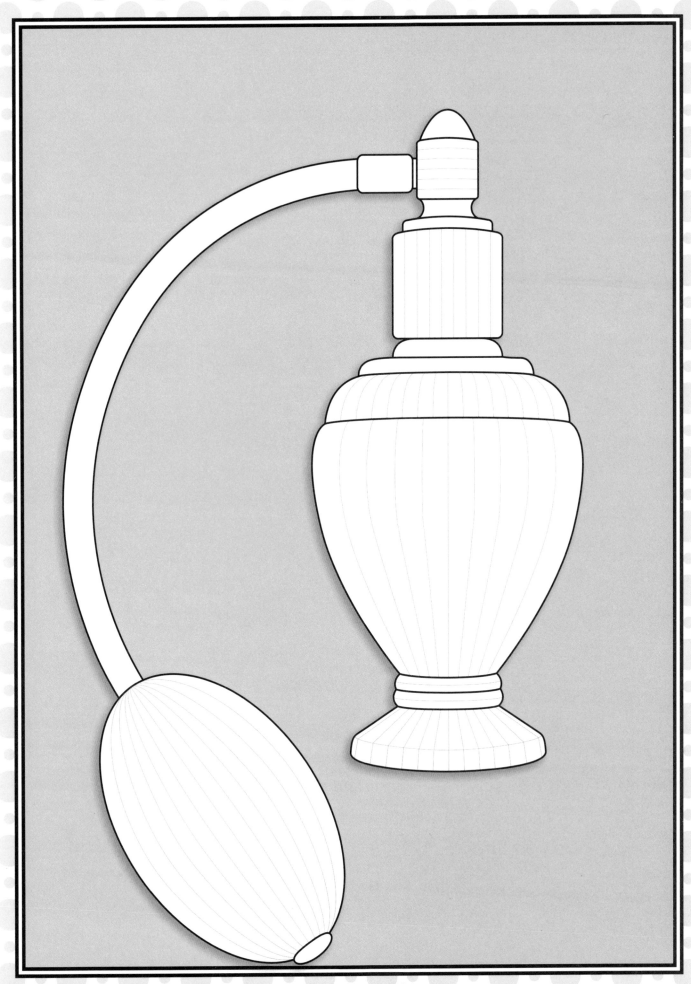

A girl should be two things: classy and fabulous.

—Coco Chanel

DO#1180, Perfume Bottle:
It is rumored that French perfumer Jean Carles
insured his nose for one million dollars.

Celebrate we will,
because life is short but sweet for certain.

—Dave Matthews Band, *Two Step*

DO#1181, Ice Cream Cone:
Before the invention of edible cones,
ice cream was eaten out of dishes or even paper.

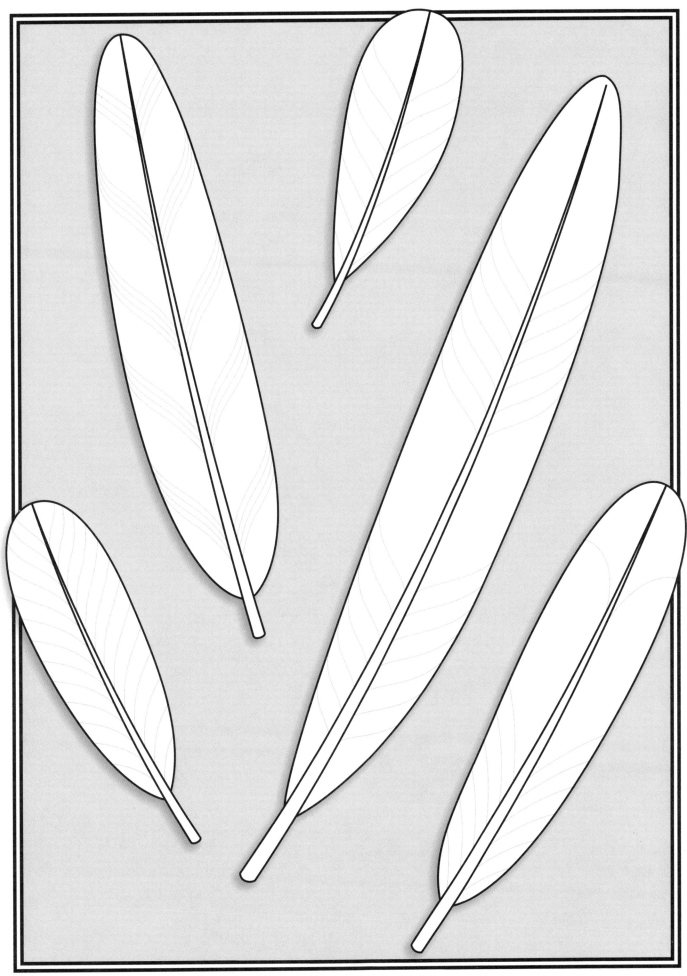

Close your eyes, clear your heart, let it go.

—Unknown

DO#1182, Feathers:
Feathers have symbolic meaning for many cultures
and are often associated with spirituality, air or wind, and freedom or lightness.

Your mind is a key, and whatever it unlocks,
the greatest treasure of all.

—Michael Bassey Johnson

DO#1183, Keys:

At one time, locks were incredibly expensive,
so a set of keys was considered a status symbol.

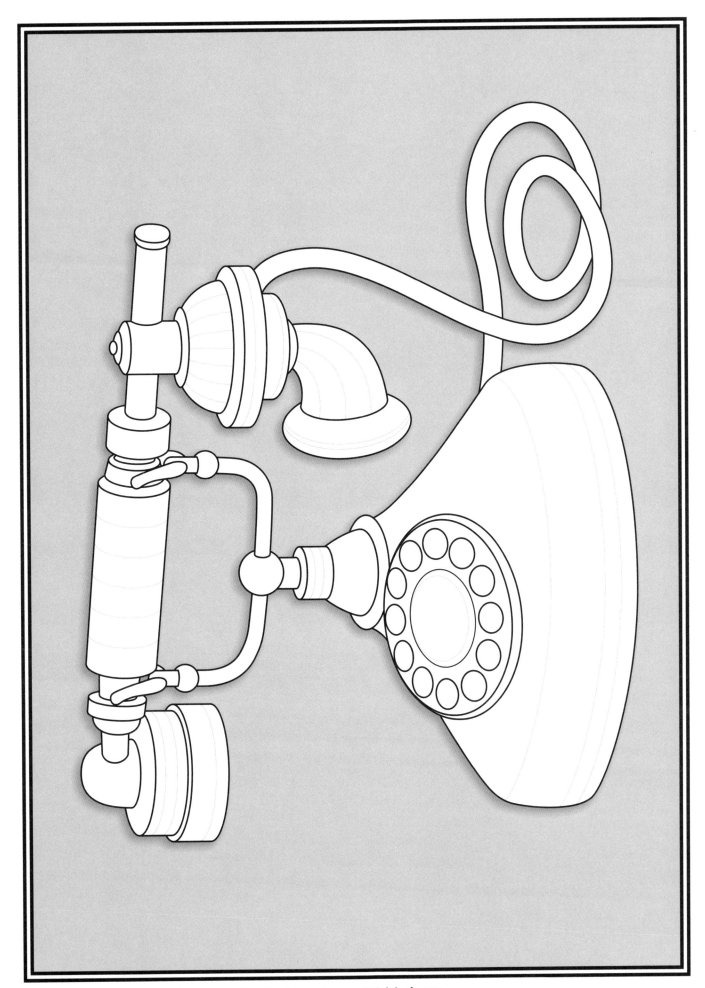

The way to get started is to quit talking and begin doing.

—Walt Disney

DO#1184, Telephone:

"Ahoy" was once a common telephone greeting.

We are all different flowers from the same garden.

—Unknown

DO#1185, Rose:

The rose is the state flower of four states:
Iowa, New York, North Dakota, and Georgia.

I am not afraid of storms
for I am learning how to sail my ship.

—Louisa May Alcott

DO#1186, Lighthouse:
Although lighthouses bring to mind coastal states,
Michigan actually has more lighthouses than any other U.S. state,
safeguarding boat traffic on the Great Lakes.

I believe in music the way some people
believe in fairytales.

—*August Rush*

DO#1187, Violin:

Playing the violin is a workout. You can burn more than 150 calories
in an hour-long practice session.

You don't need anybody to tell you who you are or what you are. You are what you are!

—John Lennon

DO#1188, Volkswagen Beetle:
Perhaps the most famous Beetle, Herbie the Love Bug
was featured in six Disney movies.